Battleground Europe

OPPY WOOD

Other guides in the Battleground Europe Series:

Walking the Salient *by* Paul Reed
Ypres – Sanctuary Wood and Hooge *by* Nigel Cave
Ypres – Hill 60 *by* Nigel Cave
Ypres – Messines Ridge *by* Peter Oldham
Ypres – Polygon Wood *by* Nigel Cave
Ypres – Passchendaele *by* Nigel Cave
Ypres – Airfields and Airmen *by* Michael O'Connor
Ypres – St Julien *by* Graham Keech

Walking the Somme *by* Paul Reed
Somme – Gommecourt *by* Nigel Cave
Somme – Serre *by* Jack Horsfall & Nigel Cave
Somme – Beaumont Hamel *by* Nigel Cave
Somme – Thiepval *by* Michael Stedman
Somme – La Boisselle *by* Michael Stedman
Somme – Fricourt *by* Michael Stedman
Somme – Carnoy – Montauban *by* Graham Maddocks
Somme – Pozieres *by* Graham Keech
Somme – Courcelette *by* Paul Reed
Somme – Boom Ravine *by* Trevor Pidgeon
Somme – Mametz Wood *by* Michael Renshaw
Somme – Delville Wood *by* Nigel Cave
Somme – Advance to Victory (North) 1918 *by* Michael Stedman
Somme – Flers *by* Trevor Pidgeon
Somme – Bazentin Ridge *by* Edward Hancock
Somme – Combles *by* Paul Reed
Somme – Beaucourt *by* Michael Renshaw
Somme – Redan Ridge *by* Michael Renshaw
Somme – Hamel *by* Peter Pedersen
Somme – Villers-Bretonneux *by* Peter Pedersen
Somme – Airfields and Airmen *by* Michael O'Connor

Arras – Vimy Ridge *by* Nigel Cave
Arras – Gavrelle *by* Trevor Tasker and Kyle Tallett
Arras – Bullecourt *by* Graham Keech
Arras – Monchy le Preux *by* Colin Fox
Arras – Airfields and Airmen *by* Michael O'Connor

Hindenburg Line *by* Peter Oldham
Hindenburg Line Epehy *by* Bill Mitchinson
Hindenburg Line Riqueval *by* Bill Mitchinson
Hindenburg Line Villers-Plouich *by* Bill Mitchinson
Hindenburg Line – Cambrai Right Hook *by* Jack Horsfall & Nigel Cave
Hindenburg Line – Saint Quentin *by* Helen McPhail and Philip Guest
Hindenburg Line – Bourlon Wood *by* Jack Horsfall & Nigel Cave
Cambrai – Airfields and Airmen *by* Michael O'Connor

La Bassée – Neuve Chapelle *by* Geoffrey Bridger
Loos – Hohenzollern Redoubt *by* Andrew Rawson
Loos – Hill 70 *by* Andrew Rawson
Fromelles *by* Peter Pedersen
Aubers Ridge *by* Edward Hancock

Mons *by* Jack Horsfall and Nigel Cave

Accrington Pals Trail *by* William Turner

In The Footsteps of the Red Baron *by* Michael O'Connor & Norman Franks
Poets at War: Wilfred Owen *by* Helen McPhail and Philip Guest
Poets at War: Edmund Blunden *by* Helen McPhail and Philip Gues
Poets at War: Graves & Sassoon *by* Helen McPhail and Philip Gue
Gallipoli *by* Nigel Steel
Gallipoli – Gully Ravine *by* Stephen Chambers
Gallipoli – Landings at Helles *by* Huw & Jill Rodge
Walking the Italian Front *by* Francis Mackay
Italy - Asiago *by* Francis Mackay

Verdun: Fort Doumont *by* Christina Holstein

Boer War – The Relief of Ladysmith *by* Lewis Childs
Boer War – The Siege of Ladysmith *by* Lewis Childs
Boer War – Kimberley *by* Lewis Childs
Isandlwana *by* Ian Knight and Ian Castle
Rorkes Drift *by* Ian Knight and Ian Castle

Stamford Bridge & Hastings *by* Peter Marren
Wars of the Roses – **Wakefield/Towton** *by* Philip A. Haigh
Wars of the Roses – **Tewkesbury** *by* Steven Goodchild

English Civil War – **Naseby** *by* Martin Marix Evans, Peter Burt and Michael Westaway
English Civil War – **Marston Moor** *by* David Clark
War of the Spanish Succession – **Blenheim 1704** *by* James Falkn
Napoleonic – **Hougoumont** *by* Julian Paget and Derek Saunders
Napoleonic – **Waterloo** *by* Andrew Uffindell and Michael Corum

WW2 **Fort Eben Emael** *by* Tim Saunders
WW2 **Dunkirk** *by* Patrick Wilson
WW2 **Calais** *by* Jon Cooksey
WW2 **Boulogne** *by* Jon Cooksey
WW2 **Dieppe** *by* Tim Saunders
WW2 **Italy – Cassino** *by* Ian Blackwell

WW2 **Normandy – Pegasus Bridge/Merville Battery** *by* Carl Shillet
WW2 **Normandy – Utah Beach** *by* Carl Shilleto
WW2 **Normandy – Omaha Beach** *by* Tim Kilvert-Jones
WW2 **Normandy – Gold Beach** *by* Christopher Dunphie & Garry Johns
WW2 **Normandy – Gold Beach Jig** *by* Tim Saunders
WW2 **Normandy – Juno Beach** *by* Tim Saunders
WW2 **Normandy – Sword Beach** *by* Tim Kilvert-Jones
WW2 **Normandy – Operation Bluecoat** *by* Ian Daglish
WW2 **Normandy – Operation Goodwood** *by* Ian Daglish
WW2 **Normandy – Epsom** *by* Tim Saunders
WW2 **Normandy – Hill 112** *by* Tim Saunders
WW2 **Normandy – Mont Pinçon** *by* Eric Hunt
WW2 **Normandy – Cherbourg** *by* Andrew Rawson
WW2 *Das Reich* – **Drive to Normandy** *by* Philip Vickers
WW2 **Oradour** *by* Philip Beck
WW2 **Market Garden – Nijmegen** *by* Tim Saunders
WW2 **Market Garden – Hell's Highway** *by* Tim Saunders
WW2 **Market Garden – Arnhem, Oosterbeek** *by* Frank Steer
WW2 **Market Garden – Arnhem, The Bridge** *by* Frank Steer
WW2 **Market Garden – The Island** *by* Tim Saunders
WW2 **Battle of the Bulge – St Vith** *by* Michael Tolhurst
WW2 **Battle of the Bulge – Bastogne** *by* Michael Tolhurst
WW2 **Channel Islands** *by* George Forty
WW2 **Walcheren** *by* Andrew Rawson
WW2 **Remagen Bridge** *by* Andrew Rawson

Battleground Europe

OPPY WOOD

DAVID BILTON

Series editor
Nigel Cave

Pen & Sword
MILITARY

This book is dedicated to the many thousands of men who fought, suffered and in many cases died to possess Oppy and its Wood.

First published in Great Britain in 2005 by
PEN & SWORD MILITARY
an imprint of
Pen & Sword Books Limited
47 Church Street
Barnsley
South Yorkshire
S70 2AS

ISBN 1 84415 248 0

A CIP catalogue record for this book is available from the British Library

Printed and bound in Great Britain by
CPI UK

Pen & Sword Books Ltd incorporates the imprints of
Pen & Sword Aviation, Pen & Sword Naval, Pen & Sword Military, Pen & Sword Select, Pen & Sword Military Classics
Leo Cooper and Wharncliffe Books

For a complete list of Pen & Sword titles please contact:
PEN & SWORD BOOKS LIMITED
47 Church Street, Barnsley, South Yorkshire, S70 2AS, England.
E-mail: enquiries@pen-and-sword.co.uk
Website: www.pen-and-sword.co.uk

CONTENTS

Some of the debris of war found in the Oppy area.

INTRODUCTION BY SERIES EDITIOR

The Battle of Arras is, as numerous historians have observed and about which Jonathan Nicholls is one of the few to have written, the battle of the Great War fought by the British which seems to have been remembered least.

It is not as though it were a small affair, with daily casualty rates higher than both those of the Somme and Third Ypres (Passchendaele). If it is remembered at all it is because of the taking of Vimy Ridge in the opening days of the offensive by the Canadian Corps, beefed up with British infantry, artillery and support troops; or the disasters that befell the Australians at Bullecourt.

In fact the opening day of Arras was really notably successful – much to the surprise of practically everyone involved. The British hoped for a short, sharp action at Arras, but the failure of the French Chemin des Dames offensive (which the British effort was meant to support) and the impact that this had on the morale of the French army, meant that the battle dragged on much longer than had been planned or desired.

Oppy Wood serves in microcosm to illustrate this point and the causes for the failure to develop initial successes: day after day of fighting based on plans speedily prepared where ignorance of the situation on the ground was common; communications were inadequate; artillery was deficient for a variety of factors and, above all, the heroic defense and the fighting quality of German troops, who endured the same sort of extreme conditions as the men opposite.

But actions such as these should not be quite so conveniently shelved. Handy for the military historian maybe, but not for those who want to know more about the men, the individuals (above all from Hull) who fought and many of whom bled, were wounded or killed here. We should come to places like this, wonder, pay our respects and ensure that we do our bit so that 'Their Name Liveth for Evermore'.

Nigel Cave
Beaumont Hamel

ACKNOWLEDGEMENTS

My youngest daughter looked at me knowingly one afternoon and enquired, 'Are you writing another book, daddy?' 'Sorry,' I replied. 'Oh,' she sighed and slowly walked away. Later, other daughter: 'Why do you want to write these books? It's not fair. I want to play Neopets®. Who cares about the war?' 'Sorry,' I replied again. Enter son, 'Another war book, dad?' 'Yes,' I said, waiting for the request to get off the computer. 'Cool!' he said, and walked off.

Writing a book such as this is a team effort and a number of thanks are in order. Firstly to my family for putting up with the insanity and secondly to the people and organisations who have helped me with the research. In France I received invaluable help from Sylvie Leclercq, Daniel Wininger, Monique Capron, André Coilliot, Jeanine Leclercq and the Mayor of Oppy. Closer to home, thanks are due to Pam Boyd of the Princess of Wales' Own Yorkshire Regiment Museum for providing access to CSM Crabtree's journal; A Richards at the Imperial War Museum for putting me in touch, wherever possible, with the copyright holders of material in their collection: E G De Caux, Captain Sir George Clark MA, Lt Pound and Private Surfleet; the keeper of the National Archive, for allowing me to use the relevant war diaries; Anne Coulson for her excellent work in proof-reading the manuscript; as always the staff at The Prince Consort's library; Graham Reddie at the Commonwealth War Graves Commission; the late Dr Alf Peacock for permission to use the memoirs of Private Aust; G Hanwell for allowing me to use material from the diary of Private Pearson and the late Lily Perkins for letting me quote liberally from Private Beeken's diary and Tam Large for allowing me to quote from the letters of Major Traill; the photograph of Lt Col Rickman is reproduced with the permission of B Wollen and the photograph of T Southworth is courtesy of D Bayliss. Further photographs were kindly provided by Owen Challans, George Hurst, B Reynolds, S Shearsmith, P Fay, Mrs H Capstick, R Thirsk and B Alden (Duke of Edinburgh's Royal Regiment). Information about the war cemeteries is copyright and is reproduced courtesy of the Commonwealth War Graves Commission. Thanks to M Hibberd for help with the maps.

Finally, thank you to all at Pen & Sword – a pleasure to work with you once again.

PREFACE

The village of Oppy and its wood, prior to the Great War, were an inconsequential part of a Department in the north of France, more famous for its mining activities than for its agricultural output. However, with the advance of the German army in 1914, the possession of Oppy, and villages like Arleux, Willerval, Fresnes-lès-Montauban, Bailleul, Acheville and Gavrelle, allowed the Germans to construct a series of strong defence lines close to Arras; each line having the name of the village incorporated into it. Closer to Arras, the main site of the fighting, commanding the heights of Vimy and Mont St. Eloi gave the Germans both the range and visibility into a crucial junction of the Western Front, allowing them to shell the city at will. Until February 1916, when British troops took over the line, this was a battle between the French and the invader; in 1917 it was the turn of the British Army to try and dislodge the Germans from their stronghold.

Oppy church before the war.

In the city of Kingston-upon-Hull, Oppy and Oppy Wood were, and still are, a symbol of grief and loss; all four City Battalions were present on 3 May, with the resultant loss of hundreds of men – many from the same street. However, for most of the remainder of the country, it represented a failed minor part of a mostly failed offensive. Although this is most certainly true, one veteran of 3 May, William Shaw, wrote in the 1970s that 'this was one of the bloodiest days of the war. Amid the roar of artillery and the crash of shells, a blood tie was forged between the City of Hull and Oppy village… For years after the battle Oppy villagers would not go near the wood even in daylight. They said it was haunted and peace had left it forever. And so it became a place of stunted tree stumps, unexploded shells and a tangle of bracken. Until 1927 when Hull's memorial… was unveiled.' One soldier of the battle, Second Lieutenant J Harrison VC, is remembered fondly in Hull; a hospital bed was named after him, as were a group of homes. And in 2004 a memorial plaque to him was unveiled at the KC Stadium in Hull – the team he played for until he joined the army.

Trapped between Passchendaele to the north and the Somme to the south, the battles around Arras have until recently been the poor relation of the major offensives on the Western Front, even though the daily casualty rate for the 1917 Arras offensive was higher than either of the other battles; casualties during the Somme offensive ran at a daily figure of 2943, while during Third Ypres they were 2323; during the Arras offensive it was 4076. Even now, in many eyes, the whole Arras offensive in 1917 is generally overshadowed by just one action, the taking of Vimy Ridge. However, the importance of the Oppy battle is shown by the naming of a mountain in Banff Park in Alberta, Canada.

The May 1917 battle for Oppy Wood provided a historic first in air to ground co-operation. On the morning of 3 May, five Sopwith 1½ strutters of 43 Squadron carried out machine-gun attacks on German troops massing at Oppy for a counter-attack. This is regarded as the first true occasion in which the Royal Flying Corps flew close air support sorties.

The battle for Oppy, in 1914 or 1918, albeit a minor part of the whole picture, was always a key part to holding the eastern part of the German fortifications in the Arras area. Unlike its neighbour, Gavrelle, it was not taken in 1917 and, when it did fall in late 1918, all the neighbouring fortified villages fell almost immediately. Its demise signified the collapse of the German army. Small in size, nevertheless Oppy was a key component in preventing the allied armies breaking the German lines.

The château before the war.

The village shortly after the Germans had arrived.

Neuvireuil church viewed from Oppy.

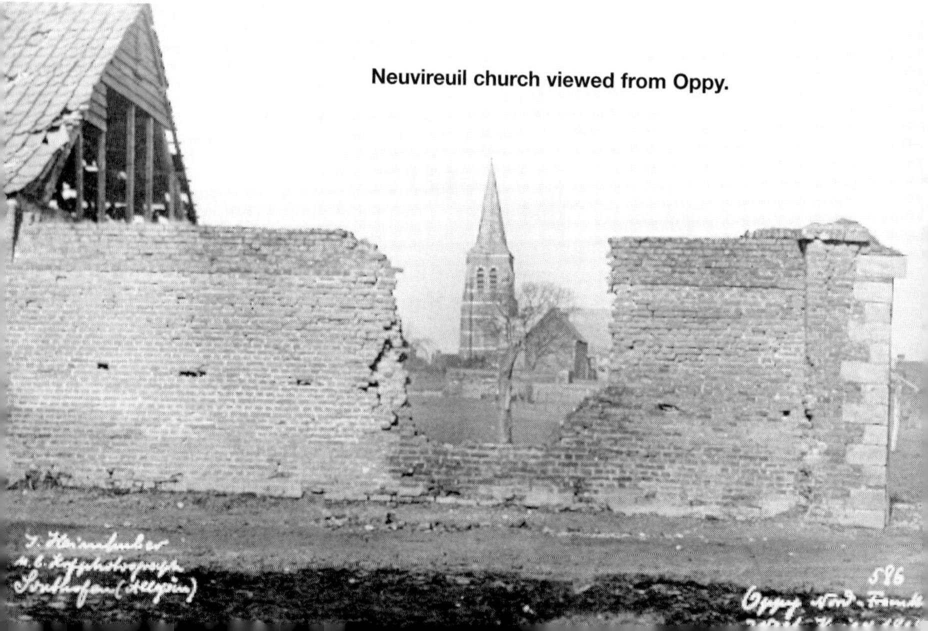

A house built during the occupation for use by officers.

Two scenes of the village during 1915.

In this book the focus will be on the battles for Oppy village and its wood, but because of the inter-relationships between the battles for the nearby villages, will necessarily also look at other areas of the battle for Arras. This will be expanded on in the tour guide where I have also included information about French sites as well.

It is also difficult to define, in some cases, which particular battle was for Oppy, so I have widened the book to include battles that overlapped. Similarly, I have broadened the tour to include general sites of interest in the area to show what is available and to allow the visitor to piece together his or her own mental image of the area and its importance. To this end I have included a number of contemporary photographs that clearly show the desolation of the whole area by 1917. In the guide I have also included all the cemeteries in the easily accessible area, whether or not they are relevant to the battle, because, while the specific battle might have finished, the war did not.

Memorial to Jack Harrison outside the Kingston Communications Stadium in Hull.

LIST OF MAPS

AUTHOR'S INTRODUCTION

The village of Oppy lies at the intersection of roads from Arleux, Bailleul-sire-Berthoult, Gavrelle, Neuvireuil and Fresnoy-en-Gohelle. Part of the Douai (or Lens) Plain, the area is essentially flat and often thought of as boring but it is good quality agricultural land producing wheat and maize. It has always been agricultural, the nearest factories being some kilometres away in Fresnes-lès-Montauban, while to the north lies Lens, a large mining area. The area was originally controlled by the Counts of Flanders (850-1180), followed by the Counts of Artois (1180-1384), the Dukes of Burgundy (1384-1516) and finally the Kings of Spain (1516-1640); it was not formally annexed to France until the Treaty of the Pyrenees in 1659. During the French Revolution it was known as Oppy the Freedom.

Looking at the area now, it is difficult to visualise what it looked like during the war as every village nearby has been completely rebuilt. In the case of Oppy, the church was rebuilt in a different position and one of the roads was slightly changed. There is no evidence of the war

The Town Hall before the war.

The Oppy Memorial when the wood was re-growing.

except for some shell holes in the wood, which is private property and unfortunately closed to visitors. At the front of the nearby church is the local French war memorial and abutting the wood is a large memorial to the men from Hull who died in the 3 May attack.

Being the major communications link in the area, the city of Arras to the west of Oppy is the main prize in the Pas-de-Calais, and, to many people, the Battle of Arras means the short action in 1940. Unlike Gavrelle, where the church has spang marks on its walls, no events of any military significance occurred in Oppy during the Second World War.

The village square in use as a remount depot.

A view of the Town Hall along the newly re-named village square, Wilhelmplatz.

The village during rebuilding.

The view from the church spire of the road to Gavrelle, taken in the 1920s.

German Christmas festivities in 1916; a tree built out of unexploded British artillery shells.

ACCOMMODATION IN THE AREA

Hotels, guesthouses, Bed and Breakfasts come and go. Therefore there is no guarantee that these will exist in a few years' time but at the time of writing (late 2004) the following are recommended by the regional tourist office. All are in relatively close proximity to the battlefield described in the book.

Arras and area

Astoria Carnot, Place Foch, Arras
Atria Hôtel Mercure, 58 Boulevard Carnot, Arras
Holiday Inn, Rue du Docteur Brassart, Arras
Hôtel aux Grandes Arcades, 8 Grand Place, Arras
Hôtel d'Angleterre, Place du Maréchal Foch, Arras
Hôtel Diamant, 5 Place des Héros
Hôtel Le Moderne, 1 Boulevard Faidherbe, Arras
Ibis, rue de Justice, Arras
Le Régent, 5 rue Anatole France, Arras
Les Trois Luppars, 49 Grand Place, Arras
L'Univers, Place de la Croix Rouge, Arras
Restaurant de l'Hôtel du Golf, rue Briquet Taillander, Anzin-Saint-Aublin.
Hôtel Campanile, ZA les Alouettes, Saint Nicholas.
Hôtel La Belle Etoile, ZA les Alouettes, Saint Nicholas

Douai area

Le Chambord, 3509 route de Tournai, Douai
Ibis Romagnant/Douai-centre, Place St. Amé, Douai
Le Grand Cerf, 46 rue Saint-Jacques
La Terrasse, 36 terrasse Saint-Pierre, Douai
Le Volubilis, Boulevard Vauban, Douai
Le Manoir de Fourcy, 48 rue de la Gare, Corbehem

Lens area

Espace Bollart, 13 route de Béthune, Lens
Hôtel de France, 2 Place de la Gare, Lens
Hôtel Gril Campanile, route de la Bassée, Lens
Hôtel Le Jardin, 29 place de la Republique, Lens

Oppy area
Hôtel de Bretagne, Vitry-en-Artois
Hôtel de la Gare, Biache-St. Vaast
L'Aquarium, 50 route Nationale, Fresnes-lès-Montauban
Le Manoir, 35 route Nationale, Gavrelle

There are also Gîtes and Chambre d'Hôtes; further information on these can be obtained from Gîtes de France du Nord at 89 Boulevard de la Liberté, BP 1210 – 59013 Lille Cedex. And for those willing to brave the elements there are also campsites, the closest to Oppy being at Biache-St. Vaast.

Chapter One

1914-1916
The Germans Arrive

On 1 August uncertainty vanished when Germany invaded Luxembourg; war now seemed inevitable. As if to further re-enforce this eventuality, the next day the German government presented Belgium with an ultimatum requiring her to let German troops march over her territory and, on 3 August, declared war on France.

In order to protect herself, to help her allies and to defend Belgian neutrality, guaranteed by treaty obligations between Britain and Belgium, Britain had no option but to demand that Germany call off her invasion of Belgium; failure to co-operate would mean that a state of war would exist between them. On having received no reply by the midnight (Central European time) 4 August deadline, the British government declared war. The stroke of

Leaving for the front.

11pm by Big Ben signified the start of the Great War for civilisation.

By this time the German army had already occupied Luxembourg and cavalry had crossed into Belgium; while on the day that Britain entered the war the German Second Army had advanced on Liege. The Schlieffen plan was now in motion; for it to succeed the deadlines it imposed had to be met.

Although Belgian resistance was stiff, the German advance was rapid and on 8 August the French had to send an infantry regiment to hold the Meuse bridges north of Dinant and link with the Belgians at Namur. Realising that the Germans were preparing a wide sweep on the west side of the Meuse, the French moved their Fifth Army to hold the line behind Namur and up the Sambre to link with the British Expeditionary Force; in turn the BEF would link up with the Belgians to form a complete defensive line. This would mean stiffer resistance than the Germans had expected and, to counteract this move, von Bulow ordered von Kluck's First Army south, instead of southwest, deviating from the Schleiffen Plan and thereby reducing the size of the western wheel of the troops.

On 20 August the Germans entered Brussels. In a show of strength the entire First Army marched through the city; it took three days and nights for the 320,000 men to pass through. By the start of the third week of August the occupation of Belgium was all but complete but this short period of time had given the Allies time to deploy and the German First, Second and Third Armies (the cream of the army) now faced the BEF and the French Fifth Army across the Sambre. Possibly more importantly, the small and weak Belgian Army, together with the

French mobilisation.

Franctireurs fighting German troops in Lowen.

civilian population, had set an example of heroism and determination to the rest of the world.

Assured that there would be little opposition from the Belgians, the Germans were both surprised and angered when, from the moment they crossed the frontier, they found themselves fired on. Their immediate response was to blame civilian snipers. Similarly, bridges, tunnels and telegraph lines that were blown up had to be the work of civilian saboteurs. The rapid advance meant that German troops did not always know who was in front of them or to their sides and as a result they sometimes fired upon each other unknowingly; looting alcohol to quench their thirst during the long marches also resulted in a number of shooting incidents. Again, believing such casualties to be the result of the work of franc-tireurs, the invaders went looking for revenge.

The shooting of civilians as a reprisal began on the first day of the invasion; convinced that Catholic priests were organising and encouraging the franc-tireurs the Germans decided that the problem was best solved by filling the civilian population with fear. Systematically the Germans began to burn villages and execute civilians. The first executions took place at Warsage (six civilians shot) and the first village to be burned was Battice.

Such reprisals had been planned by the Germans before the war; they had even had posters printed before the invasion that listed the offences that would be punishable by death. The posters also warned that not just individuals, but the whole area, where a hostile act took

Priests were suspected of inciting civilians to violence – a priest going off to war.

place, would be considered responsible; hostages would be taken at random and shot. Behind them, the advancing armies brought a trail of burning and death with mass executions replacing individual executions. On 19 August, the town of Aerschot suffered the first mass execution. After rounding up the population in the town square with men on one side and women on the other, 150 individuals were picked out at random and shot; the process was repeated at Andenne, Tamines and Dinant (612 executed, one of whom was a three-week-old baby).

Visé had been occupied on the first day of the invasion and the German army had moved on. However, on 23 August there was a

The site of a mass execution in Dinant.

report of sniping and in response the Germans sent an infantry regiment to execute a selection of the population and then set fire to the town. Similar occurrences happened all over Belgium but events in the city of Louvain stand out above them all.

A satirical view of the executions.

Until 18 August, Louvain had been the tactical Headquarters of the Belgian Army. It was a medieval city, famous across the world for its library that had been founded in 1426; housing some 230,000 volumes it also contained a unique collection of medieval manuscripts. The city also boasted many fine examples of Gothic architecture and a collection of Flemish masters. On the second day of the occupation a German soldier was shot in the leg; the occupation forces claimed it was the work of a sniper. Believing that government and local officials were encouraging resistance, executions began and the Germans selected hostages from the population. To make matters worse, on 25 August, Belgian troops carried out a raid on German rearguard troops at Antwerp who fell back in confusion on Louvain. In the city shots were exchanged, again the Germans claimed they were result of civilian action.

German reaction was as swift as it was horrific. They went through the city on a wanton rampage of looting, burning, shooting and general

The ruins of Louvain.

Anti-German propoganda – hiding behind the white flag.

destruction. The next day General von Luttwitz, the Military Governor in Brussels, calmly announced to the horrified American and Spanish Ambassadors that the Germans would destroy the city the next day as a reprisal. Starting on 26 August, the library was destroyed with its valuable contents, while the church of St. Pierre and the Town Hall were damaged. Whole streets were set on fire and civilians shot. The pillage ended abruptly on 30 August, the day after the first reports appeared in the world press.

Back at the frontiers the German advance continued and the Allied line moved back towards Paris. In the west the BEF was fighting the German First Army at Mons in a battle where the khaki-clad men of the British Army came into their own. However, like the Belgians, they were overwhelmed by numbers and fell back. However, this battle held up von von Kluck's army for a day and gave the Allies a short breathing space because the Germans did not press on immediately, believing that the British would fight as they had at Mons. When they did realise that it was a retreat it was too late for the BEF to be encircled. To the east the French Fifth Army was also pulling back from its positions on the Sambre.

On 24 August 1,000,000 Germans invaded France; the great retreat had begun.

During the 13 days of the retreat, five of the seven German armies scythed down towards Paris on a 75 mile front. For the troops on both sides they were days of endless marching under a scorching sun; marching until nearly every man seemed to have nails sticking through the soles of his boots into his blistered feet, and the horses had worn their shoes wafer-thin. Every movement was hampered by refugees. Order and counter-order plagued both sides, communication by wireless and telephone was often desperately slow. Each side had its special troubles. The French were subject to unaccountable panics, and inclined to see spies everywhere. The back areas of formations which had suffered severely were infested with pillaging deserters.

The Germans, as has been previously mentioned, saw franc-tireurs lurking behind every bush. Their advance had been so rapid that supply lines were stretched beyond coping with the consequence that there was a good deal of marauding and drunkenness, with the usual deterioration of discipline. Their heavy-handed treatment of the civilian population during this period helped to foster the 'Campaign of Hate'.

The German advance continued but the position was about to change with the Marne Manoeuvre or, as it is more popularly called, the Battle of the Marne. False German intelligence reports indicated that their western flanks were exposed and that there were large numbers of British troops landing in Belgium. Responding to von Bulow's urgent appeals, von Kluck had altered the direction of his First

A wishful view of the German retreat on the Marne.

Army to swing east of Paris instead of west as originally planned in order to follow French troops thought to be moving in a southeasterly direction. This exposed his right flank to Gallieni's fortress troops in Paris. On 5 September Gallieni struck at the exposed flank of the German II Corps (part of First Army) with the hastily composed French Sixth Army. This threat to the flank was so serious that von Kluck was forced to halt his advance and face west to meet it, thereby creating a gap between the German First and Second armies; a gap into which the BEF marched. By 9 September the Germans were in retreat; their swift bid for victory had failed.

Further north the German Army was pushing towards Arras and on 6 September German cavalry entered the city. After an occupation of just three days, French Saphis (light cavalry) pushed the Germans out. Apart from looting, the occupation was not violent but the Germans did requisition large amounts of money and goods.

French troops defending Arras.

Almost immediately after their departure, what became known as the 'Martyrdom of Arras' began. The retreating German troops quickly dug themselves in, in some cases only four kilometres away from the city and invested the city from north to south; a siege that was to last for thirty-one months, ending with the Battle of Arras on 9 April.

A view of an entrance to Arras sent home by Gefreiter Franz Magg.

The German bombardments began on 6 October and in the next two days over 1000 shells were fired into to the city (only the station and the barracks were in French military use). Most damage was done to the central quarters that contained the finest buildings in the city. The Hotel de Ville was burned down on 7 October and a few days later, sixty-nine shells destroyed the Belfry. Afterwards, the bombardments slackened but each day the city was shelled. At times the shelling would break out with great fury; 6000 shells, mostly incendiary, fell on 9 July 1915, setting fire to the Cathedral and the Abbey of St. Vaast. By the time the siege was lifted, 962 buildings had been completely destroyed, 1595 destroyed beyond repair and 1735 badly hit. Out of the 4521 houses in the city, only 292 went undamaged.

A view of the damage caused by the German shelling of Arras.

Germany's hopes of a decisive victory now came to rest on the right wing of its army and its ability to outflank the Allied troops. This resulted in a series of battles that moved north and towards the coast. The object was not to get to the sea, but to get behind the Allies.

When the French Second Army failed to outflank the Germans, Falkenhayn, on 26 September, launched an attack against the French on his central flank; attacking against prepared positions the German troops were repulsed with heavy losses. Joffre in the meantime shifted XI Corps to Amiens and by 1 October had two further Corps plus three infantry and two cavalry divisions in transit for Amiens, Arras, Lens and Lille. The Second French Army, now consisting of eight corps, held a 100-kilometre front with orders to hold rather than outflank. At the same time, two infantry corps and one cavalry corps moved on Arras and took up positions between Vimy and the Scarpe valley.

> *To the east of Arras, Conneau's Cavalry Corps was being pressed by the 2nd German Cavalry Corps and the I Bavarian Reserve Corps. These had occupied Douai on the evening of the 1st of October, and the next day were continuing their advance north-westward and westward when they came upon French infantry in position on the rolling downs between Monchy-le-Preux and Arras; these were the first units of the detachment of the Second Army* (later to become the Tenth Army), *under Maud'huy, which had been formed on the 30th of September from the X and XXI Corps and a Provisional Corps (consisting of the 45th, 70th and 77th Divisions). This Army being incompletely concentrated, Maud'huy had thrown forward two divisions of the Provisional Corps to gain time, and this they succeeded in doing, despite the superiority of the enemy.*

The German view of the cavalry attacks around Arras.

French cavalry in Vimy.

On the 3rd of October the X Corps was ready for action and moved forward south of Arras against the German IV Corps. On this and the next day there was hard fighting both here and farther south, where the Territorial Group was in action against the Guard Corps.

To the north-east of Arras the I Bavarian Reserve Corps pressed back the left of the Provisional Corps on the Vimy Ridge, and by the evening of the 4th the situation appeared to be critical and even the arrival of the 45th French Division on the following day failed to restore matters entirely. However, though on the north of Arras the Germans were still advancing, the progress of the Guard and IV Corps to the south was definitely checked towards evening. The near approach of the Germans to the town rendered necessary the evacuation of the inhabitants, which was carried out on the 6th, despite a heavy bombardment that continued intense (sic) *for three days. The front lines installed themselves in the eastern suburbs of Arras, and the battle gradually died away without either side being able to make any important progress.*

Ehre dem Andenken
des Herrn
Franz Stempfl
Unteroffizier
im Kgl. Bayer. 1. Reserve-Infanterie-Regiment
gefallen am 6. Oktober 1914
bei Arras, Nordfrankreich
„Mein Jesus, Barmherzigkeit!“

A German casuality of the attack on Arras.

On the 4th of October, Foch was entrusted by Joffre with the task of coordinating the actions of the Second and Tenth French Armies, the Territorial Group and the two Cavalry Corps under Conneau and de Mitry – in a word, of all the French forces north of the Oise. Foch took up his headquarters at Doullens. He found that on the north of Arras, as well as on the east and south, the battle was becoming stabilized. Since the

Zum frommen Andenken
im Gebete
an den tugendſamen Jüngling
Johann Grill,
Unterbutter-Sohn, Pfarrei Inzell,
Infanteriſt im 1. Reſ.-Inf. Regt.,
12. Kompagnie,
welcher am 4. Oktober 1914 bei Arras
in Nordfrankreich im Alter von 25
Jahren den Heldentod fürs Vater-
land ſtarb.

Haſt fürs Vaterland geſtritten,
Haſt den Heldentod erlitten;
Und als wahrer Tugendheld
Schau'ſt Du nun die beſſ're Welt.
Süßeſter Jeſus, ſei mir nicht Richter, ſondern
Erlöſer! (300 Tg. Ablaß).

A German casualty.

1st of October the German 1st and 2nd Cavalry Corps had been struggling for supremacy with Conneau's and de Mitry's horsemen between Arras and Lens; on either side infantry had later been brought into action, the German I Bavarian Reserve Corps, followed by the German XIV Corps and the French XXI Corps. On the 6th, the Germans reached the front Carency-Notre Dame de Lorette, which proved to be the high-water mark of their advance; the French counter-offensive commenced on the 7th, and after three days heavy fighting the XXI Corps retook Carency and installed itself firmly on the line from there to Loos. Here, too, the fighting subsided as the battle spread farther and farther to the north, and on the 10th of October the opposing cavalry had become engaged in the Lys plains. The battle front of the Tenth French Army, held from south to north by the X, Provisional and XXI Corps, ran from Wailly through the eastern suburbs of Arras by Carency and Loos. Facing the Tenth Army were the IV and XV German Corps (from the Aisne) *and the I Bavarian Reserve Corps* (from Lorraine).

Falkenhayn had directed the Sixth Army, commanded by Rupprecht, to attack Arras on 28 September with a plan to hold the French troops at Arras and wheel north round the city; however, to the south the

The defenders of the Oppy/Gavrelle area were local men.

A French barricade on the road from Arras to Lille.

resistance of the French territorials was weakening. By the evening of 4 October the French positions at Arras were threatened with encirclement. However, the appointment of Foch as Chief of Staff for these northern operations galvanised the commanders of the units involved and by 5 October the Allied line from the Oise to the north of Arras was secure. The war was now to move north to Flanders.

The area around Oppy played a small part in the October battle for Arras. During the early morning of 2 October French and German troops clashed along a line between Méricourt, Fresnoy, Oppy, Gavrelle, Roeux and Monchy. Losses were heavy on both sides. One notable action occurred at Gavrelle, the next village south of Oppy, when a scouting party of French Dragoons came in range of a German machine gunner sited in the window of the local windmill. Twelve French soldiers were killed, including the officer in charge. The windmill was destroyed during the fighting in 1917 and was not rebuilt after the war.

Fighting continued around Arras until almost the end of the war and attacks by the French and British to the north of Arras in 1915 resulted in the Germans building a three part defensive system; the first line

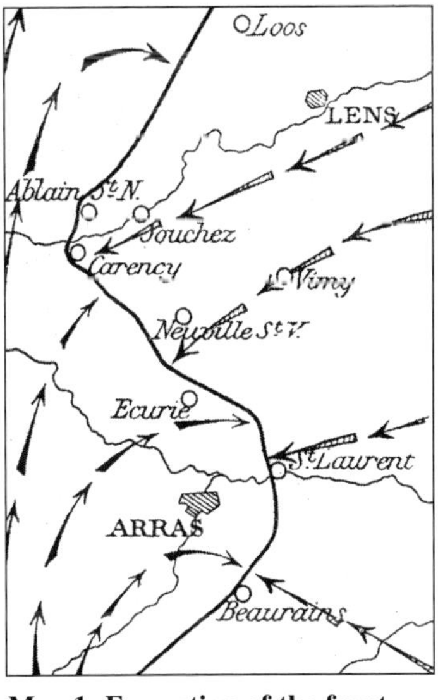

Map 1: Formation of the front – October 1914.

To spur his troops on the Kaiser visited the Arras front on 4 October 1914.

being close to Arras, the second line in front of Vimy, running south through Athies, while the third line ran south in front of Méricourt, Arleux, Oppy, Gavrelle and Fampoux. Later a fourth defensive line was added, the Drocourt-Quéant switch.

In spring 1915, Foch launched an offensive against heavily-fortified trenches to the north of Arras with the aim of breaking through to Loos and Douai. On 9 May after a violent artillery bombardment with 75

Map 2: Panorama of the Oppy area of the Western Front.

and 155 cm guns, lasting several hours, the French Tenth Army attacked on a frontage of four miles. Advancing rapidly in the centre, the French troops advanced 4½ kilometres in an hour, leaving the troops on the right and left behind. Such a rapid penetration had not been expected and the French were unable to send up reinforcements in time, allowing the Germans to rush their troops to the front in trucks and stop the advance. The battle continued until 19 June by which time the Germans had been forced back at Notre Dame-de-Lorette, Ablain-St.-Nazaire, Souchez and Neuville-St. Vaast. Captain Humbert noted the unpleasantness of the new trenches the French now occupied:

> *Countless dead lay buried in the parapets of the trenches, dug in the thick of the battle during May. At every step, protruding through the wall, one saw here a hand or foot, there a tuft of hair or a piece of a tunic. Corpses on every hand... We were living among the dead.*

A French counterattack just outside Arras.

The next offensive was a joint Anglo-French attack, on 25 September, again to the north of Arras. In liaison with the French Tenth Army the British troops attacked near Loos with the French attacking further south at Vimy and Souchez. The French attack force consisted of seventeen infantry divisions on a twelve mile frontage, supported by 420 heavy guns and 670 field guns; two 'cavalry divisions were to be ready to press through any gap made in the German defences'. To the north the British attack was to be on a frontage of six miles with six divisions supported with 114 heavy calibre guns; in reserve were three divisions of infantry and the Cavalry Corps and Indian Cavalry Corps.

French trenches at Mont St. Eloi near Arras.

With heavy artillery the Germans were able to shell Arras from a considerable distance.

An inhabitant of Gavrelle with some of the occupying troops – relationships were not always poor.

French trenches outside Arras.

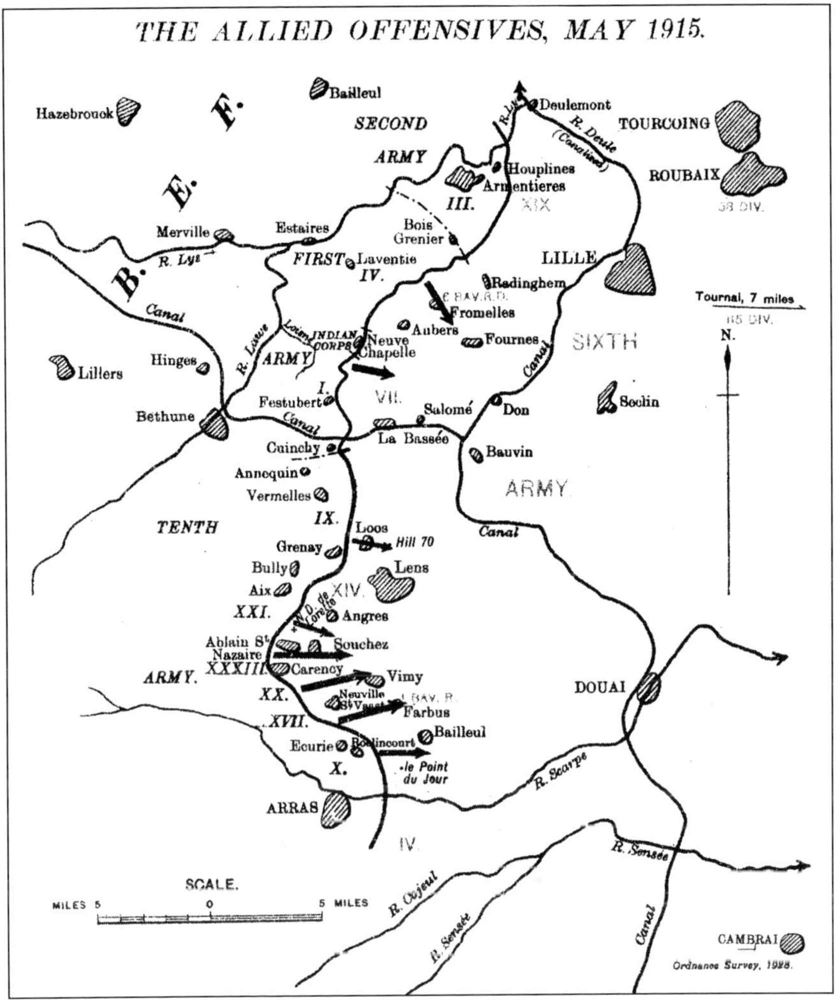

Map 3: Allied offensives – May 1915.

After much desperate fighting, progress was halted by German reinforcements and much of the liberated territory returned to German occupation.

Even though the British Army took over the Arras front in March 1916 there was no big breakout battle; although in May 1916 there was a significant attack by the Germans at Vimy ridge. Until April 1917 there was little change to the position of the front-line and as a result Oppy was a quiet area where troops could rest and even fraternise with the local population. However, in March 1917, the population was moved out and sent to un-occupied France through Switzerland and the

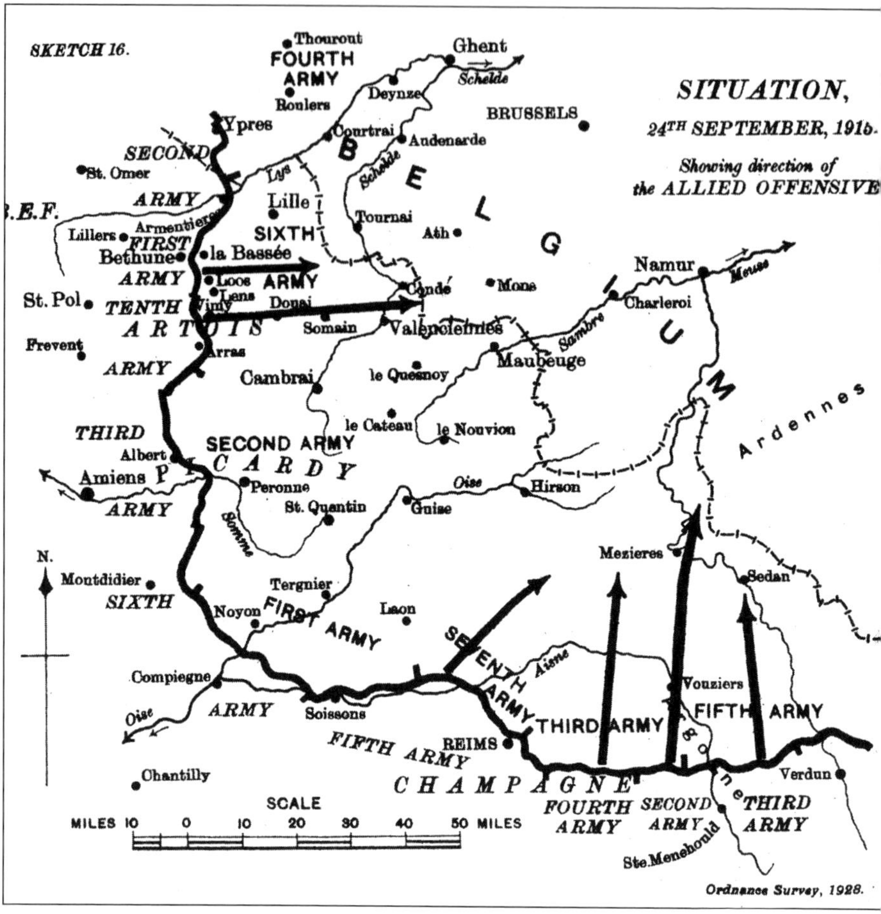

Map 4: Franco-British offensive – September 1915.

whole area became a potential battle zone.

While the initial stages of the German advance were taking place in France, tens of thousands of men in Britain and Ireland were volunteering for the armed forces. One particular group of these men would find themselves in the trenches at Oppy, two and a half years after they first enlisted – they were the Hull Pals.

Formed between September and November 1914, the Hull Pals consisted of four front-line battalions and a reserve battalion; nearly five thousand men who had enlisted for a variety of reasons; some no doubt in order to avenge Belgium and make the Germans pay for the atrocities they had perpetrated on defenceless men and women, others

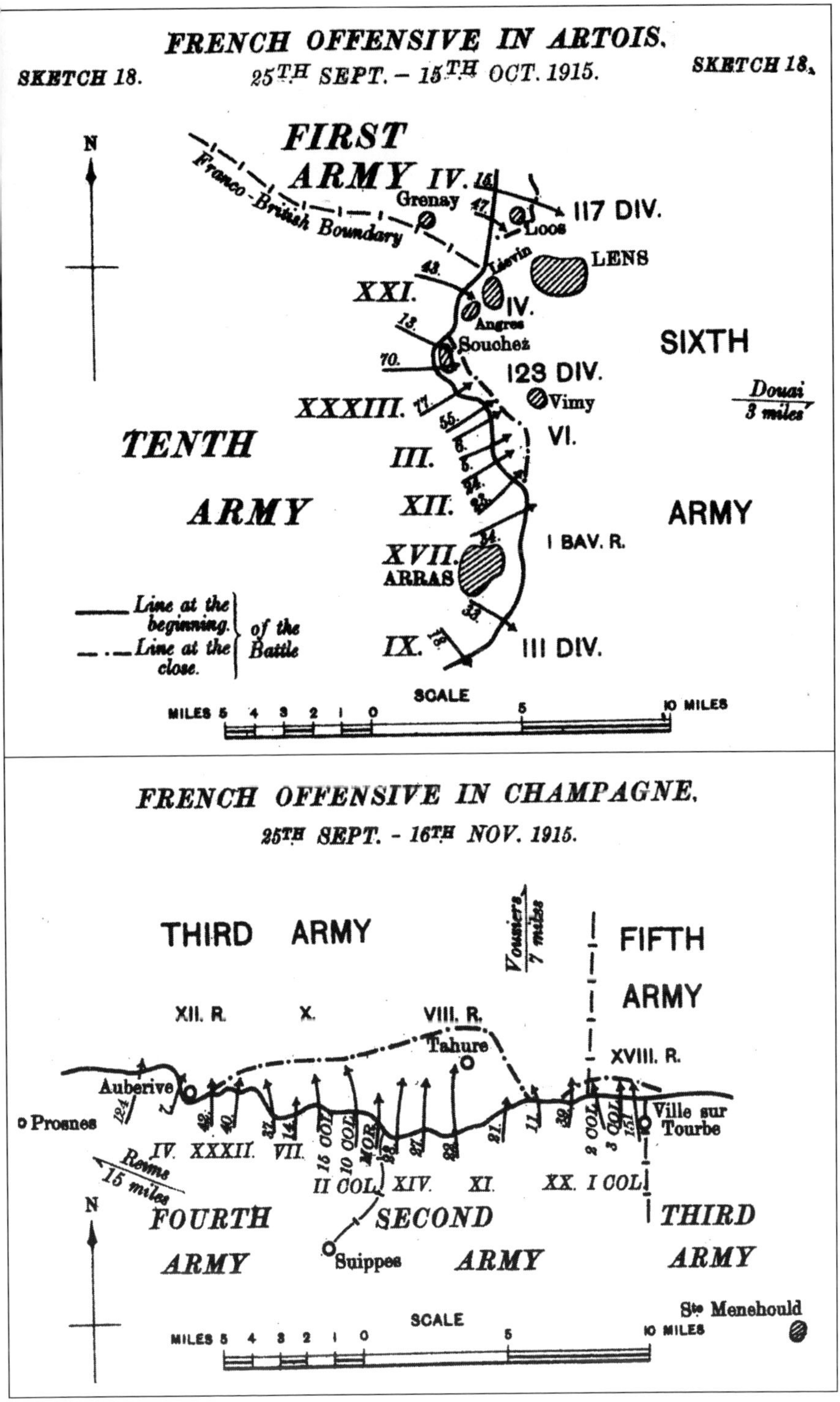

Map 5: French offensive in Artois and Champagne – September-November 1915.

The Hull Pals in training.

out of a sense of duty to the King and Empire, but mostly out of a sense of adventure and not wanting to be left out of the war.

After training in and around Hull, they moved out to the East Yorkshire coast to guard it against a German invasion. After further training in and around Ripon they moved south to Salisbury Plain for final training prior to overseas service. At the beginning of December 1915, an advance party was sent to France but quickly recalled. Instead of fighting the Germans they had joined up to fight, they were to be sent to the Suez Canal to guard against a Turkish attack. It was not until March 1916 that they arrived on the Western Front. After service on the Somme for a year, they moved north to the Arras battlefront.

Joseph Hartl , of the 1st Bavarian Reserve Infantry Regiment, killed during an attack on the British lines near Arras on 5 June 1916.

Chapter Two

April 1917
The First Battle

Remaining on the defensive, the Germans, determined to prevent a breakthrough had 'strengthened their positions with new lines of deeply echeloned defences, protected with wire entanglements and blockhouses in reinforced concrete'. Between Arras and Douai, besides the old defensive lines of 1914 and 1915, there were three new positions collectively forming the Hindenburg Line. As well as the new positions the Germans had, in accordance with von Bulow's instructions, improved their defensive tactics by organising their reserves for immediate counter-attacks at specific points; points at which the Germans felt the attacking troops would lose their cohesion after taking the initial positions.

Gavrelle windmill showing shell damage.

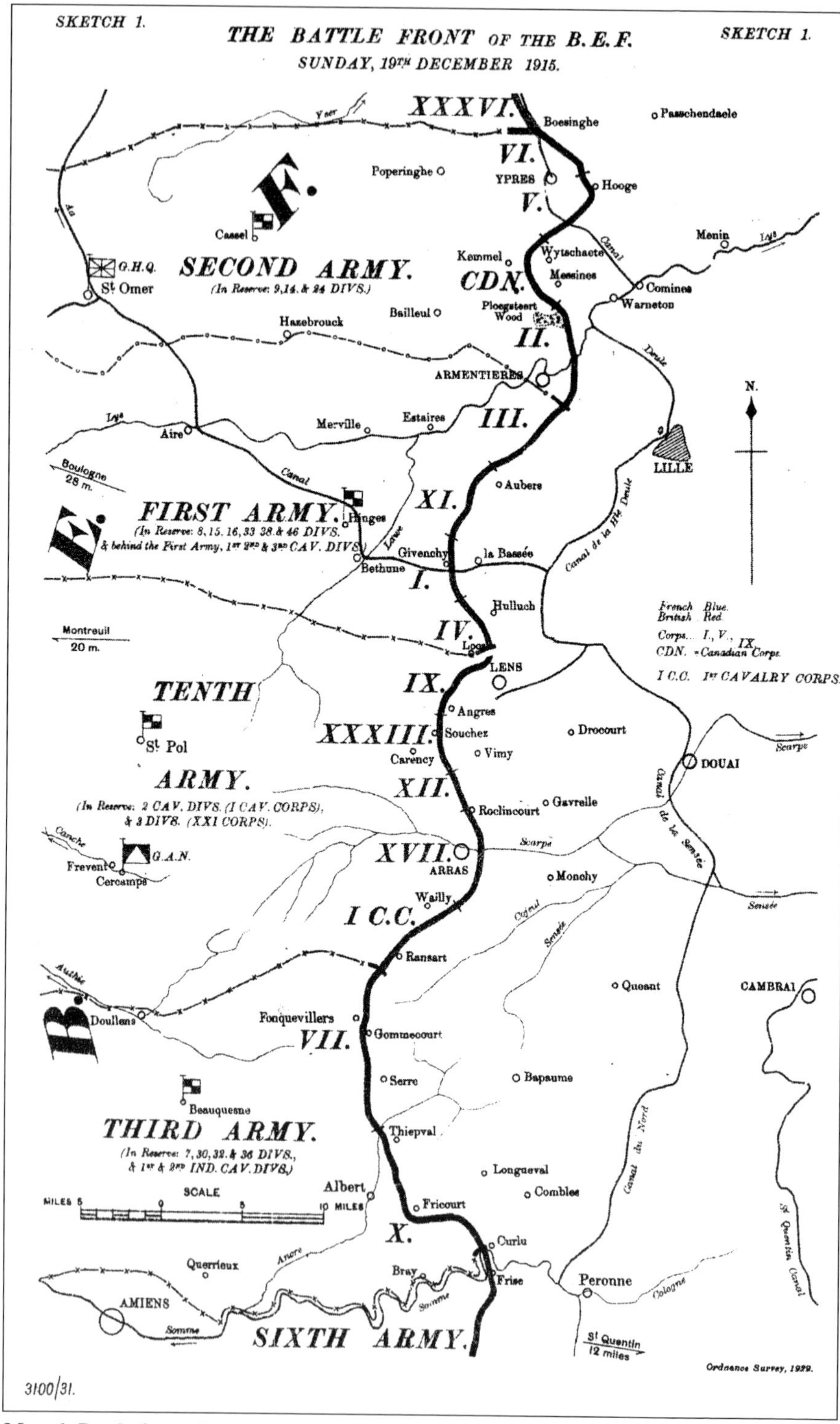

Map 6: Battle front, December 1915. (note the Tenth and Sixth armies are French)

Timed for 8 April 1917, the original Arras plan had been produced by Haig in cooperation with Joffre and had been designed as a major offensive by the British First and Third Armies in the Vimy-Arras area. However, with Nivelle becoming the French Commander in Chief, the British contribution was to be subordinated to the main effort: the French attack on the Chemin-des-Dames.

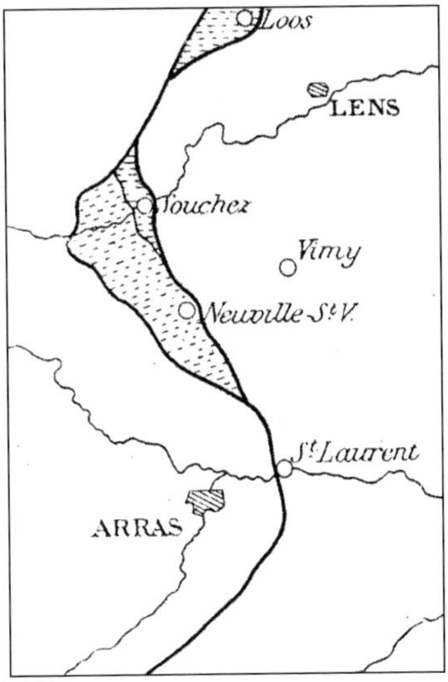

Map 7: Battle front around Arras, 1916. Shaded areas indicate allied advances made in 1915.

The initial sector for the British attack was unique. Vimy Ridge, a significant objective, was honeycombed with tunnels and caves, giving the Germans safe shelter. On the British side of the line, underneath the city of Arras, was a labyrinth of tunnels and caves and a large sewer system that followed an underground stream. Discovered by the British shortly after taking over the sector, these were quickly seen as a way to provide a safe, covered approach to the front line. Throughout the winter of 1916/17, in great secrecy, the caves, tunnels and sewers were joined together and by March 1917 it was almost complete; the construction work provided access to No Man's Land near the Cambrai and Bapaume roads. In the caves there was accommodation for 30,000 men, with lighting, proper drainage, a power plant, administrative centres, ventilation and a hospital.

Reserve troops in the village of Billy-Montigny close to Oppy.

Maison-Rouge near Arras. This clearly shows the damage done by British bombardments before the offensive.

On 2 January Allenby, Gough and Horne received their orders from Haig for an attack to commence on 8 April (later changed to 9 April). Third Army (Allenby) was to be the centre of the attack, advancing due east, while to the north was First Army (Horne) who was tasked with taking Vimy Ridge. In the south was Gough's Fifth Army; its rôle in the planned attack had been reduced by the German withdrawals in February and March.

On the sixth day of the artillery bombardment the offensive began. Easter Monday was a day of sleet and snow, after a winter of atrocious weather; each man was chilled to the bone; the infantry advanced weighed down with heavy packs and the weight of the water they were absorbing from the weather. Regardless of the conditions, the

Vimy was reduced to rubble well before the attack – the church in 1916.

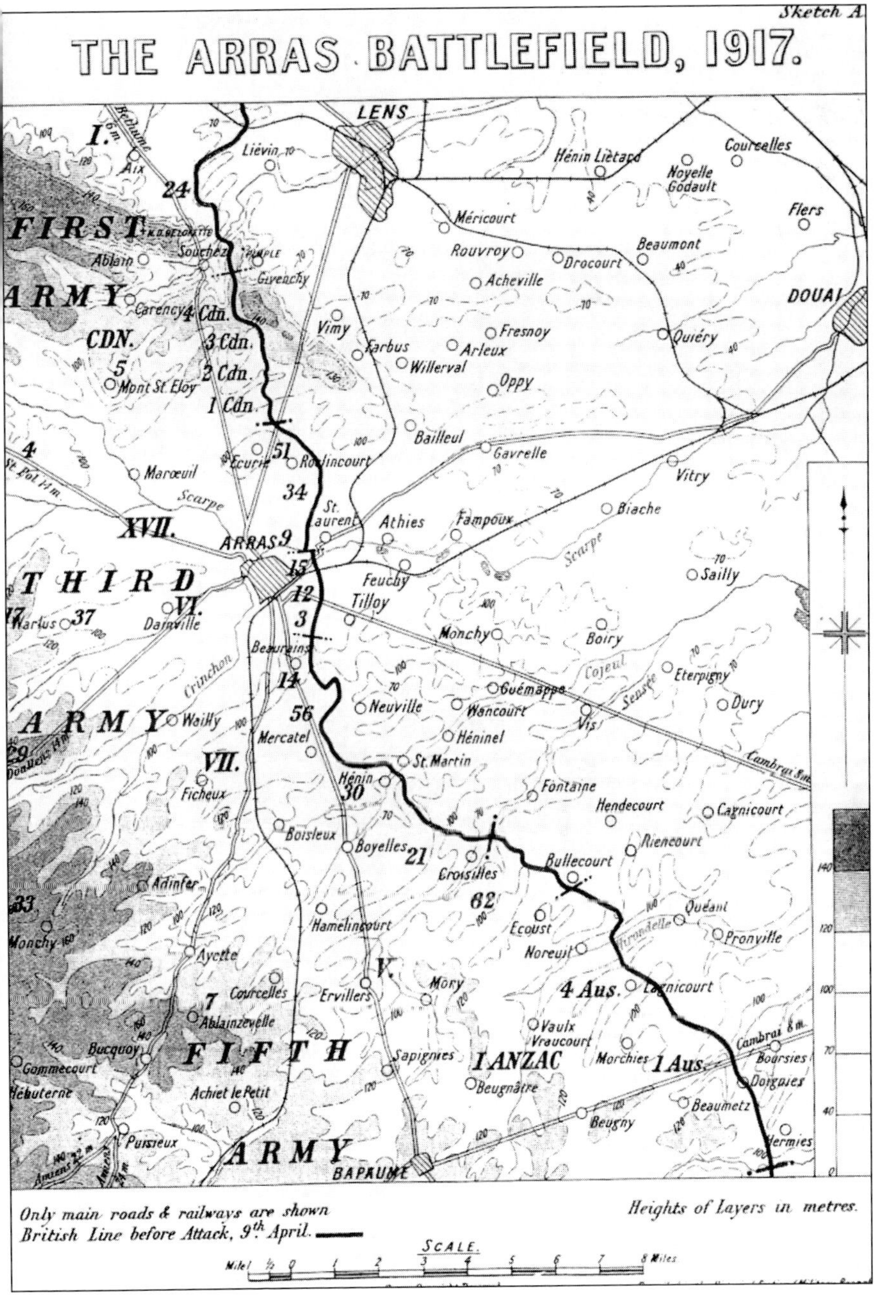

Map 8: The Arras battlefront, 1917.

A 1917 aerial photograph showing Gavrelle; the road to Oppy is at the middle top right.

Canadians on the left flank quickly took their objectives while on the right flank – 51 (Highland) Division – the attack did not proceed as planned. However, the problems on the right did not stop the advance in the centre.

Three days later the British Army had taken Neuville Vitasse, St. Martin, Wancourt, Monchy, Feuchy, Athies, Fampoux and the Point-du-Jour; the Oppy-Méricourt third line defences had been breached. The road lay open for the advance to move in the direction of Oppy.

> *In spite of the great victory achieved by the British armies in the opening phases of the Battle of Arras, Sir Douglas Haig never believed that 'any great strategical results were likely to be gained' by following up this success.*

He would have preferred to move the men and material north for the coming offensive. However, Haig was not a free agent. The Arras offensive was a part of Nivelle's strategic plan for a decisive breakthrough on the Western Front in 1917 but was subsidiary to the French attack on the Aisne. The much-vaunted French offensive was launched on 16 April. It began indifferently and quickly gave rise to concern and disappointment.

On the same day as the French offensive, Haig conferred with his army commanders over the next assault that this time would directly involve Oppy. By 18 April it was clear that there was opposition, by a number of corps and divisional commanders, to the plan and, as a result, the attack on the Oppy-Méricourt line was changed to a local attack south of Lens. The main thrust would now be south of Oppy along a nine-mile front from Gavrelle, Roeux, Guémappe and Fontaine-lès-Croisilles, starting on 23 April.

After twenty-four hours of heavy fighting during which the Germans had launched continuous counter-attacks, the British line had advanced from one to two miles across the whole front. British troops remained in possession of Gavrelle and Guémappe, and the high ground overlooking Fontaine-lès-Croisilles and Chérisy. They had also made progress to the east of Monchy-le-Preux on the western slopes of Infantry Hill and had gained a foothold on Greenland Hill.

On 26 April, at GHQ, Lieutenant General Kiggel, Haig's Chief of Staff, informed Generals Horne and Allenby that the offensive would be continued.

> *Objectives would again be limited with no deep penetration intended, partly because the existing front line was considered an unsuitable base for a major offensive, and partly because Haig had decided that no fresh divisions were to be brought in to reinforce the tired and under-strength formations.*

Prior to the next major assault, two minor operations would take place on 28 April; Third Army would take Roeux, the Chemical Works and the spur east of Monchy-le-Preux while First Army would capture Oppy and Arleux. The main offensive would follow on 3 May and would be launched along the whole front.

German photograph showing Canadians preparing for the offensive.

The Third Army operations of 28 April were even less successful than those of 23 April but, at the northern end of the front, the attack was a limited success. Of the three divisions involved, 63 (Royal Naval) Division, to the south of Oppy, failed completely, leaving 2 Division with no protection on its right wing. Despite heavy fighting it too failed in its objective to take Oppy. On the left flank of the attack, 1 Canadian Division achieved the only tangible success of the operation, capturing Arleux.

The First Army attack on Arleux and Oppy – 28 April

The German third line made a big loop round the village of Arleux and from the eastern side of the loop a switch joined it to the next line of defence, the Rouvroy-Fresnes position, west of Neuvireuil. First Army had been ordered to break through the Oppy line which was already in British hands to the north of Gavrelle and capture the villages of Oppy and Arleux, putting the British troops over half-way across the Arleux loop.

A German casualty of the British offensive on 9 April 1917.

The boundary between XIII Corps and the Canadian Corps ran from 300 yards south of Arleux to the southern corner of the wood south of Fresnoy. 63 Division was on the right flank of XIII Corps attack and was to form a flank that protected the right of 2 Division. Previous attacks on Gavrelle by 63 Division had resulted in its capture but their success had created a salient that had ramifications for the attack. The plan called for an attack in echelon with one battalion advancing from Gavrelle for a distance of 750 yards north of the Fresnes road where it would establish its right flank along the road. Another battalion would form up west of the Oppy line and, in the area previously occupied by 2 Division, advance due east until it was aligned with the first battalion. Such a

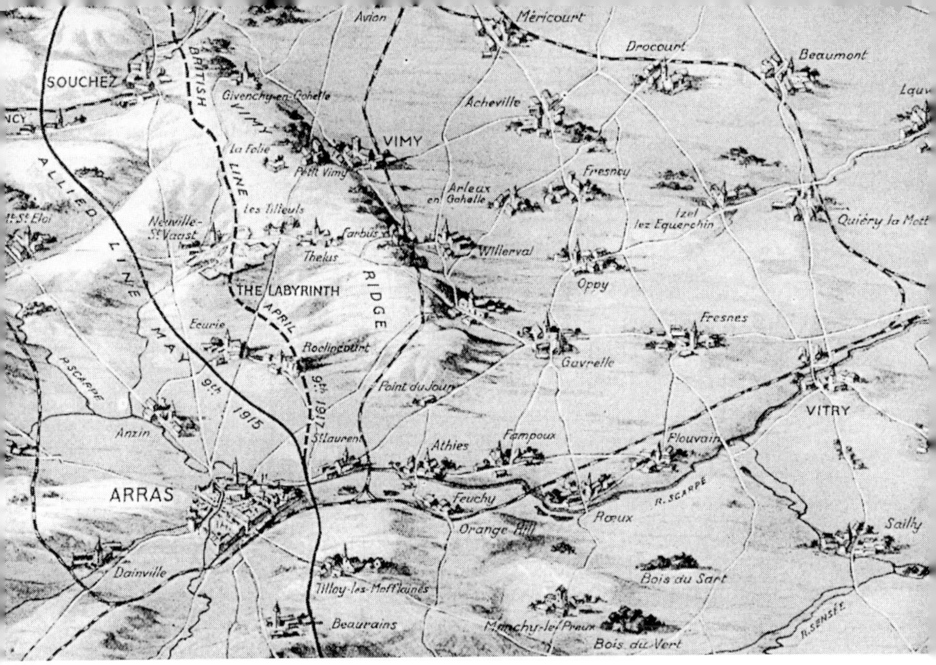

Map 9: Contour map of the Arras battlefront, 1917.

plan was not without risk because both attacks were to be separate, starting from bases a thousand yards apart and with separate barrages and only coming into contact at the final objective, one thousand yards ENE of Gavrelle. The attack on the northern sector by 1 Royal Marines was a complete failure; that of 2 Royal Marines was a partial success. It gained 'a good deal of ground and beat off a succession of counter-attacks, but suffered from artillery fire and fell back to almost its original position at dusk', leaving behind a small garrison at the windmill. The German counter-attacks actually regained some ground in the Oppy line that had been lost on 23 April. As a result of this failure there were no troops covering the right flank of 2 Division.

The task allotted to 2 Division was made even more difficult by its lack of manpower; attacking would be two brigades with a total fighting complement of less than a full strength brigade. With around 3500 men, its first objective was to break through the strongly-wired Oppy line, then take Oppy Wood (now a mass of shell holes and collapsed trees) before moving on to the village of Oppy, a total frontage of a thousand

Victorine Capron, an inhabitant of Gavrelle was killed by a British shell.

yards. Artillery support was in the form of a double 18-pounder creeping barrage, with one half moving ahead of the other by 200 yards, the inner barrage being shrapnel and the outer high explosive. Holding the German lines was one battalion of 75 Regiment (17 Division), a relatively fresh unit.

As usual there was an air of optimism. The War Diary of 17 Royal Fusiliers for 26 April, the day after orders had been received for the attack, records that the 'day (was) chiefly spent in equipping & fitting for Hun hunt'.

On the right, 6 Brigade did comparatively well at first. The War Diary for 13 Essex records this initial success:

> *...at 4.38am the 1st wave crossed the enemy's front line trench, with the exception of the extreme right of the Battalion, which was held up by uncut wire and lost heavily from Machine Gun fire in endeavouring to get through it.*

They then lost contact with the division on its right and had to detail a support company to protect that flank. However, the advance continued under the barrage to a line of practice trenches at the eastern end of Oppy Wood. All the while the attackers were under heavy machine gun and rifle fire from Oppy village and German bombers on the right flank; large numbers of the enemy advanced down the sunken road near Crucifix trench. The heavy barrage and machine gun stopped the attack short of its destination; they got no further than the British front line.

Enemy resistance in the village was stubborn and firing from loopholes cut in the walls prevented 17 Middlesex from advancing any further than the east side of the wood. Around 5.50am they were heavily attacked from the front and left flank by enemy troops

A view of the wood from the approximate positions of the British trenches.

Oppy was relatively undamaged until the attacks of April 1917.

Aerial view of Oppy Wood in 1917.

An artists impression of the struggle for Oppy Wood.

The German garrison of Oppy pose outside the Town Hall.

advancing through Oppy Wood who got into the rear of the line and reoccupied parts of the German front line.

Heavy fighting continued until around 9am when the troops were ordered to fall back, hold and consolidate the German front line. With only small, detached parties being able to do this, there were insufficient men to deal with the number of enemy who were holding the trench. By this time all the officers and the majority of the NCOs had become casualties and

> *'what was left of the Battalion was quite disorganised and exhausted. Small parties held out but eventually retired to the old British line, running from shell hole to shell hole at dusk.'*

The narrative of this operation is clearly told in the 17 Middlesex War Diary.

> *The Battn marched from Roclincourt on the evening of the 27th and formed up in its battle formation on the front allotted to*

Map 10: Trench map to show the German positions before Oppy became a position that needed taking.

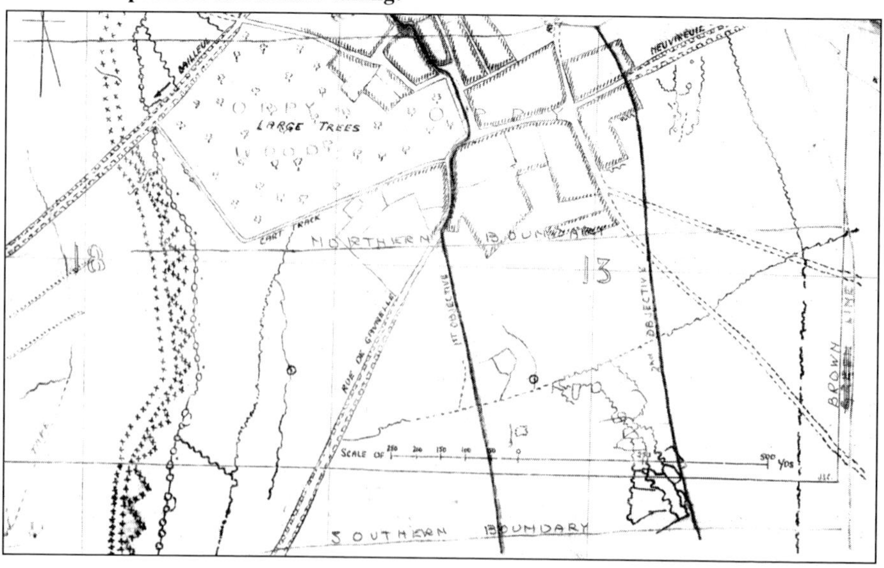

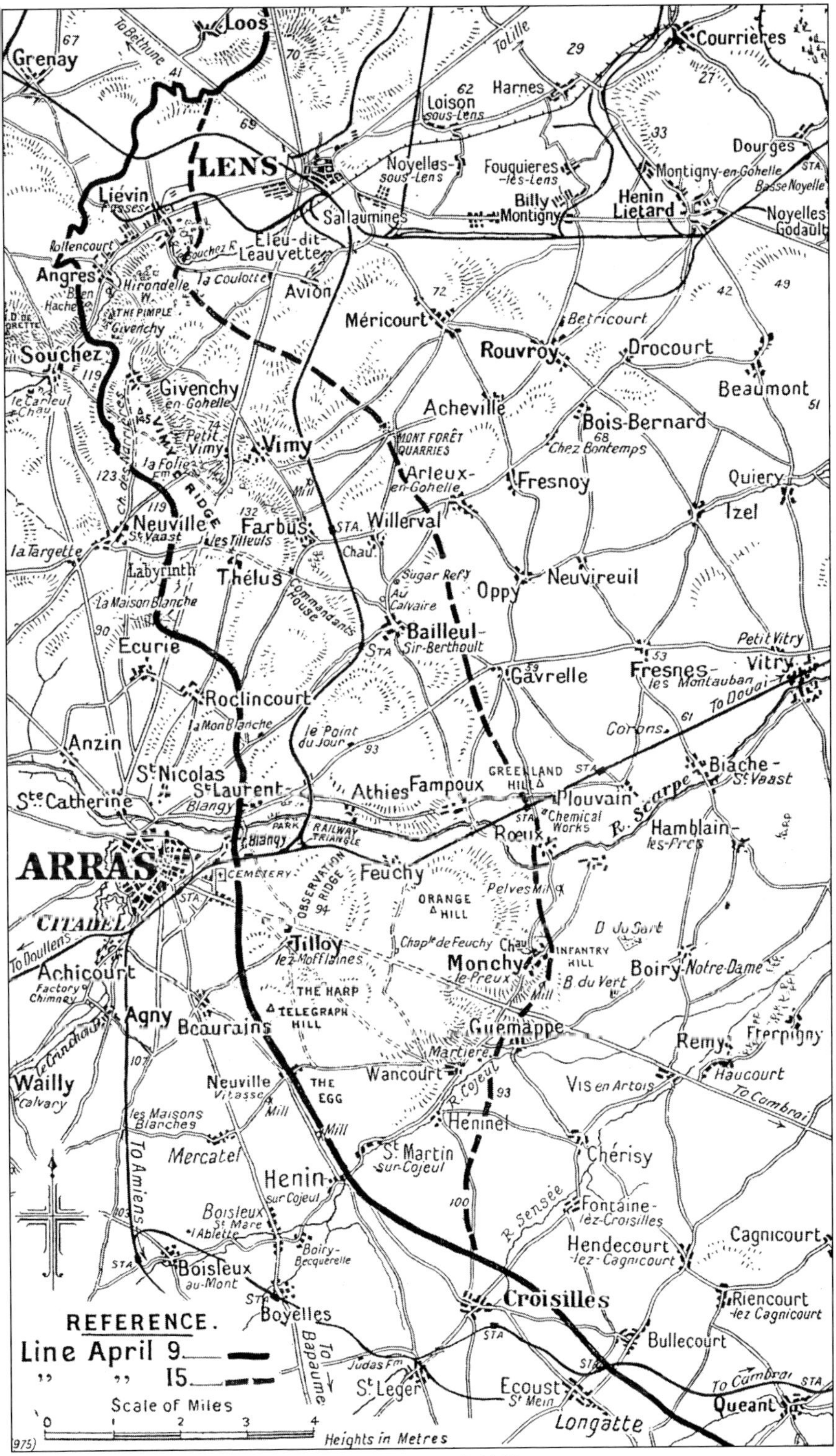

Map 11: Area of the British Offensive, April 1917

the battn, opposite wood & village of OPPY. The forming up was carried out without hitch and in perfect silence in spite of steady shelling of the front area... at 4.25am our barrage came down and at 4.33am the leading wave entered the enemy front line trench – wire was found to be perfectly cut and the trench practically empty. The Battn. pressed forward behind the creeping barrage and the 1st objective was reached with only few casualties – shortly after the advance commenced the O.C. A Coy on the left noticed that the Battn. on our left had either lost touch or had been unable to make progress. He thereupon placed a Lewis Gun Section and some bombers in the enemy Front Line Trench with instructions to block the trench and prevent any movement by the enemy against the left flank. The right flank during the advance to the 1st objective appears to have kept well in touch with the 13th Essex. Fighting became much heavier on reaching the line of the 1st objective, very heavy machine gun & rifle fire being opened from the houses in the village. Capt. Parfitt of D Coy had been specially charged with the consolidation of the 1st objective and this was taken in hand by the 1st wave, while remainder pressed on towards the 2nd objective. Very heavy fighting now ensued on the Right (sic)*, but on the left the German Trench running North & South... was reached. The fighting had now become so serious that both the 2nd & 3rd waves were fully involved in the struggle for the 2nd objective while the 1st objective was still being consolidated. Up to this juncture reports from wounded men and reports by runners had been received confirming the capture of the 1st objective and of the struggle for the 2nd objective, but owing to the hostile shelling all reports were somewhat late in reaching Battn. H.Q. and the situation on the left did not seem clear as although A Coy were known to have gained ground a report came in from the H.L.I. on our left to the effect that they were hung up by fire in the Sunken Road in the neighbourhood of the Crucifix. A senior officer was now sent from Battn. H.Q. to clear up the situation on the left and to locate a suitable forward position for Battn. H.Q. to move to. It was now nearly 8 o'clock and a few minutes later a report came in from the O.C. A Coy, the left Coy. to say that the enemy were working round both his flanks. The only available reserve inside the Battn. viz: the moppers up of the 1st Objective (who had reported the completion of their task) had already been sent forward to strengthen the right in the hopes that the 2nd Objective might* *still be reached. Capt. Edwards, the officer who had been sent out to clear up the situation, found that the enemy had pressed down in strength from the North both down the German Front Line Trench and by the Crucifix Road on the flank of out two left Coys and had driven these back through the wood to the enemy Front Line Trench. Here these two Coys were making a stand but had by now sustained very heavy losses. The enemy also appear to have counter attacked against the front & right flank as well and had succeeded in re-entering the wood and getting in between the troops consolidating on the 1st Objective and those who had been driven back to the OPPY Trench. The enemy had also worked up the OPPY Trench from the South and were bombing up from that direction also. All communication with the remnants of the troops in the 1st Objective was now cut off and runners who attempted to get through to the troops still holding the OPPY Trench were either killed or wounded.*

Lt. Col. Martin 13th Essex Regt commanding sent forward a Company of 1st Royal Berks to endeavour to relieve the situation, but these could not get beyond the O.B. Line [Old British Line]. *The remnants of the 2 Coys still holding on to the Oppy Trench finally exhausted all their bombs and when reduced to about 10 all told made a dash for the O.B. Line. 1 officer and 3 men succeeding in getting through. The troops on the 1st Objective were not heard of again until a wounded officer succeeded in making his way back during the night. His evidence made it clear that these troops had fought till they were*

British Prisoners of War captured during the offensive.

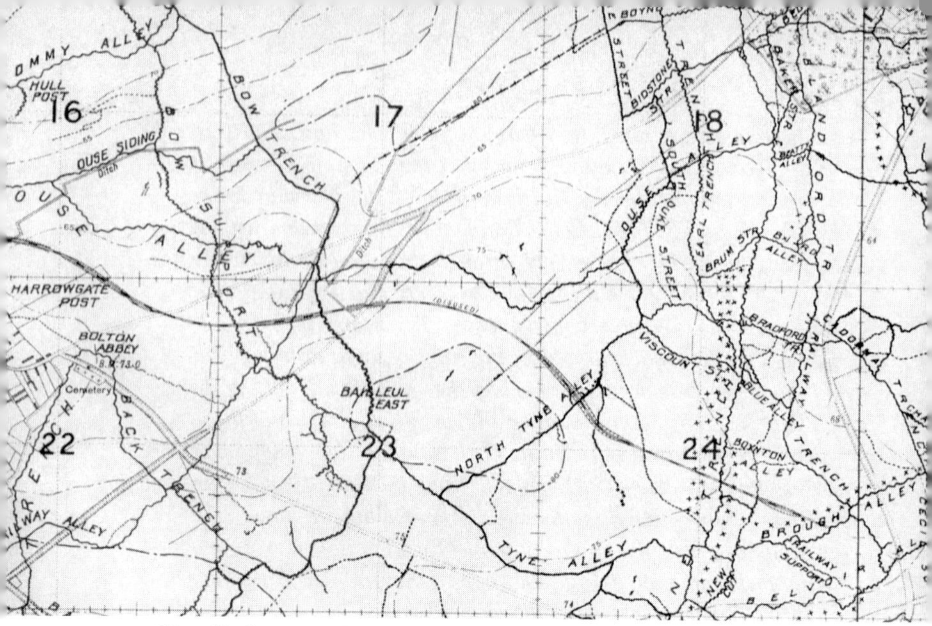

Map 12: Large scale map showing the objectives for 28 April 1917.

practically exterminated by the superior pressure of the enemy; the few survivors probably surrendered. The remaining few men of the Battn. with some of the So. Staffs [South Staffs] *carrying party remained for the rest of the day in the O.B. Line until relieved at night by the 23rd Fusiliers.*

Of the troops who went over the top in the morning 1 officer & 41 unwounded men eventually found their way back while 3 wounded officers & 106 wounded O.R. were able to get back in the early stages of the fight.

The two other battalions of the brigade, 1 King's and 2 South Staffs, were employed as 'moppers up' and carrying parties, leaving 23 Royal Fusiliers, detached from 99 Brigade, to clear Oppy. However, the battalion was not ready to attack until around midday and by then the enemy had already forced the brigade back to the German front line, which was evacuated in the evening. The Germans had moved their troops to the flanks, allowed the advancing British troops to enter the wood and then moved back in their rear. There was no shortage of German troops as 'reinforcements came up in columns by rail and bus, and troops from Neuvireuil (a nearby village) filtered into the wood and the groups of houses near the white manor house to reinforce the garrison'.

On the left of 2 Division the attacking units were 2 Highland Light Infantry (right flank) and 2 Oxford & Bucks Light Infantry; 17 Royal Fusiliers were to act as carriers. The officers and men of 2 Highland Light Infantry were to start the attack with a disadvantage. On 27 April a German bombardment of the sugar factory HQ resulted in the wounding of their commanding officer, Lieutenant Colonel J Grahame, DSO, Major W Stewart, DSO, Captain R Whistler and four other ranks; the same bombardment killed five soldiers.

The artillery preparation had not thoroughly cut the wire and there were only three gaps for the troops to attack through until the HLI cut a fourth with wire cutters. Indeed the War Diary for 2HLI mentions that the 'enemy barrage came down within 1 min of our own which was very irregular' and that several casualties were caused by poorly cut wire. The troops also quickly caught up with their own barrage. All the time there was constant sniping and machine gun fire from the wood and by the afternoon the Germans were shelling the newly consolidated positions. However, two counter-attacks were beaten off. The attackers also had to contend with considerable sniping from the roofs of the houses in Oppy.

Both battalions (HLI and Ox &Bucks LI) reached the sunken Oppy to Arleux road, however the withdrawal by 6 Brigade from Oppy Wood resulted in the HLI being forced back to the German second line where it beat off two further counter-attacks. With the Canadians on the extreme left, 2 Ox & Bucks LI was secure in its new positions as the Canadians had successfully taken Arleux.

A detailed account of this action is contained in War Diary WO95 1345 at the National Archives.

> *Before ZERO hour the attacking Battalions were formed up in the front line which was used as an assembly trench. ZERO was at 4-25 am. The attack was made in normal formation. The Barrage opened according to timetable and the troops moved forward. By the time they reached the German wire the enemy's M.Gs. opened fire and then he laid down an intense artillery and minenwerfer barrage about 150-200 yards behind our front line.*
>
> *5-30 am. Message from 2nd Oxf.&.Bucks L.I. Right Front Coy., stated:- 'My Coy has reached 1st objective... 50 prisoners*

German reinforcements.

taken... We have a good many casualties... We are held up by M.Gs.... Enemy made fair resistance... I am in touch with 2nd High. L.I. on my right and am in front of Canadians going towards Arleux.'

6-45 am. Left Battalion report they have consolidated Green Line in touch with Canadians but not with 2nd High. L.I. Held up by M.Gs. from C.l.c. and C.7.a. Casualties appear to be heavy.

7-20 am. A wounded Officer from Right front Coy., of Left Battalion stated that they had only found one gap in the wire and the whole of his Coy., had to go through this. He was of opinion that they were over Green Line.

8-55am. 2nd Oxf.&.Bucks L.I. report that the enemy is massing apparently with a view to making a counter attack: in B.6.d. and B.l2.b.

9-5 am. Left Battalion report that they are not in touch with 2nd High. L. I. on right and that they had reached Brown Line but had to fall back because they had no supports and their right flank unprotected. During this time the 2nd High. L.I. on the right had reached the Sunken Road but owing to heavy M.G. fire and bombing had to fall back on to the 1st objective. The 6th Brigade on our right had established themselves in OPPY WOOD and village but owing to the 63rd Division on their right being forced to retire and also to number of casualties they were receiving had to fall back. Our Right Battalion had therefore to fall back on the Blue Line, Block (sic) *the trench, and so far as possible form a defensive flank.*

1-35 pm. B. Coy., 17th R. Fus., reports:- '2nd High. L.I. have retired and joined us in GERMAN FRONT LINE. My right flank is in same position but all connection with 6th Inf. Bde. has been lost. 8th Inf. Bd. appear to have retired from OPPY. We are being heavily shelled.

2-10 pm. Divisional observers report that German counter attack reached trench running N.W. and S.E. through Square C.7.a. and d. There it was caught by our M.G. fire and shrapnel. Some Germans dropped into the trench, the others fled in disorder towards NEUVIREUIL, followed by our shrapnel.

During the operation the enemy snipers were very active. Machine Guns were being fired from the church and houses in OPPY and from OPPY WOOD. The heavies were got on to these places. The enemy apparently did not move away any of his guns

A German trench mortar in one of the many sunken lanes around the area.

Reinforcemens in a nearby village wait to be called.

as he was firing at quite short range.

At 3-40 pm it was definitely established that the enemy was holding OPPY LINE from B.18.b.2.5. to B.12.d.3.0. and the sunken road from this line to the CRUCIFIX. Orders were received that the 6th Bde. would attack OPPY TRENCH and establish themselves there, shoving out posts into the wood. The 5th Bde. were to co-operate and clear up the situation on the south of their front and gain touch with 6th Bde. in O.G. (old German) front line. This attack never came off. The situation remained much the same till 7pm, when the Artillery Liaison Officer reported that the Arty. Observation officer had seen Germans in squares B.23.a and d, and in our front line in B.24.

The Bde. on our right was at once asked what the situation was on their front, and replied that as far as they knew none of their men were in this old front line and that they had lost touch

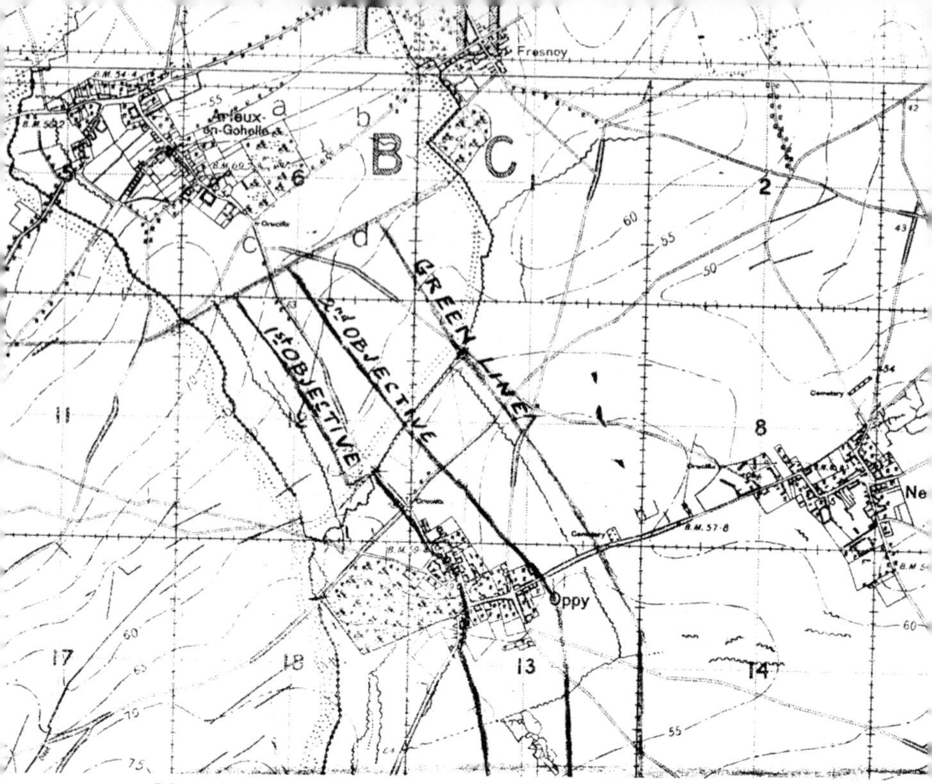

Map 13: 6 Brigade objectives, 28 April 1917.

with the division on their right.

The 24th R. Fus, were then ordered to take up a defensive flank from our old front line in B.18.a through B.17.a. and c.

This Battn. moved out from its position in the Support trenches and took up their line, reporting that it was in position and digging in at 11pm.

The 99th Bde. had taken over the 6th Bde. on our right at 5pm and were ordered to attack and capture OPPY Support trench at 4am and to push out posts in to the wood on the 29th. The 5th Bde. were ordered to co-operate and clear up the situation to their southern boundary.

The 24th R. Fus. were ordered to move up two Coys., from the defensive flank they had taken up to the old British Front line in B.12.d. and moving forward with 99th Bde., establish a line from the Sunken road at B.18.b.6.9. to join up with the 2nd Oxf.&.Bucks L.I. in the Sunken Road about B.12.d.5.9. The latter pushing down to this point. The actual number to be employed was left to the discretion of O.C. 24th R. Fus. This order was issued at 12-45 am on 29th.

Aerial view of the wood just before the attack, clearly showing the trenches.

The two Coys had barely time to form up in the old British line before ZERO hour, but advanced catching up the barrage at the support line, they had a good many casualties coming up to the forming up trench from shell fire, but from there to the Sunken Road at the Crucifix very few. They were not in touch on their right and owing to the darkness pushed on further than their objective. They captured 1 officer and 68 prisoners in OPPY line.

These two Coys were followed by a supporting Coy of the 24th R. Fus. who remained in the O.G. (Old German) *Front line and were in touch with their Battn. All day.*

The two leading Coys in the Sunken Road N.W. of the Crucifix were completely cut off being in touch with no one, and after losing heavily from snipers in OPPY VILLAGE and OPPY WOOD, and from OPPY TRENCH N. of them, they returned to the O.G. Front Line in B.12.d.0.4. remaining in this line South of the Block until the Bde. was relieved on the night of the 1st/2nd.

The wood after the bombardment had started.

The battle statistics show the severity of the fighting. Casualties up to the evening of 27 April were 3 officers killed, 5 wounded and 1 missing with 22 other ranks killed, 127 wounded and 35 missing. From then until relief during the night of 1/2 May the casualties were 34 officers killed, wounded and missing with 135 other ranks killed, 520 wounded and 127 missing.

At 7pm XIII Corps commander (Lieutenant General Congreve) issued orders to the two divisions to capture that part of the Oppy line still in German hands. The 3am start was moved to 4am and was preceded by a series of heavy artillery bombardments during the night.

On 63 Division front 188 Brigade reached its objective but was driven out almost immediately. During this attack Captain (acting Lieutenant Colonel) J S Collings-Wells, was awarded the DSO. The citation reads:

> *...on the 29th April he was placed in command of a composite battalion with orders to attack and capture the Oppy line of trenches between the ground then held by the 188th Brigade and the 2nd Division. It was chiefly owing to his leading, coolheadedness and disregard for personal safety that the battalion reached their place of assembly, and formed up under shellfire in darkness on practically strange ground, and subsequently achieved its objects. His courage on this occasion inspired all ranks, and was greatly instrumental in carrying the operation though successfully.*

However, a further German counter-attack south of Gavrelle was successfully repulsed.

Writing home on 28 April, Captain Stone explained that the next day the battalion would be in action.

> *We have had a very busy anxious day and now we are off for a fight. Of course, you needn't worry about me as I shall be at the bottom of a deep dugout all the time living in foul air and probably much discomfort. But it will be nothing to what the rest go through and I shall be thankful when we get the battalion out again. We have been a week in dugouts and trenches now with little or no kit, and it's chiefly absence of sleep and good food, and the incessant tinned food that exhaust the men – far more than the actual excitement of shell fire and fighting.*

At 4am on 29 April, 22 Royal Fusiliers, so seriously under strength that they had to combine four companies to form two weak companies of about 125 men each, attacked the German positions in Oppy Wood. To bolster their strength they were reinforced by one officer and fifty men of 1 King's Royal Rifle Corps.

The night before the attack had been nerve-shaking on account of the cries of the wounded from the attack the day before. Even so, Captain Valentine of C Company 1 Royal Berks noted that his men looked as though,

> *...going over the top were an everyday occurrence, even though they were loaded down like a lot of furniture removers with all the implements of war, utensils, sandbags, food, and ammunition.*

The 99 Brigade attack (22 Royal Fusiliers and 1 Berkshire) fared little better than the southern attack when:

> *...the fusiliers failed to penetrate the second belt of wire, except at two points, where parties of about a platoon in each case forced their way into the trench.*

Here their supplies of ammunition quickly ran low because German shelling had destroyed two of their three battle stores dumps.

On the right of 22 Royal Fusiliers Second Lieutenant S F Jeffcoat (a recent arrival in the battalion), after finding a gap in the wire on the extreme right, divided his party into two groups, one to bomb its way up the trench in a northerly direction under CSM Hogan with the other, under his direction, to bomb the trench in a southerly direction. After bombing 400 yards south of the divisional boundary they made contact with men of 63 Division who were bombing northwards independently. CSM Hogan and his group bombed for about 100 yards and then set up a block to stop the Germans.

Further north 1 Royal Berkshire Regiment and 24 Royal Fusiliers were initially successful in capturing a section of the Oppy line but after six counterattacks were forced out. The German attack then moved south to take Second Lieutenant Jeffcoat's party in the rear.

Troops in the front line at Oppy.

Upon hearing that Second Lieutenant Jeffcoat was under attack, Hogan took some of his men to help him beat it off. When he returned he found that his block had been pushed in. Out of ammunition he took his fifteen or so men back to the British positions to replenish supplies before preparing to retake the position.

Responding to Second Lieutenant Jeffcoat's message that it was possible to get men to him in small parties along the railway, Lieutenant Colonel Barnett-Barker sent one company of 23 Royal Fusiliers to press the attack. Making their way into the Oppy line by the railway, supported by soldiers from 63 Division, they cleared the trenches up to a point 200 yards from the southwest corner of Oppy Wood – a distance of nearly a thousand yards. Shortly after the arrival of the reinforcements, Second Lieutenant Jeffcoat was mortally wounded.

D company, attacking on the left, found that the wire was uncut. Of the four platoons (13, 14, 15 and 16 platoons), three were cut down with only Second Lieutenant Palmer VC managing to survive in a shell hole in the enemy wire. 13 Platoon succeeded in getting into the enemy trench and making contact with 1 Royal Berks, with whom they fought.

> *The Royal Berks set up blocks and defences on their flanks and placed snipers in Oppy Wood. Three German machine-guns were used against a fleeing enemy and some prisoners were taken. The right flank of the battalion was under considerable pressure but managed to beat off a counter-attack. Over a period of four (?) hours the Germans launched no fewer than five counter-attacks and they were repelled by the 'splendid marksmanship of the Berkshires'. At the fifth attempt the Berkshires' supply of bombs ran out but as they moved back they came across a German bomb dump which allowed them to continue the desperate fight.*

As their numbers dwindled it was inevitable that they would have to pull back to their start line.

> *Initially they moved back to the sunken road that ran south-westwards from the western corner of the wood. C Company, the left-hand company, was to the north of the sunken road and was down to thirty-five men; they were now able to join up with the 5th Brigade of their own division.*

With their left flank still open, the remaining Berkshires retired to their front line and held their ground. During this fighting 8763 Lance Corporal James Welch of B Company, who was in charge of a Lewis Gun, won the Victoria Cross. The citation read:

> *For most conspicuous bravery. On entering the enemy trench he killed one man after a severe hand-to-hand struggle. Armed*

with an empty revolver, Lance Corporal Welch then chased four of the enemy across the open and captured them single-handed. He handled his machine-gun with the utmost fearlessness, and more than once went into the open fully exposed to heavy fire at short range to search for and collect ammunition and spare parts, in order to keep his guns in action, which he succeeded in doing for over five hours till wounded by a shell. He showed throughout the utmost valour and initiative.

Lance Corporal Welch,. VC

The Regimental History recorded that:

It had been a fight to the death with no quarter given and heavy casualties on both sides. Shortages of men, uncut wire, a determined skilful enemy and, above all, a shortage of grenades and ammunition, were the downfall of the 22nd which fought itself into the ground. When it was relieved, only the headquarters officers and forty men marched out, although a few others, like 2nd Lieutenant Palmer, struggled in later.

On 30 April, Captain Stone wrote home to his wife about the attack.

We have had such a terrible twenty-four hours, and another page of glory added to the battalion's history at the cost of far too many lives: and of course no sleep for two days and nights, and only the scrappiest of food – and thank God the Colonel and Adams and I have come through another strafe, which proved the advantage of being at headquarters... The remnants of the battalion will come crawling out tonight, ready to drop with fatigue and exposure; but nothing can make up for the men who are left out there dangling on the German wire or lying in shell holes. God grant that saner counsels may soon prevail, and that our object may be gained without all this slaughter. But it's a wonderful battalion and deserves all the praise it gets.

Later in the day he recorded that

...the men came back with fine stories that make one ashamed of being alive. Our losses are not so heavy as feared, and the shell holes have given up a certain number of men that we counted as lost. But it's bad enough, God knows.

Of the twelve officers in the attack, only three returned unwounded and of the approximately 240 men involved in the assault, 144 were listed as killed, wounded or missing. The assault on Oppy Wood was

British troops working their way up a trench at Oppy.

probably the bitterest action seen by 22 Royal Fusiliers and, in commemoration of the attack, the battalion produced the 'Oppy Cross' that after the war was moved to a church in Kensington. The 13 Essex War Diary recorded their casualties as seventy-nine other ranks and four officers wounded (one of these, A R Sacre, had previously been under arrest for withdrawing his men from the front line trench without orders on 21 April while they were under fire) with eight officers and 240 men missing. Further proof of the severity of the losses incurred during the fighting in the Oppy area is shown by 1 Royal Berkshire Regiment figures. By 1 May there were only enough men left to form two companies of four officers and 100 men each which was joined with 23 Royal Fusiliers to form a composite battalion. After the second Oppy battle they were down to two officers (both wounded) and 94 men; it was not until the end of August that they were up to a strength of 700 officers and men.

The Times History of the Great War blamed the failure on insufficient British troops and an excess of German soldiers:

> *...at Oppy and in the wood which screened it an even fiercer struggle had been proceeding. In the branches of the trees platforms for machine-guns had been constructed and the English troops could only move slowly and carefully through the wood to the village. At last the wood was cleared, but in the cottages there were desperate hand-to-hand conflicts. In the German background lines of motor-omnibuses could be seen racing for Neuvireuil, whence streams of reinforcements were*

poured into Oppy and towards Gavrelle. Counter-attack succeeded counter-attack, and at nightfall we were still only on the outskirts of the village. Our advance, too, from Gavrelle on Oppy had been checked.

The Commanding officer of 22 Royal Fusiliers in his narrative of the battle blamed the failure of his battalion on uncut wire and the difficulties in finding any gaps in the dark; lack of bombs of which the Germans were never short; the barrage of six minutes did not allow sufficient time for men to advance over 150 yards and get through two belts of wire – the barrage had lifted before the men had reached the second belt of wire.

Then there was the problem of the quality of the Germans:

...the enemy were guardsmen and fought magnificently... and their counter attacks appeared to be splendidly trained and organized.

The War Diary of 1 King's Royal Rifle Corps also highlighted the German artillery as being problematic, describing two barrages put down at 2am and at 3.30 am as 'terrific, quite reminiscent of DELVILLE WOOD'.

Of the attacking battalions only 17 Royal Fusiliers details its recommendations for bravery: four Military Crosses, one Distinguished Conduct Medal and five Military Medals and this was from a battalion that provided carrying parties, strong point troops and 'moppers-up'.

Reinforcements at Acheville, a nearby village.

The only real success of the day was achieved by 1 Canadian Division. Taking the German front trench, 8 Canadian Battalion crossed the Arleux to Oppy road and made contact with 2 Ox & Bucks L I on its right. With assistance from 7 Canadian Battalion it overcame resistance from a strongpoint in the embankment of the sunken track south of the village and attacked the southern section of the village, taking two officers and a hundred men prisoner. They then proceeded to consolidate their position along the objective east of the village, through Arleux Wood.

Attacking in the centre, the advance of 10 Canadian Battalion was held up by two machine guns concealed near wire entanglements. After bombing and shooting the crews, the battalion then moved on into the village where further resistance was encountered; this time the machine gun was silenced by rifle grenades. When they reached the eastern part of the village, the Germans were seen retiring in such good order that in the poor light they were thought to be part of the British attack. Only three minutes later than planned, the battalion had taken all of its objectives in two hours.

On the left flank the battle did not progress as well. While the centre and right units took the front trench and crossed the open ground north of the village, the left flank was held up by uncut wire. Not until the support company had bombed up the trench from a previously cleared area could any form of progress be made towards the objective, the sunken Arleux-Méricourt track north of the village.

Protecting the left flank was 25 Canadian Battalion from 2 Canadian Division. Delayed, its assault companies then met uncut wire and stiff opposition that was only overcome after heavy fighting,

Waiting in the frontline.

resulting in a further delay. To further compound the problems, they then discovered that they had not actually reached their objective but were about 600 yards short. Their position offered no protection to 5 Battalion on their right who consequently suffered casualties from two machine guns and were forced to fall back to the German front trench.

The German writer and soldier, Ernst Junger, was in Fresnoy during the battle. In his book, *Storm of Steel,* he recounted what it was like on 28 April waiting to receive the order to counter-attack. At midnight on 27 April he received the coded message '67 beginning 5a.m.' that indicated a heightened state of alert. After receiving the telegram he 'promptly lay down right away, so as to be up to the anticipated exertions' but just as he was on the point of sleep, 'a shell struck the house, smashed the wall against the basement steps', and filled the room with rubble.

> *We leaped up and hurried into the shelter. As we sat on the steps, by the light of a candle, tired and sullen, the leader of my light-signalling troop, whose station had been destroyed that afternoon, including two valuable signaling lamps, dashed in to report: 'Lieutenant, the basement of No. II has taken a direct hit, there are some men buried in the rubble!'*
>
> *Since I had two bicyclists and three telephonists among them, I hurried over with some of my men.*
>
> *In the shelter, I found one lance-corporal and one wounded man, and received the following report: As the first shells began to land ominously close, four of the five inhabitants decided to take to the shelter. One of them ran down right away, one of them stayed in his bed imperturbably, and the other three sat down to pull their boots on. The most cautious man and the most carefree, as so often in the war, survived, one of them being quite uninjured, the sleeper receiving a splinter in the thigh, while the other three were torn apart by the shell that flew through the basement wall and blew up in the far corner.*
>
> *Following this account, I lit a cigar and entered the smoky room in the middle of which was piled almost to the ceiling a bolus of straw sacks, smashed bedsteads, and other furniture. After we had set down a few candles in niches in the wall, we set about the sorry task. We seized hold of the limbs sticking out from the wreckage, and pulled out the corpses. One man had lost his head, and the end of his torso was like a great sponge of blood. Splintered bones stuck out of the arm stump of the second and his uniform was drenched with blood from a great wound in his*

A British heavy shell that failed to explode.

chest. The intestines of the third were spilling out of his opened belly. As we pulled him out, a splintered piece of board caught in the wound with a hideous noise. One orderly passed a remark, and was rebuked by Knigge with the words: 'Shut up, man, you don't waste words over something like this!'

I made an inventory of their personal belongings. It was a ghastly job. The candles flickered reddishly in the dusty air, while the men handed me wallets and rings and watches, as if we were a bunch of gangsters. Fine yellow brick-dust had settled on the dead men's faces, and gave them the rigid appearance of waxen effigies. We draped blankets over them, and hurried out of the basement, having first wrapped the wounded man in a tarpaulin. With the stoical advice, 'Better grit your teeth, comrade!' we dragged him through wild shrapnel fire to the dressing-station.

Then the barrage increased in ferocity.

The terrain between the edge of the village and the dressing-station was receiving a total artillery barrage. Light and heavy shells with impact-, fire- and time-delay fuses, duds, empty cases and shrapnels all participated in a kind of madness that was too much for our eyes and ears. In amongst it all, going either side of the witches' cauldron of the village, support troops were advancing.

Fresnoy was one towering fountain of earth after another. Each second seemed to want to outdo the last. As if by some magical power, one house after another subsided into the earth; walls broke, gables fell, and bare sets of beams and joists were sent flying through the air, cutting down the roofs of other houses. Clouds of splinters danced over whitish wraiths of steam. Eyes and ears were utterly compelled by this maelstrom of devastation.

Fortunately for Junger his troops were not required and on 30 April he and his regiment were moved to Flers.

The effect of heavy artillery on a house.

As the Fresnoy line was regarded as more important, there were no German counter-attacks against the Arleux loop. The next afternoon, after an artillery barrage, the left of 5 Canadian Battalion and the whole of 29 Canadian Battalion advanced and occupied the original objectives. Total casualties for each of the four divisions involved were respectively, 3910 in 1 Canadian, 3044 in 2 Canadian, 3081 in 2 Division and 3794 in 63 Division.

During the attacks of 28/29 April, three Victoria Crosses were won. The one directly relevant to Oppy (that of Lance Corporal Welch) has already been detailed. Both of the other two awards went to officers in the same battalion, 1 Honourable Artillery Corps, for bravery in the Gavrelle area (2/Lieutenant R L Haine VC, MC + Bar and 2/Lieutenant A O Pollard VC, MC + Bar, DCM).

Chapter Three

May 1917

The First Army Attack on Arleux and Oppy 3 May

The next attack on Oppy and its feared wood would take place on 3 May as part of an offensive previously agreed upon with the French to assist their attacks scheduled on 4 and 5 May. It was arranged that Fifth Army would attack and secure Riencourt and Hendecourt, Third Army would take Fontaine, Chérisy, St. Rohart Factory, the Bois du Sart, Pelves and Plouvain station while Oppy and Fresnoy would be taken by First Army.

The Australian commanders in Fifth Army pressed for the attack to start in the darkness with a start time of 3.30am with Third Army setting off at 4.05am. Deciding that all the attacks should be simultaneous, Haig ordered a start time of 3.45am for the whole operation. According to the *Official History* this was both an unfortunate and disastrous decision for First and Third Armies. This change in time was not given to divisional commanders until the afternoon of 2 May, allowing them no time to prepare for an assault in the dark.

> *A night attack was therefore carried out, based on dispositions suited to an attack at dawn. The sun did not rise till*

Map 14: The Oppy and Vimy front.

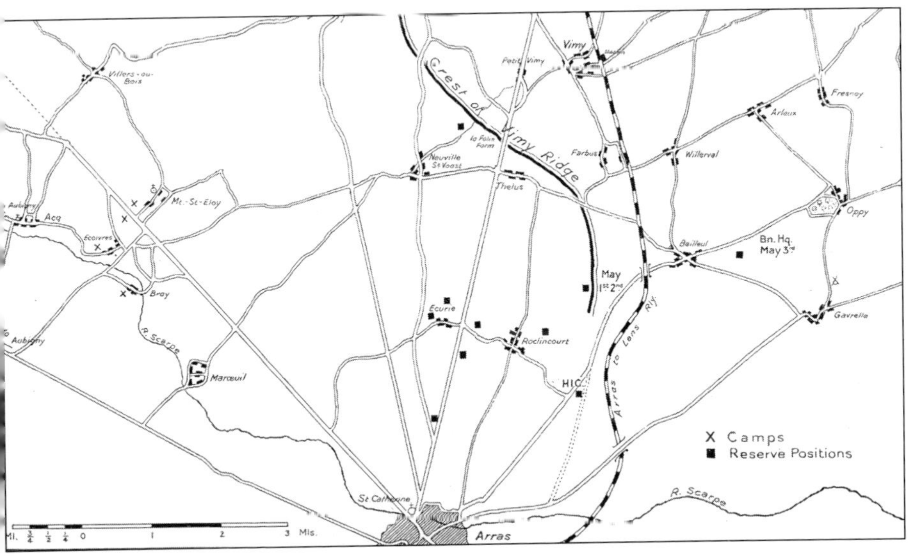

5.22am, and it was impossible to distinguish a line of men at a distance of fifty yards until 4.5 A.M. – the original Third Army Zero.

To make the problems of the attack worse, the moon was nearly full and was due to set sixteen minutes before the revised zero hour. This gave the defending Germans a distinct advantage.

On large stretches of the front the troops assembling for the assault were silhouetted against its light as it sank behind them, their appearance giving warning of the attack and drawing heavy fire, which caused serious loss and confusion.

Only the attacking Empire forces seem to have been able to make use of the darkness in a successful way.

Ground operations on First Army front were preceded by air attacks on German observation balloons in order to decrease their intelligence gathering about the forthcoming offensive. There were also a number of successful bombing raids against German targets in the attack area.

The XIII Corps attack was to be on a front from the southern outskirts of Gavrelle to the southern corner of the wood south of Fresnoy, a front of about 4600 yards. Two divisions were scheduled for the assault: 31 Division, fresh from Corps reserve and 2 Division that had previously attacked Oppy on 28 April. The latter division, according to the *Official History*, 'had been reduced to a shadow of its former self'; 63 Division on its right was also exhausted so 31 Division took over its front and also the right half of 2 Division's front – 3500 yards against the 1100 yards held by the latter. Any attack on this front was hampered by the German tenure of the Oppy line west of Oppy Wood.

Facing the two British divisions, the German positions were held by experienced and, in some cases, rested troops. The trenches from the southeast of Gavrelle to the Oppy-Bailleul road were garrisoned by 1

Typical French trenches in the area, before the British took over.

Guard Reserve Division with the central section of this front being held by 28 Reserve Regiment (185 Division). All of these regiments had been heavily engaged in the previous attacks. However, 15 Reserve Division, holding the line from the Oppy-Bailleul road to halfway between Fresnoy and Acheville had not previously been engaged; along the whole front to be attacked, sixteen miles in total, only two British divisions were fresh, compared to seven new divisions on the German order of battle.

The frontage to be attacked by 31 Division was too long for it to be successfully shelled by its own artillery so it was allocated the field artillery from both 2 and 63 Divisions and a further four independent artillery brigades – because of the nature of the terrain all of these guns would be firing at very long ranges. Similarly to assist its machine-gun companies the division was loaned sixteen Vickers guns from 63 Division and eight Hotchkiss guns from the 1/1st Northumberland Hussars.

In front of the Hull Pals, when they attacked, was Oppy Wood; a difficult prospect because the felled trees provided both cover and unseen strong-points, providing a series of fortifications in which the branches would be entanglements to hamper movement. Described in *The Great War* as 'a more difficult position to assail' than Arleux,

> *...it was farther removed from direct observation from the ridge and from the British batteries around the conquered heights. The key to Oppy was a wood beside the village, and this wood the enemy had fortified in an amazing manner. It was a grand rookery of machine-guns. The guns were mostly placed in the budding boughs twenty to thirty feet above ground, and the gunners took shelter during a bombardment on ladders running down the eastern side of the trunks. On the ground, the deep dugouts placed behind barricades were concealed and strengthened by felled trees. And even after a heavy bombardment the manor house survived, with its broken roofs and empty windows clearly visible through a fringe of dead tree.*

Through gaps in the shattered wood, observers on the ridge could see 'the Oppy trenches, filled with dead Prussians and wrecked machine-guns'.

As the division formed up it could be clearly seen silhouetted against the setting moon and as a result met with much artillery fire. In spite of this 93 Brigade, (15, 16 and 18 West Yorkshire Regiment) on the right flank of the attack made good progress, with some companies reaching their final objective. However, faced with strong

The ruins of Oppy just before the attack.

counter-attacks and the failure of 92 Brigade on their left flank, they had no choice but to retire; in the process the Germans re-took the windmill but a counter-attack by a company of 18 Durham Light Infantry (the brigade reserve battalion), gallantly led by Second Lieutenant H E Hitchin, recaptured it.

The attacking force of 92 Brigade also consisted of three battalions – 10, 11 and 12 East Yorkshire Regiment. A tremendous German artillery barrage on their assembly positions before zero hour

> *...caused serious disorganization, and in the darkness – here increased by the black mass of Oppy Wood in front – the troops could not see when the barrage lifted.*

German barbed wire defences.

Advancing upon Oppy Wood, the men found themselves among trees in the darkness with criss-cross lacings of barbed wire from the branches in every direction and under heavy fire. The battalions got completely mixed up. On the right flank 11 Battalion failed completely while in the centre and left progress was made and troops passed through the wood in the darkness but were eventually either killed, captured or driven out in spite of a strenuous resistance by the East Yorkshires. One act of bravery was rewarded with a posthumous Victoria Cross – Lieutenant John Harrison of 11 East Yorkshire Regiment. In total the division suffered around 1900 casualties to all ranks.

The above is all taken from official sources and gives the dry facts about the attack. Fortunately there were soldiers in 10 and 13 East Yorkshire Regiment who kept diaries at the time or recorded their experiences later. Private Surfleet described what it felt like to be there in *Blue Chevrons: an Infantry Private's Great War Diary*, while Privates Aust, Beeken and Pearson wrote up their experiences after the war.

After wintering on the Somme the brigade set off, on 8 April, in the snow for Marles-les-Mines and the trenches near Vimy Ridge. Before their arrival, the Canadians had taken Vimy Ridge so it was obvious to the rank and file that they were not there by coincidence, especially when, for the rest of the month, they were involved in training for an attack or cleaning up after somebody elses. When they did move to the front it was to see the failure of the 28 April attack on the very place they themselves had been brought up to attack. Initially all was relatively easy, as Private Surfleet recorded in his diary, written up, usually, a few days after the events.

> *April 18th: Still here and having a grand time. This district has the Somme and Pas-de-Calais (and most other places we have been to) absolutely 'sewn up' and Camblain-Chatelain must rank high in the 'rest places' we have had; certainly the people here must come very near the top of the list of 'friends we have found in France'. Rumour (that bête-noir) says we shall soon end this life of bliss and we expect to go up the line any day now for the 'Big Show' which is in the offing for the P.B.I.*
>
> *April 21st: Our A Company went off on a working party today to Vimy Ridge; heard they were doing salvage work and burying the dead. They were fed up at missing any of this wonderful rest period. Rumour says we may follow at any time, a rumour which enhances the pleasures of Camblain-Chatelain. Had a payday: one (not-to-be-mentioned) N.C.O. did a tour de ville, 'one' in each estaminet, for a bet. A man of considerable capacity who, I*

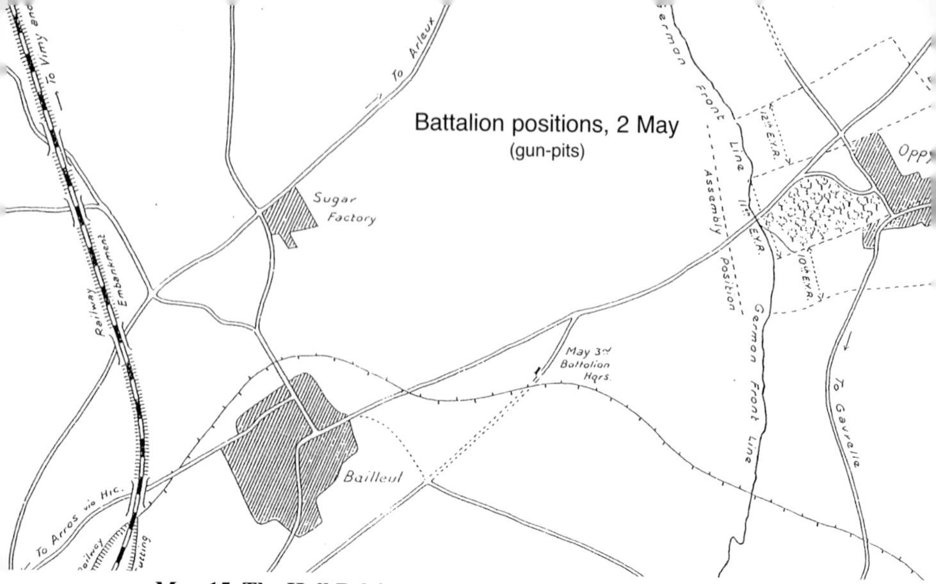

Map 15. The Hull Pals' attack positions on 3 May.

am told, left the field standing, with not a few 'casualties' on the way. (A fool's game, to my mind.)

April 22nd: Still here and likely to stay; Battalion Sports are being arranged for next week... great news! We are all thoroughly enjoying life and have fallen in love with these kind-hearted folks. (Have since heard that A Company are now road-making in the captured area: at least it is an improvement on burying the dead.)

After a relatively quiet introduction to the area, the Brigade now found out why it was there; on 30 April each man in the brigade learned of his part in the coming attack. As the brigade was new to the front, they all found it difficult to believe that they were supposed to attack over unknown ground. To the men who would be making the attack this had the makings of a disaster. For the men of 10 East Yorkshire this would be their first real battle; the other battalions of the brigade had been blooded during the November 1916 attack on the Somme. Given four days' warning, there would be precious little time for preparation.

Certain officers and NCOs from each company went on the night of May 1st to see the assembly position in front of Oppy...returning on the 2nd, they spent the rest of the day issuing wire cutters, bombs, etc., to their respective companies. The same night they were back again leading their respective parties to the jumping-off position, and many officers and NCOs were in poor physical state to meet the strenuous conditions which were to begin in a few hours' time.

Being unfamiliar with the terrain and tired were two factors that would count against them in the forthcoming battle. Given their specific orders the men moved forward, under cover of darkness, to disused trenches and gun pits near Maison de la Côte on 1 May. Throughout the next day they watched counter-battery duels and waited until it was time to move to their jumping-off positions. Private Beeken, who was to be in the assault, recalled the period just before the attack.

The artillery on both sides, was active all night and at dawn it was intensified. The German heavies dropped just in front of us. An enemy aeroplane was brought down with the first shot from an anti-aircraft gun.

The weather on 2 May was good and with nothing else to do but wait he found the time to read a book.

In the evening we moved forward in 'battle order' during which we had enemy shells dropping round us. At last we arrived at support trenches near Bailleul.

As they were about to go into combat there were no tents to rest in and they had to make the best of the 'funk holes' (a hole dug in the side of the trench) for cover. So as not to inform the Germans of the attack the troops were not allowed to walk about on the top, yet contrary to this order working parties carrying bombs, lights and rockets were walking about in the open all afternoon because there were no trenches for them to use; severe German artillery fire during the 28 April attack had destroyed them. The ground was also covered in the debris of war left behind by the British attackers during the Battle of Arleux. Private Pearson recalled his impressions of the proposed attack and battlefield,

...no great results were expected, the same objective had been unsuccessfully attacked only a few days previously & all around was the evidences & chaos of that abortive attempt.

German heavy artillery responding to the British attack.

During the night the British put down an intense bombardment on the German positions but fortunately for the waiting infantry the Germans only replied with a few shells. At night, pack mules carrying 18-pounder shells made their way to guns.

In the evening they were kept busy receiving instructions for the attack. Although it was to be the battle for which the Hull Pals were to be best known, it was a very minor operation in the Battle of Arras, intended to give the French time to recover from their failed 16 April attack on the Chemin des Dames. As an attack to keep German troops around Arras no great results were expected. The objectives were simple: clear the Germans from the wood and take their support trenches. Private Pearson explained what he knew about the attack:

> *Our task was to attack the enemy in the front of & rear of Oppy wood, an objective of no special value or military significance whatsoever but further south we learned that the enemy had given the French a severe mauling – there were even rumours of mutiny in the French army & something had to be done to relieve the pressure on them & so our Higher Command had ordered a series of diversions to draw the Germans away & this was one diversion.*

The battalion left the relative security of the 'funk holes' for the uncertainty of the front at 9.25 pm in order to be ready to take up assembly positions around 11.30 pm. What they found when they got there was not a portent of success. Their jumping off position was a

> *map reference rather than an actuality, for the taping party of May 1st had found it to be merely an isolated untraversed length of trench barely four feet deep, with no communication to the rear, nor any means of contact to left or right.*

The position was so exposed that, in two days, the battalion holding this section had suffered 100 casualties.

As the battalions moved to the assembly trenches, guided by men from 13 East Yorkshire Regiment, the moon, which was low in the sky, silhouetted the movement of the troops, while, during the assembly period, a German aircraft flew over the assembled troops. George Cotton who was already in position ready for the assault noted how easy it was for the Germans to know what was about to happen.

> *On the night of May 2nd we could see other Battalions moving up for the onslaught. It was moonlight and I could have counted the men coming over the ridge. No wonder Jerry was waiting for them.*

The assembly trench was only about 250 yards from the German

A soldier's view on moonlight.

German machine gunners.

Troops in the front line south of the wood, just before the attack.

trenches and Very Lights fell amongst the battalion while it was waiting. As if this was not enough, around midnight a German patrol of between four and six men was spotted; they immediately retired. At 12.30 am the Germans commenced a twenty minute bombardment of the assembly area and after a short lull re-started the bombardment at 1.30; this time it was fiercer and continued until zero hour. Fortunately, casualties were few, but confusion reigned among men tired from carrying stores during the afternoon. Private Beeken later recorded that:

> *...we moved off at 9.25 pm and arrived at our assembly places in front of Oppy Wood at midnight. The enemy guns were very busy but luckily we were not caught by them.*
>
> *My home now was a little shell hole which I shared with Bob Smith. We took off all our equipment for we badly needed a rest for we were worn out with carrying shovels, telephones and more, besides other odds and ends e.g. more ammunition and bombs.*
>
> *At 12.30 am May 3rd an intense German barrage fell on the almost non-existent assembly trench. Bob and I set about making our shell hole deeper when the shelling stopped. Then at 1.30 am an intense 'strafe' was put on us. It lasted for about twenty minutes.*

Company Sergeant Major Crabtree was also concerned.

> *What I saw staggered me. As I looked down into the German lines I could see a line of helmets as they showed up in the chalk trench. Looking to the right I could plainly see in the wood machine-gun posts in the trees. Barbed wire stretched from the ground to the posts. Looking east across the plain of Douai I could see lines of troops, transport and guns all making for Oppy village. This was no evacuation but a massing for attack...The Germans were massing for attack and it was a case of who got in first...and the troops we were to meet were...Prussian Guards. So we were up against something...and we were taking into the attack a draft of youths from the Army Pay Corps who had never even been in the trenches before.*

To assist the attackers, senior members of each battalion were issued with a map of the trenches about to be assaulted. CSM Crabtree noted in his memoirs that his map was handed to him at about 2am on 3 May as he approached the trenches for the attack. His comment written on the map was that 'it was of course useless.'

Private Pearson also felt let down:

> *The preparations were very haphazard & intelligence almost nil, we weren't even sure where the enemy line was & there were no outstanding marks or features to help one keep course & no trench or land contour to give a scrap of cover from enemy observation and rifle or machine-gun fire.*

For some of the attacking troops food was a problem. George Cotton recalled:

I was only 150 yards from the wood but our mates could not get up with rations. We had nothing to eat or drink for 48 hours. All we had was a bit of candle which served as chewing gum.

The 3rd Battle of the Scarpe was scheduled to start when the British barrage commenced at 3.45 am. At zero hour the men were occupying a maze of shell holes 100 yards deep that were being pounded mercilessly by the Germans. Responding to the British barrage, the Germans increased the intensity of their own bombardment:

Barrages were put on us at 2.30 am and at 3.30 am. We were having a hectic time. While this was going on, our bombardment opened out and the Germans immediately intensified theirs.

German field artillery just behind the front line.

In four waves, the troops set off in the dark, through the fumes and mist, into a murderous machine-gun fire, while overhead enemy rockets and Very lights lit the sky. In later life, ex-Private Beeken recalled the chaos:

We advanced to the attack. It was hell. Our shells were shrieking over us and bursting just in front. It was a creeping barrage advancing as we moved forward. The German shells were shrieking over us and bursting behind. Machine-gun fire swept the whole front. Different coloured Very lights and rockets went up over the German lines.

As we moved forward Bill Smith said to me, 'Isn't it a pretty sight!' I replied with, 'Yes it is, but isn't a lot of stuff missing us?'

Everything looked so weird in the fumes from the shells.

Although we were only about 100 yards from Oppy Wood I couldn't see it, for a mist had descended. The fumes almost choked us and I had a splitting headache. As we walked on we saw a number of dead lying about. Eventually we met the sergeant major and his party who were lost. I was not surprised for we couldn't see where we were going. All we could do was to walk towards the lights.

George Cotton was in the first wave of the attack and, like Private Beeken, soon found himself isolated, and decided that the best thing to do was ask God for help.

One of our big naval shells went over, and then our barrage started and we were all out of the trench and running. I found myself in a shell hole by myself. So I took my life in my hands and asked God to help me. I put my rifle on my shoulder and walked from the shell hole across No Man's Land back to a disused trench. I was expecting death at any moment. I was able to link up with other Hull men, but the road of escape was shattered and limbers and horses were blown to pieces...We had not been able to send up Verey lights to guide the artillery as all the men carrying the lights had been killed or wounded.

It was not only the men who were disorientated. Captain Traill had the same problem during the attack. On his way across No Man's Land he was blown up by a shell just before he reached the German line, and when he regained consciousness he had completely lost his sense of direction. He wandered about in the semi-dark unable to recognize any landmark or to find his men. However, once it became light, he rounded up a group of stragglers, and, instead of retreating to safety he took his men forward into the thick of the fighting on the right of the battalion sector; for this action he was awarded the Military Cross.

The reamins of the village as seen by the attacking troops who got through the wood.

The Battalion Medical Officer, Captain Deacon, described what happened in a letter home,

> *...you have probably heard how well he did on the 3rd, and how the C.O. of the Battalion on the right reported that it was entirely due to Traill that his left didn't go phutt, and how he went forward with just a handful of men until there remained of his Company* (sic) *only himself and another man – the latter he sent back with a message, but as no reply reached him he returned himself. He was badly concussed that day having been thrown over by a 5.9. He ought to have got a D.S.O.*

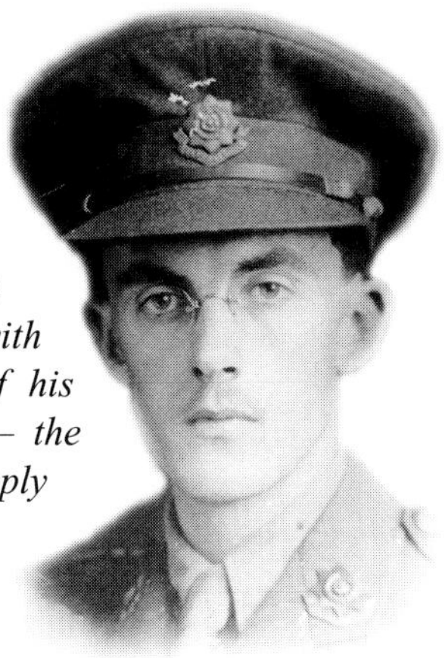

Captain Trail was concussed during the attack but continued to lead the men forward.

Instead of going to hospital on 2 May after Trail had been hit in the face by a shell splinter, he stayed with his men and on 3 May suffered from shell concussion. In hospital in Paris Plage he wrote home to tell them what had happened. The experience was obviously quite dramatic:

> *I seem to have lived a thousand years in the last four days... We moved that night to an unpleasant German trench a bit nearer up, where we spent a rotten 24 hours. At about 6p.m. on the 2nd, I stopped that unfortunate piece of 5.9., so that when we moved up into our assembly positions my head was all swathed up like a mummy. We reached the positions about midnight. The Bosche* (sic) *spotted us and put up S.O.S – twice – so that we had to sit under his barrage (about an hour each) with no better protection than shell-holes. I lost about 20 men each time; so when zero at length arrived (it was still quite dark) you may imagine the waves were not as tidy as they look in a diagram.*
>
> *I got blown up just as we reached the Bosche* (sic) *trench, and when I came to my wits the whole company had gone on. I was horribly fuddled, and wandered off quite in the wrong direction, for about a mile. Then the sun began to rise, and I had just wit enough to remember that it usually appeared in the East. After a few wrong turnings and adventures I finally met a party of some 60 – 80 of our men, from all four companies, without an officer. It would take too long to tell the whole business, even if the censor and my woolly wits would let me. Anyway, I finally found only four of the 10th men left with me, and about two o'clock we staggered back to H.Q. My skin was a little messy by this time, and I collected a good old bruise or two and some small*

scratches. My voice had gone altogether. I could get no news at H.Q., and gave as little. I struggled along to the Casualty Clearing Station. Here I had dinner and a partial wash, got into the hospital train, and was awakened at 7 a.m. on the 4th, to find myself here (Paris Plage).

Upon recovery he was sent to serve in the Humber Garrison until he was fit to return to France. His award of the Military Cross appeared in the *London Gazette* of 18 July 1917. It read:

For conspicuous gallantry and devotion during and after an attack. Although wounded in the head, and later blown into the air by a shell, he refused to retire, displaying the greatest courage and resource, and it was only when the critical period was over that he went to the dressing station.

He was killed in action by shell blast on 26 June 1918 as a major, commanding C Company, 10 East Yorkshire Regiment.

Little was going right for 10 East Yorkshire. In the sector being attacked by The Commercials, the wire had only been cut in a few places, making the men easy targets for the machine-gunners as they funnelled through the few gaps. All four company commanders were wounded and the smoke and dust made it impossible to see where anyone was going. To make matters worse, while the troops were struggling forward, the barrage moved on more quickly than they did, allowing the Germans to become active with machine-gun fire.

Private Beeken was fortunate not to be in the first wave and so did not start immediately and by the time he was scheduled to move

A view of the wood today from 11 East Yorkshire's positions.

Two of the German defenders before the attack – both are machine gunners.

forwards things had got even worse. Even before he and his comrades had crossed No Man's Land they met the earlier waves coming back:

We then met men who were falling back. Our forward movement was checked at 5 a.m. We lay down and fired at groups of Germans who appeared out of the mist. They withdrew. We sat in a shell hole to decide on what we should do. It was decided that we should go back. Out went the men but a machine gun opened out and of course there were casualties. I was left alone. Looking out from the shell hole I saw a machine gun & crew directly in front and only about 30 yds away. I fired at the man behind the gun and then fired at the one who was on his left as he bent over his fallen comrade. Immediately I left the shell hole and was able to look round for any of the wounded men but I couldn't find them. Voices were calling me to go to them. I eventually found some of our party in a shell hole. Later we learned that three of our wounded men were with a party in a shell hole not far from us and that they had been bandaged. They were Smith, Summers and Clark. They were with a machine gun crew.

Sergeant Richardson after his release from Germany.

Neither was it going too well for 12 East Yorkshire Regiment, as Sergeant John Richardson later recalled:

On the night before the attack, which was timed for about 5 o'clock on the 3rd May, we had assembled in a railway cutting. When it was dark, we were taken out of the cutting to a post in the front line where there was a guide who would go forward with us. We were told that in all probability there would be nothing in front of us. We were lying out in the open all night and the Germans were shelling us unmercifully. We had no cover. I don't know how many were killed – we couldn't tell. We were going over and there was a young officer in our platoon and our objective was the left hand edge of Oppy Wood. Before we had got very far, I could see that we were swinging right away from the line and I went to this officer and said, 'Excuse me, but the attack should be concentrated on the edge of the wood there and we are going away from it.' He was very nasty and said he was going to report me.

Lying out in No Man's Land were hundreds of men, some wounded, some dying, some dead; for all but the dead and dying, the day ahead was to be both dangerous and very long as they waited for darkness and the chance to return to British lines:

We couldn't get back to our trenches for the German barrage cut us off. When at last it ceased it was too light for us to move about so we decided to wait until it became dark.

Unable to move because of snipers hidden in the wood, machine-gun fire and artillery, they had to lie there in shell-holes and hope that the Germans did not counter-attack:

There was always the possibility of the Germans coming forward so we kept a sharp look out. We had plenty of excitement during the day for a sniper would persist in firing into our shell hole. He must have been in a tree but we couldn't see him. It turned out to be a very fine day but it was very hot. Aeroplanes

How the wood looked to attacking troops.

of both sides flew over us and of course the guns blazed away at them. At 5pm after having had something to eat I was hit in the shoulder by a piece of shrapnel from the German guns firing at one of our aeroplanes.

Private Pearson was also caught in No Man's Land:

> *We could see the other battalions held up as we were & that day, spent in shell holes, out in no mans land & at the mercy of the enemy shells and machine guns was sheer nightmare.*

While the men waited in No Man's Land, Headquarters needed information. Lying in their shell holes the men could see battalion and company runners, running, creeping and dodging backwards and forwards from shell hole to shell hole, trying to ascertain whether any of the positions could be consolidated.

But it did not all go in favour of the enemy. Private Pearson noted during the battle one soldier walking back to the British lines with eight prisoners.

With darkness there was some safety from detection; slowly men began to leave their shell holes and make their way back to the assembly trenches where assistance awaited:

> *At 9 pm the machine-gun crew informed us that they were going out. We asked them about the three wounded men who had dropped into their shell hole and were informed that one of them had died, but that Summers and Smith were going with them. I told them that we were going back and I would send stretcher bearers to them, but they told me the wounded men were going back with them. We set off and eventually reached the scarcely recognisable trench of our company and then started to dig in. News was passed down the line to me that Summers had passed through our lines. Many wounded men came to our trench and all the time Fritz kept up his shelling.*

There was to be no safe bed in a clean hospital for Private Beeken. His wound was never treated other than with a drink of rum and tea and an inoculation when he returned to the battalion. However, it did get him excused from trench and any other general duty for a short period of time.

Company Sergeant Major Crabtree was also wounded in the attack when the Germans shelled his position:

> *Men began to fall. How can you explain what happens at such a time. We were nearing our objective, and I was along side that lying devil* [his Company Commander], *when a shell dropped right amongst us. Something heavy hit my foot and down I went. What*

happened to him I don't know, but he was never heard of again. Missing believed killed. Jerry had at least done one good deed.

I found I could not put my foot to the ground so I hopped to the nearest trench and as I dropped in, a shell came, and nearly buried me. How long I crept round I cannot tell for I lost count of everything. Could one have gone to sleep in all the noise of the battle?

But I seemed to wake up to hearing someone say, 'Take the legs', and I felt myself placed on a shelter. It was Padre Tindall and a Sergt. of the R.A.M.C. who were carrying me. It was not far to where our M.O. was stood out in the open field. A quick dressing and I was off again.

Lance Corporal Reynolds of 11 East Yorkshire survived the attack unscathed.

All was looking good until the next disaster struck.

The padre and Sergt. carried me about 200 yards, and then handed me over to two R.A.M.C. men. They would carry me shoulder high and it was then I was hit again. Then on to the Field Dressing Station for further dressings.

In relays I must have been carried at least half a mile, as no ambulance could come over the ridge. I found myself in a mass amongst hundreds more laid out in rows. The last I remember was being carried by two German prisoners, but where to I did not know.

I woke up to look at a white roof above my head, there was a rushing sound, and I thought, 'This is Heaven'. And I was more convinced that I had arrived there, when I heard a voice the likes of which I had not heard for months.

It was the voice of an English nurse coming along the train to ask if we were alright. I was in a top bunk on my way to the Base Hospital. I was there for weeks.

While he was there he was shown something that he was carrying that would have got him shot if he had been captured.

Lance Corporal J. Busby was killed in the attack.

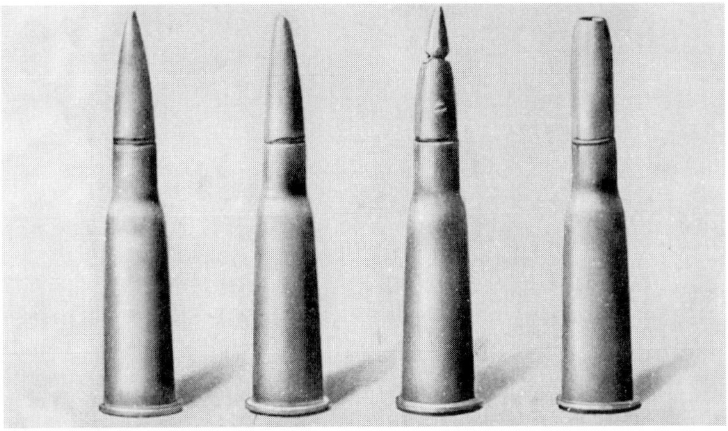

A German propoganda card showing the use of illegal ammunition.

I was shown what was taken from my pouch. In my pouch was found six rounds of revolver ammunition the noses of which were cut flat. I remember cutting these one night when I was bored. If one of these had struck a bone it would have made a terrible wound. In fact it could have destroyed the part of body hit. And if Jerry had captured me with them in my possession, well that would have been the end.'

Sergeant Richardson would not be so lucky:

Soon after that a big shell fell behind me. I didn't feel any pain at all. I was simply stopped in my tracks and fell into a shell hole. I knew I was hit. I couldn't move at all. It turned out to be a blazing hot day. It would be about mid-day. The attack was over and the Germans were coming out beyond their wire. They were out to pick up anyone, and they picked me up and took me to their line.

I must have been conscious because I can remember hazily everything that happened. They took me into their front line and one of them – I don't know whether he was a field orderly – collected a number of field dressings. The shell which had fallen behind me had caused a number of wounds which must have been bleeding profusely. They took my tunic off and patched up these wounds with the field dressings. From there they carried me in a water-proof sheet to a field dressing station and I was left there until they carried me in a conveyance to Douai. That would be about three miles behind [sic] *Arras. As far as I can remember, the place looked like a converted chapel or place of*

Private Hurst and four friends before the attack; only Private Hurst was not wounded on 3 May.

worship. It was a big hall and there they operated to remove some of the shrapnel. There was none in my head fortunately and, of course, a lot of the wounds were superficial. The shrapnel, they could nearly hook it out! There was one piece near the backbone, embedded in the bottom of the back. After a few days we were taken from Douai and taken right into the heart of Germany to Cassel. It was a mountainous place, although we didn't see much of it.

The other two attacking battalions had fared no better; insufficient progress had been made for the troops to consolidate any gain they had made. Attacking through thick belts of wire and with visibility obscured by thick, choking dust and smoke, the creeping barrage moved

Lance Corporal Sharpe, MM, 11 East Yorkshire, survived the attack but was killed in action on 12 April 1918.

on faster than the men, leaving them exposed to heavy machine-gun fire. Two attacks by B Company were repulsed with heavy losses. Rallying behind their officer, the men of 6 Platoon made a further attempt to get through the German wire but were pinned down by machine gun fire from the southernmost point of the wood. With the area being swept by rifle and machine-gun bullets as well as shell splinters, high explosive and shrapnel balls, the platoon would not have survived for long if it had not been for the action of their officer.

> *Telling his remaining men to keep the machine-gun position under constant fire and, armed only with a pistol and Mills bomb, he hurled himself towards the source of the enemy fire… Dodging and weaving from shell hole to shell hole, he got sufficiently close to the machine-gun pit to hurl his grenade. By the light of star shell and flare, the men of 6 Platoon saw their officer fall forward as soon as he had thrown the bomb. The machine gun was silenced.*

Another survivor of the attack was Lance Corporal Arthur Moody.

The officer, Second Lieutenant John Harrison, MC, ex-England Rugby International, won the Victoria Cross for single-handedly attacking the machine-gun post and losing his life in the attempt. The citation for the award appeared in the *London Gazette* on 14 June, by which time he had been reported missing, believed killed. It read:

> *For most conspicuous bravery and self-sacrifice in an attack.*
>
> *Owing to darkness and to smoke from our own and the enemy's barrage, and to the fact that our objective was in a dark wood, it was impossible to see when our barrage had lifted off the enemy's front line.*
>
> *Nevertheless, Second-Lieut. Harrison led his Company against the enemy trench under heavy rifle and machine gun fire, but was repulsed. Reorganising his command as best he could in No Man's Land, he again attacked in darkness under terrific fire, but with no success.*

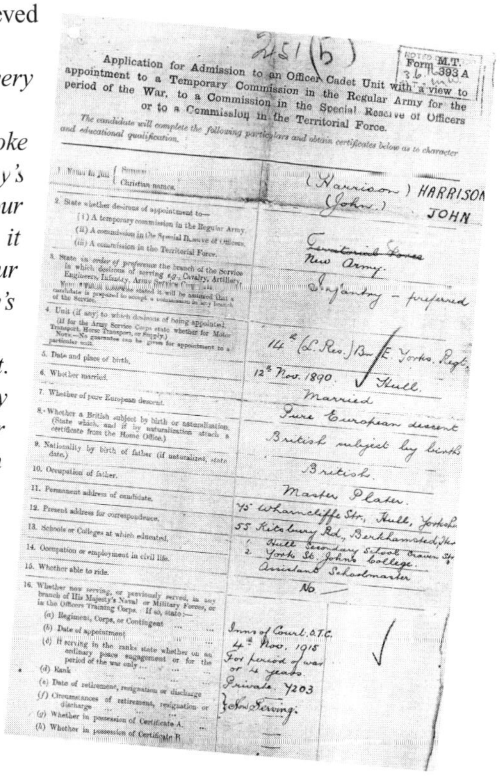

251 (b)

Form M.T. 393 A

Application for Admission to an Officer Cadet Unit with a view to appointment to a Temporary Commission in the Regular Army for the period of the War, to a Commission in the Special Reserve of Officers or to a Commission in the Territorial Force.

The candidate will complete the following particulars and obtain certificates below as to character and educational qualification.

1. Name in full { Surname / Christian names. — (Harrison) HARRISON (John.) JOHN
2. State whether desirous of appointment to— (i) A temporary commission in the Regular Army. (ii) A commission in the Special Reserve of Officers. (iii) A commission in the Territorial Force. — ~~Territorial Force~~ New Army.
3. State in order of preference the branch of the Service in which desirous of serving e.g., Cavalry, Artillery, Engineers, Infantry, Army Service Corps ... candidate is prepared to accept a commission in any branch of the Service. — Infantry – preferred
4. Unit (if any) to which desirous of being appointed. (If for the Army Service Corps state whether for Motor Transport, Horse Transport, or Supply.) Note.—No guarantee can be given for appointment to a particular unit. — 14th (L. Res.) Bn E. Yorks. Regt.
5. Date and place of birth. — 12th Nov. 1890. Hull.
6. Whether married. — Married
7. Whether of pure European descent. — Pure European descent
8. Whether a British subject by birth or naturalization. (State which, and if by naturalization attach a certificate from the Home Office.) — British subject by birth
9. Nationality by birth of father (if naturalized, state date.) — British.
10. Occupation of father. — Master Plater.
11. Permanent address of candidate. — 75 Wharncliffe Str., Hull, Yorks.
12. Present address for correspondence. — 55 Kitsbury Rd., Berkhamsted, Herts
13. Schools or Colleges at which educated. — 1. Hull Secondary School Craven St. 2. York St. John's College.
14. Occupation or employment in civil life. — Assistant Schoolmaster
15. Whether able to ride. — No
16. Whether now serving, or previously served, in any branch of His Majesty's Naval or Military Forces, or in the Officers Training Corps. If so, state:—
   (a) Regiment, Corps, or Contingent — Inns of Court O.T.C.
   (b) Date of appointment — 4th Nov. 1915
   (c) If serving in the ranks state whether on an ordinary peace engagement or for the period of the war only — For period of war or 4 years.
   (d) Rank — Private. 7203
   (e) Date of retirement, resignation or discharge — } Now Serving.
   (f) Circumstances of retirement, resignation or discharge
   (g) Whether in possession of Certificate A.
   (h) Whether in possession of Certificate B.

Second Lieutenant Harrison's application form to join an Officer Cadet Unit.

A future Victoria Cross winner, John Harrison, before the war.

Then, turning round, this gallant officer, single-handed, made a dash at the machine gun that was holding up his Company, hoping to knock out the gun and so save the lives of many of his men. His self-sacrifice and absolute disregard of danger was an inspiring example to all.

The Battalion History scathingly commented that little appeared to have been learned from 1 July 1916; divisional headquarters had assumed that the attack would be a walkover because of the previous battle over the same piece of territory and the artillery barrage. They thought that:

...the attack of May 3rd would be met by shaken and demoralised troops, whereas events showed that our attempt followed immediately upon the strong reinforcement of the enemy lines by fresh troops.

Due to the confusion caused by smoke and mist, the battalion war diaries concluded that it was not possible to give a really accurate account of the battle but that:

...a considerable number of men undoubtedly crossed the German line and got some way forward and possibly in places reached the first objective.

After the war it was discovered that the majority of Commercials who had been taken prisoner were actually captured in Oppy Village.

Penned anonymously, 10 Battalion History contains an account from a soldier who was taken prisoner near the village. He had a painless passage through No Man's Land across flattened German trenches:

Killed in action on 3 May, either Sergeant Cubley or Dawson.

Still walking forward [he had parted from his friend to go round a shell hole – his friend disappeared] *in the growing light, I became aware of a small party from A Company, under Lieutenant Akester. Under his order, we took up a position in an old trench, with Oppy village sixty or seventy yards away on our left front. We appeared to be isolated, and the sound of firing and bombing from a considerable distance to the rear seemed to indicate that the enemy's front line had not been taken.*

The officer left us to endeavour to make contact with some other party which might have also broken through and, as our position had now been discovered, we engaged in a machine-gun duel with an enemy party about 150 yards ahead. I was with the gun on the extreme right of and somewhat detached from our party, and so was not aware of all that took place. When a group of the enemy left their cover and advanced towards us, I prepared to open fire on what appeared to be the best target yet presented. A yell, 'Cease fire!' however, caused me to pause, and I learned that some sign of surrender had been made further to the left. And so an action which would have been dubbed 'base treachery' was narrowly averted.

Private Knight, a reinforcement from another regiment, survived the battle but was killed in the March offensive.

The writers of 11 Battalion East Yorkshire Regiment's History described the whole battle, considering the losses, in comparatively few words. They recalled the moon low in the sky and the very heavy barrage while waiting to attack. Their objective was the wood and village which was bad enough but when they

...moved forward it was found that the enemy was himself massing for an attack on us, and also that the wire on the south-western corner of the wood was uncut. D Company, on the left, succeeded in making their way through to the village, but few of them returned, while B and C Companies made desperate but vain endeavours to overcome superior numbers and dense masses of wire. B Company made at least three successive attacks, all of which were repulsed, but all alike showed the utmost heroism. Lieutenant J. Harrison here earned the V.C. for an heroic effort to destroy the machine gun that was holding up his company, and in addition Lieutenant H. W. Cowling received the M.C., C.S.M. Woodall and Sergeant J. W. Clayton the D.C.M.,

and many other N.C.Os and men were awarded the Military Medal. Our losses in this attack amounted to about eleven officers and 350 N.C.Os and men, among whom was one of the most devoted servants of the battalion, Captain E. W. Reeve, M.C., beneath whose somewhat grim exterior there lay hid a large store of kindliness, and who gave all of us an example of stern devotion to duty that can have seldom been surpassed.

The 13 Battalion History dismissed their involvement very briefly.

In April and May the Battalion was in occupation of trenches in the neighbourhood of Oppy and Bailleul, in reserve, when the remainder of the Brigade attacked the enemy May 3rd (sic).

Private Tottle of 11 East Yorkshire survived the battle and the war.

Private Aust was one of the fortunate ten per cent normally left out of the attack to act as a cadre around which to build the battalion if it was destroyed. He summed it all up:

As we were waiting for night-fall before moving into our assault positions our sergeant came up and said he had instructions to keep ten per cent of our company out of the attack and that my pal and I were to be part of this.

Two days later, we realised our luck when the scanty remnants of our company rejoined and the roll call took place. Our battalion's memorial at Oppy Wood on Vimy Ridge is a memorial to our good fortune as well as to the misfortune of all who died there. That was how you survived. Just being in the right place at the right time. You only had to be in the wrong place once.

Shortly after this Private Aust improved his chances of survival by re-joining the Company Signal staff – he had previously been returned to the infantry because of his indiscipline. He was very pleased with this as it meant from now on:

Instead of guns on the front-line fire-step or in shell holes I was now in the support trench perhaps 100 yards further to the rear and usually under some sort of protection.

As is usual in the heat of battle there were many acts of bravery, most of which were not witnessed by officers. Private Green of A Company was seen doing his bit and was awarded a medal for it. He was in the first wave of the attack, suddenly finding himself alone and, approaching a German machine gun with a crew of twelve men, had a split second to decide what to do:

They had stopped firing for a moment and I threw a Mills bomb which wrecked the gun, killed four men and wounded one, and the others then threw up their hands. Just then, Captain J C Addy jumped into the trench and when he saw the prisoners he said, 'You'd better take them back. Green, you seem to have done your bit for to-day'.

Captain Addy was killed shortly afterwards. For his heroism Private Green was awarded the DCM.

Private Challans was awarded the Military Medal for his work during the battle.

Total honours awarded for the attack amounted to two DCMs (Sergeant Sendall and Private Green), an MC to Captain Traill, and five Military Medals, while Corporal Crooks was Mentioned in Dispatches; 11 Battalion also received an MC, two DCMs, four Military Medals and three Mentions in Dispatches. Only five Military Medals were awarded to 12 Battalion. While the other three battalions had been attacking, 13 Battalion for once had been holding the line, and for their work they received five Military Medals and three Mentions in Dispatches.

The battered remnants of 10 East Yorkshire marched away from the battlefield to huts near Ecurie that they reached around dawn on 4 May:

Exhausted and depressed and even more so when we heard of the total casualties... later in the week we heard that the flags in Hull were flown at half mast when eventually news of the disaster reached the city.

After the attack, battalion casualties were estimated as being:

	Killed	Wounded	Missing
Officers	1	7	6
Other ranks	7	103	107

When stragglers had returned and Field Ambulance returns had been studied, this was later amended to four officers killed and seven wounded with two dying of wounds and three missing. The other ranks' casualties were sixty-eight killed in action, forty-six missing and an unknown number who died of wounds (for the rest of the year there were fewer deaths in action than deaths from wounds; a not inconsiderable number of the latter were probably a result of the fighting at Oppy Wood).

The losses meant that there were insufficient men to maintain a four

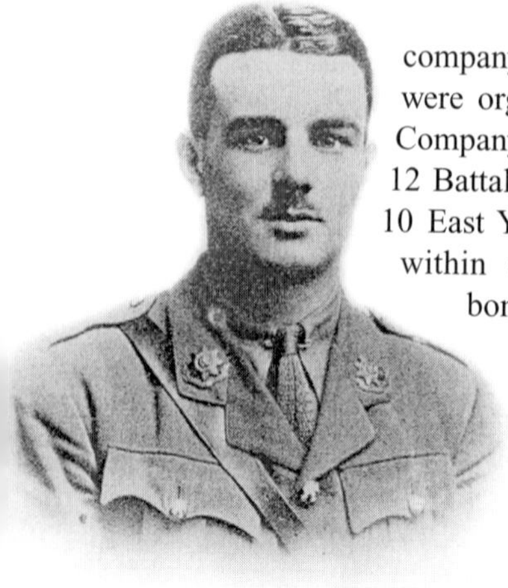

Captain Leech was wounded during the attack and sent to hospital where he died.

company system and as a result the battalion survivors were organised into three companies, A, B and D; C Company was reformed by borrowing a company from 12 Battalion. Even with these losses, within three days 10 East Yorkshire was back in the same trenches, and within a day of arrival the Germans launched a bombing attack that was successfully repulsed. During this short tour, enemy artillery fire was heavy and on the first day the battalion suffered a further three men killed – although *Soldiers Died in the Great War* only lists one – and fifteen wounded. For some reason the War Diary does not record the following:

> *A 5.9" fell on a Battalion ration party, killing five of them and leaving the rest dazed and apparently not capable of making any attempt to go on. The arrival of the RSM and an NCO, however, galvanized them into activity and such of the rations as had escaped the effects of the shell-burst were taken on their allotted journeys.*

Needless to say, rations were short that day!

After nine months of service Private Knight had two battles under his belt. Like so many other soldiers who had experienced the horrors of battle, aware of both the censor and the sensibilities of those at home, his letter to his sister after the battle was about the mundane things of life with just a hint of his predicament:

> *Well dear sister I am quite well at present but having a very rough time and the weather is hot. I am sorry to tell you I have lost nearly all the pals that came with me from the N.S.* [North Staffordshire Regiment].

Further south, 93 Brigade fared little better. Private Oxtoby of 18 West Yorks Regiment wrote home after the battle. His letter, fortunately for historians, had been poorly censored:

> *Our battalion was in an attack, and after gaining their objective they had to retire, and give it up again.*

In the letter he sent home some photos that he used to illustrate the losses:

> *Our platoon officer is killed, and the sergeant is wounded and quite a lot of the men are killed, wounded or prisoners. This time in the trenches has been the roughest of my experience so far, and they tell me that it is the worst the battalion has had.*

12.5.17

POST OFFICE TELEGRAPHS.

(Inland Official Telegrams only.)

No. of Telegram 80 / P123

Prefix Code

Office of Origin and Service Instructions. | Words. | Sent

O. H. M. S. M.S.3 C.AS.

At M. To By

I certify that this Telegram is sent on the service of the WO

(Signature) W. Dowding

Attention is called to the Regulations printed at the back hereof

Dated Stamp.

TO { Wm? Leech – Lindenhurst Bourne End – Buckinghamshire

The Army Council express their sympathy on hearing of the death of Capt N.B. LEECH East Yorkshire Regt.

FROM { SECRETARY, WAR OFFICE

The Name and Address of the Sender, IF NOT TO BE TELEGRAPHED, should be written in the space provided at the Back of the Form

Telegram to Captain Leech's parents informing them of his death.

After the battle, Private Surfleet recorded his experiences, as a non-combatant, of the battles for Oppy on 28 April and 3 May.

> *May 8th: This is awful; we are now in the Saint-Catherine suburb of Arras and it is a long time since I felt so uncertain of life and depressed. We got here yesterday, met by our Band as we marched from the trenches and played into our billets here. I hardly know how to write about what we have gone through since we left Camblain-Chatelain; a more hopeless outlook would be hard to imagine.*
>
> *We were suddenly wakened on the morning of April 28th and ordered to pack at once. Moved off at 8 a.m. in London General omnibuses. Of course, the sports and a concert which had been arranged were cancelled. It was about 52 kilos, to Ecurie, a one-time village on the outskirts of Arras, just off the main Arras – Lens road and I don't mind saying we all cheered when our poor old bus broke down... which it did frequently... and more than one old-timer expressed the opinion that it would be a good idea if it fell to pieces altogether... so that we should have to march all the way. Such was the keenness of the troops to be at the foe. At first, I enjoyed those long, tree-lined Routes Nationales; it was quite pretty, but we soon left the peaceful*

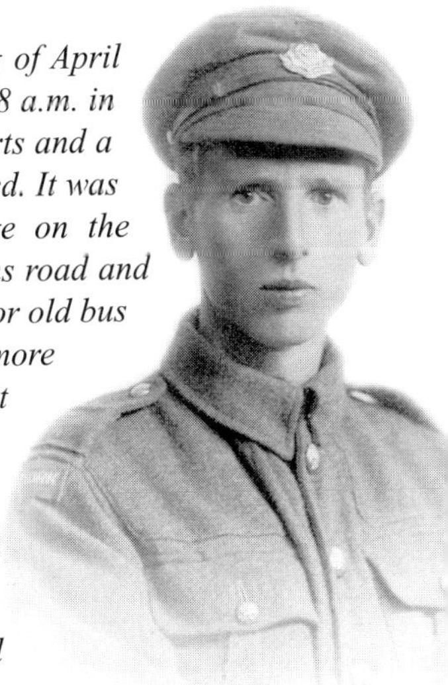

Private Beeken survived the battle and became a teacher after the war.

countryside and entered an area of dreadful devastation which had, obviously, suffered some terrible bombardments.

There was not much jocularity left when we bumped into Saint-Catherine; all the houses battered and torn, some with the roof off, some with great gaping holes in the walls though an odd one, here and there, had escaped damage. Most of the former inhabitants had gone, save a few indomitable old souls who seemed to care little for life now that the war had destroyed most of the things they ever had. They looked too sad to bother to leave their homes in their failing years; how they existed there I cannot say, unless the Army helped them with food. The spectacle, as we arrived, was one to chill the very marrow in one's bones and I felt very sad as we rattled over the cobbles out on to the road to Lens. We soon turned off this road and after missing many telephone lines hurriedly run out by the signalers (lines which stretched across the road from house to house), we pulled up just outside what had once been Ecurie. The road was lined with guns of all calibres, being fired as fast as they could be loaded; the place was alive with ammunition wagons, lorries, mules, drivers, artillery and infantrymen: a horribly lively scene! We were formed up and marched to some old German trenches and dugouts just in front of the disintegrated village; we have never seen so completely razed a place before; not a single house standing and nothing to show there had been any form of human habitation, except the huge, shell-torn boilers of the one-time sugar refinery. Our first night at Ecurie was impressive; looking over the waste into the blackness of the night, a red flash or two would attract your attention and in a second, these flashes, accompanied by an ominous roar, spread across the front as if some great devil away on the right had set a light to a fuse and it had spread for miles like an electric spark. It was another of those hellish barrages; almost immediately, the sky was alive with a thousand flares... red, green, white, yellow, 'golden rain', rockets: every conceivable type of signal, each with its special message to the gunners behind. One of the boys said to me as soon as we got here it was like being taken by motor-bus from Heaven to Hell, and that about described my feelings.

Next morning we were sent out to make a road from Arras to the village of Bailleul. There was not much left of the original road and our first experience of road-making under shellfire was

Three survivors from 10 East Yorkshire, from the right, Private Catron, Lance Corporal Routledge and Private Butler.

repeated so often during the next few days that that damnable game became too exciting for most of us. Jerry bumped the road vigorously and frequently; our routine was the same each time: collect gear and march to the scene of action, spread out, each take a section and get busy. It was a matter of luck where you were placed. A salvo of 5.9s would shriek over at the end of the road where a few, forlorn trees still stood, giving the signal to those more favourably placed to take cover, if any was available. Whether we could take the signal from our pals or vice versa was a matter quite beyond our control, but these little strafes were far too frequent around there. Plane scraps were pretty common. I saw an old R.E.8 (those slow but persevering observation planes) calmly droning over the line one afternoon when a bosche (sic) *scout dived from the clouds and poured a deadly hail of bullets into the poor old bus. To our horror, the machine burst into flames and nose-dived to earth. I have never seen the boys out here more horrified; it turned me nearly sick to see those two poor fellows fling themselves out of the burning inferno and spin, top-heavily, to certain death: seemed to stop the blood in one's veins. God knows this sort of thing is getting far too frequent these days. Surely we must have something faster and better to cope with those German scouts? I can*

Looking towards the British lines from the German front line near the wood. The ground is very flat and now, as then, has no natural cover.

truthfully say we returned to our trenches that afternoon very sad at heart and more than depressed by the whole situation. In fact now, here at Saint Catherine, everyone looks as worn out, fed up and depressed as it is possible for fit men to be.

That road progressed fairly well except near those trees where any new work was blown up and almost as soon as it was done; I am jolly glad that the section I was with was mostly a good distance from that 'windy corner'. Early one morning whilst working on the road, we saw a Jerry plane slide down out of the very low clouds and dive on a kite-balloon which was up near our camp. He must have missed with his incendiary bullets, swerved and flew round and round it at about 200 feet as cheekily as you like until, with a final swoop, he almost ran into the fabric, still blazing away. Then, in a flash, he was up again, lost in the clouds. Anti-aircraft 'archies' wowed (sic) *like angry terriers at his tail, but he was well away: the old balloon smoked, burst into flames and slid, a blazing mass, earthwards. As the envelope burned away the mass gathered impetus until the car, freed from its ropes and impedimenta, dropped like a stone to the ground. A black cloud like a patch below the clouds marked the place where an R.F.C. Observer had been 'spotting'; he had escaped a horrible death by jumping out with his parachute a few moments before Jerry arrived.*

On the third day of these miserable working parties we were suddenly recalled to camp and told to prepare for going into the line at a moment's notice. We tramped back through the devastated village of Roclincourt and met hundreds of wounded coming out of the line: walking, limping, on trolleys, on stretchers, in lorries and cars, in ambulances, some helping others worse than themselves, and all wearing an expression of utter exhaustion and horror. Poor devils: I cannot forget them and we have seen a bit of what they went through since then. It was not a very cheering sight prior to our going in. We also saw lots of German prisoners coming through near Roclincourt; fine specimens of manhood, most of them, though here and there was an absolute weakling. How happy they looked! God! The more I think of this blasted war, the more I realise what fools we must all be. Jerry is fed up with it all; so are we, yet we shall go on blowing each other to pieces until some high-browed devil who has never seen a shell puts his hand up and it all stops; and that doesn't seem likely, in our day. I feel dreadful here and wish we could move to some other part of the line. Why...when we walked into Arras this morning and stopped for a café at a broken-down little estaminet on the roadside, poor old Charlie Bush had a super fit of the blues and I could see he was having a hell of a time to keep from crying! That's how it can get you out here. Bush seems to have the idea firmly fixed in his mind that he will never get back home, and when a soldier gets that idea in these parts, there is always the distinct possibility of his being credited with presentiment; I try not to think of such things, but I must admit that, nowadays, I often find myself muttering little prayers for safety and I cannot claim to be a deeply religious chap. I suppose it is always the same: people turn to God when they are frightened.

May 10th: We are still here at Arras; no one knows how long we shall stay. Feeling a bit more cheerful, though we are standing-by to move up the line if required. So much has happened since we were recalled from that road-making job on the Bailleuil – Arras road, I hardly know where to start. We were certainly let in for a lot we never expected, setting off about 6 p.m. that night and walking miles along "overland" tracks. On the way, we were ordered into some long, dark tunnels; I think we were lost and they put us down there until the officers found out where we were supposed to go. Anyway, we were soon

Private John Mann of 13 East Yorkshire. After going through the whole war he was to die a few days after the Armistice.

called up again and plunged blindly after the man in front, stumbling into shell-holes, disused trenches, tripping over wire (both barbed and telephone) until, exhausted and dejected, we waited in a trench. No sooner in than we had orders to hurry out: dangerous instructions to troops in our state of mind and body! Full of doubt, and rapidly losing faith in our guides, we followed on, in and out of trenches, across open ground, along sunken roads, until shell-bursts and flares were so near it was obvious we had nearly reached the end of our trail. A long trench, fall of holes, wires, duck-boards and gun-bridge crossings led us into the open, across which we hurried, with orders to take cover on the "home" side of a railway embankment (which I have since found was part of the Arras – Lens main line). We have to thank our I.O. [Intelligence Officer], *Lt. John, that we got to our appointed place safely; we were about opposite Oppy Wood and got there just before the barrage put down for the 2nd and 63rd Divisions (who were attacking for Oppy Wood and village) opened out. All the forward guns were just behind us; we had a tottering time when the retaliation set in a few minutes later.*

When the show started, in real earnest, Charlie Gold and I, like the rest of the boys, set out to look for some little cover and we were very bucked to find an old wire bed which had formed the roof of a bivouac at some time; it would not have stopped an egg-shell and how we came to feel so safe crouched under it I am at a loss to explain. The inferno lasted until daybreak: three men were killed within ten yards of our spot and four others wounded. We felt we had been very lucky. I shall not attempt to describe that night and dawn: that is beyond me, but I know the tense excitement, the awful nerve-strain, the dreadful 'breeze' have so deeply impressed the tearfulness of this place upon our minds that we hate the thoughts of going anywhere near that area. Fritz certainly had that Railway Embankment taped to a nicety!

After daybreak, we had orders to take cover from aircraft in a huge dugout which we found, built into the embankment and into this (a German strong-hold a few days ago) we packed. Sardines in tins have a roving commission compared to Tommies down that hell-hole. I was almost at fainting point when we got orders to go aloft and proceed, in small parties along the 'home' side of the embankment to some dugouts in a big railway cutting adjoining the embankment. An intermittent bombardment by both sides added to our difficulties but it was good to get fresh air.

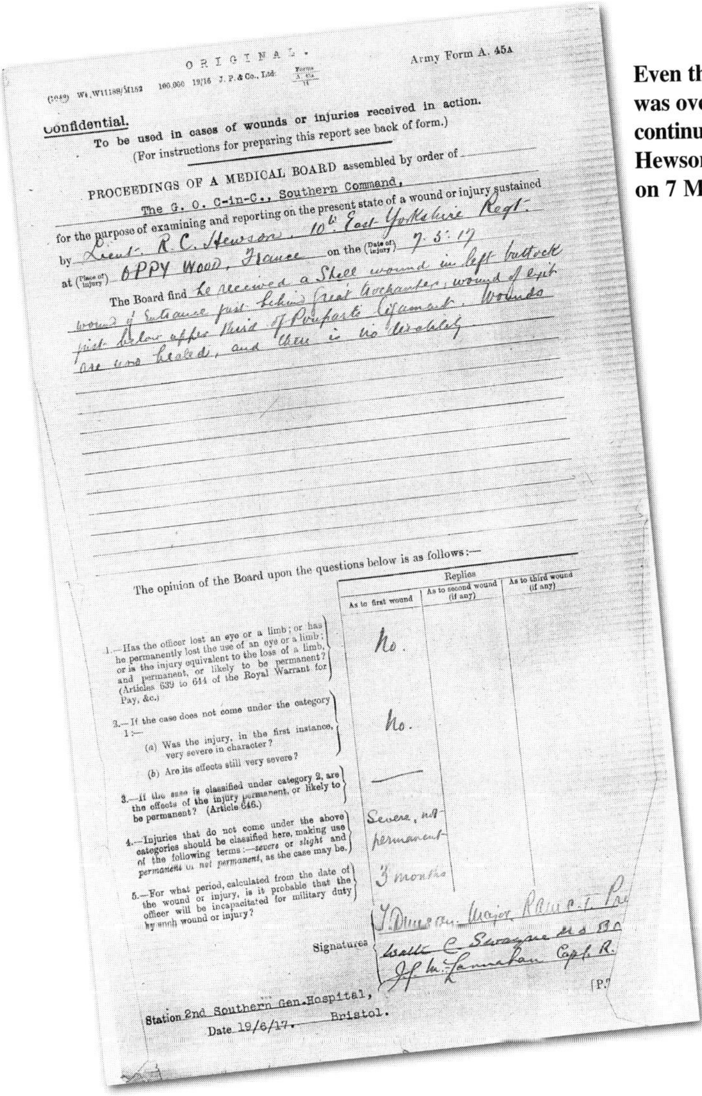

ORIGINAL. Army Form A. 45A

(5049) Wt. W11189/M152 100,000 12/16 J. P. & Co., Ltd. Forms A 45 / 11

Confidential.

To be used in cases of wounds or injuries received in action.

(For instructions for preparing this report see back of form.)

PROCEEDINGS OF A MEDICAL BOARD assembled by order of The G. O. C.-in-C., Southern Command,

for the purpose of examining and reporting on the present state of a wound or injury sustained by Lieut. R. C. Hewson, 10th East Yorkshire Regt.

at (Place of injury) OPPY WOOD, France on the (Date of injury) 7.5.17

The Board find he received a Shell wound in left buttock wound of Entrance just behind Great trochanter, wound of exit just below upper third of Poupart's ligament. Wounds are now healed, and there is no disability.

The opinion of the Board upon the questions below is as follows:—

	Replies: As to first wound	As to second wound (if any)	As to third wound (if any)
1.—Has the officer lost an eye or a limb; or has he permanently lost the use of an eye or a limb; or is the injury equivalent to the loss of a limb, and permanent, or likely to be permanent? (Articles 639 to 644 of the Royal Warrant for Pay, &c.)	No.		
2.—If the case does not come under the category 1:— (a) Was the injury, in the first instance, very severe in character? (b) Are its effects still very severe?	No.		
3.—If the case is classified under category 2, are the effects of the injury permanent, or likely to be permanent? (Article 646.)	—		
4.—Injuries that do not come under the above categories should be classified here, making use of the following terms:—*severe* or *slight* and *permanent* or *not permanent*, as the case may be.	Severe, not permanent		
5.—For what period, calculated from the date of the wound or injury, is it probable that the officer will be incapacitated for military duty by such wound or injury?	3 months		

Signatures [illegible] Major RAMC T. Pres.
[illegible] M.O. Bd.
[illegible] Capt. R.

Station 2nd Southern Gen. Hospital, Bristol.

Date 19/6/17.

[P.T.

Even though the battle was over the casualties continued. Lieutenant Hewson was wounded on 7 May.

To get to the cutting, we had to pass the open space where the Bailleul-Oppy road ran through the embankment and the sight, looking through the bridge was amazing. The little village of Bailleuil, almost within stonesthrow (sic), *was smouldering and diminishing as the bosche* (sic) *heavies crumped and crashed into it, but, beyond that was a wonderful panorama, with the little, chalk trenches showing deathly white against the fearful background of Oppy Wood: little white lines which smoked and split and flew to dust as the heavies made their mark. We hurried past, but it was a sight we are not likely to forget. In the Railway Cutting, we took over old German dugouts which faced their new Oppy-Gavrelle line; they had only been driven out of these dugouts a day or so previously and we spent the rest of that day and the night there. Had our first meal since leaving Ecurie; how welcome dear old bully stew was that time!*

The atmosphere was tense; stragglers from the two attacking Divisions kept coming through and had some terrible tales to tell, though we are getting too old at this game to be worried (or should I say to be visibly impressed) by such yarns. All the same, I did not like their news; was glad to get orders to move. The Railway Cutting, through which the Arras-Lens expresses thundered in the days before the war, ended in an embankment at a point about a hundred yards from the bridge over the Bailleuil road which I have mentioned; a more ill-used bridge I have never seen. During our few days there, hundreds of shells, mostly five-nines, dropped within a radius of fifty yards of it and the ground around was a maze of shell-holes (mostly new ones); the railway lines on both sides curled upwards to the sky in a most fearsome manner. A battered railway truck perched precariously in the middle of the partially- demolished bridge and I expected to see it crash to the ground each time a shell whined over; it was still there when we left.

Company Sergeant Major C Thirsk was commissioned shortly after the battle.

The move took place at dusk. There had been a steady bombardment all day at the entrance to the Cutting and we were all debating upon our chances of getting past that danger point when one of those unaccountable things happened: as soon as we started to file out of the Cutting, the heaviest shelling died down and Fritz started one of those 'one-every-two-minutes' sort of stunt which, if trying, is not too difficult to dodge. We got past safely and took the track which skirted the village of Bailleuil; after much excitement we reached our appointed place, a feat for which I shall always give our C.O., Lieutenant Col. Moore, full credit. The track was ominously quiet, so that it added awe to our uncertainty. There were no trenches as such about here; simply short lengths of trench varying in length and often joined by two or more shell-holes. There was only one, deep German dugout which was used for Battn. H.Q. and the officers' mess (though, later, we found another half-completed one away to the right).

We waited in these narrow bits of trench for an awful long time, knowing nothing of our job or how long it was to last. The battalion we were relieving failed to get out; a grumbling, cursing, clattering mass of humanity bunched and barged in that bit of cover until, without warning, a salvo of 5.9s split the blackness and the dallying 'relieved' disappeared, with astounding speed, across the overland track in a cloud of smoke. We had to duck to avoid flying splinters from some shells which burst about thirty yards away, but these were only fore-runners; almost at once, a hurricane bombardment of heavies and whizz-bangs started: a nasty mixture which put the fear of death into all of us. The bombardment lasted about half an hour and was immediately followed by a steady, gas-shell bombardment on our light artillery just in our rear. The 'whirring' of these shells passing overhead and the dull 'plonk' of their landing (sounding like a host of 'duds') was very weird and as our guns stopped firing, we got a peculiarly isolated sort of feeling, as if we were left on our own in those strange and insecure surroundings. The wind was blowing from the rear, so we soon got the gas coming over our bits of trench. The signal went round in a flash and we pulled on our box-respirators as quickly as possible. Some of us were not at all sure of the necessity and took them off to see how things were going on: we did not take much convincing then! Shortly after this show commenced, a number of chaps staggered across the top coughing and spluttering: 'I'm gassed! I'm gassed!' and even in such trying circumstances I was amused at the muttered and muffled advice from the helmet next to mine: 'Well, put your bloody helmet on, you fool!' ...not much sympathy

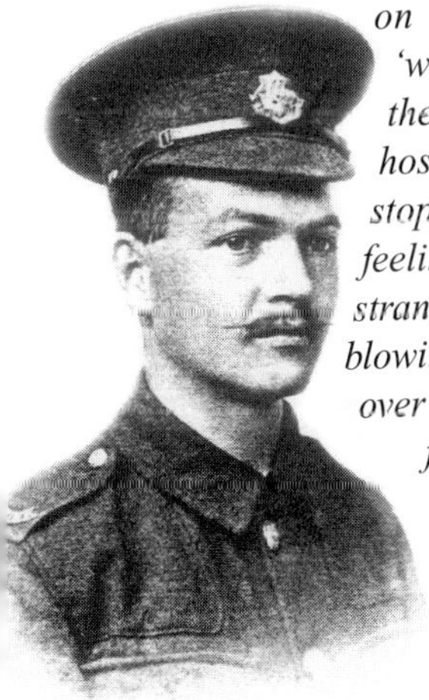

Private Carter of 10 East Yorkshire who was also later commissioned.

there! After that, Fritz kept up a steady bombardment with one of his 5.9s firing with great regularity and, thank goodness, accuracy, on a point about thirty yards to our right; we were kept busy dodging pieces of flying metal which came our way at intervals.

There were frequent cases of gassing, due, I think, to carelessness.

Everyone blessed his respirator and I know now I have a profound respect for mine. I found little discomfort during those hours we wore them, apart, that is, from the pinching of the nose-piece and the silaverang (sic) *from the mouth-piece. It certainly was not nice to feel the silava* (sic) *trickling down your chin and neck to form a sticky mess on your chest, but that was only a little discomfort in a world full of pain and distress and, honestly, I almost dozed off once or twice with my respirator on! We took the helmets off about 6.50 in the morning; everything reeked of gas, everything tasted of gas...even those 'Red Hussars' (and, goodness knows, they tasted bad enough anyway!)* [a type of cheap cigarette]. *Dawn had already 'broken fine and calm': something like the calm after the storm, it seemed and, save for an occasional crump in the distance, all was quiet. Then one of our front-line companies sent up an SOS; our artillery replied magnificently; then all was quiet again. The wounded had been hurried away over the top under the cover of darkness; we survivors had breakfast prepared by the company cooks under the most trying conditions: they used finely shaved pieces of wood which burned quickly and smokelessly, for any sign of human habitation was relentlessly shelled.*

After this, we had a careful look round; I believe we were about eight hundred yards from Oppy Wood which looked singularly well-foliaged and pleasant in the early morning sunshine. Whilst we were gazing at this peaceful scene, we noticed a chap stretched out on the strip of road, the Bailleuil – Oppy road, which ran by the end of the bit of trench we were in. He waved an arm in our direction: Whole, Hurste, Bridge and I took a stretcher from the pile outside the M.O.'s [Medical Officer] *place and ambled along the road to him. Until we got right up to him we did not realise he must have been in full view of the enemy: he was just over the rise nearing Oppy Wood. We put him on the stretcher and brought him back to our Aid Post: he had been out there two days and nights with his leg shattered and had been trying to get back to our lines, using an old rifle as a crutch. I shall never forget that man's expressions of gratitude* when we got him safely to the shelter of the Aid Post; the tears in his eyes gave us just an inkling of an idea of the hell he had been through. I know I had a peculiar feeling of exhilaration as he waved goodbye when the stretcher-bearers took him away over the overland track. I felt glad we had done something for him, though, to be quite honest, not one of us realised how risky our rescue had been. Ignorance was indeed bliss on that occasion; we now know what a store of trouble and distress that road can hold for pedestrians even after night has cast its welcome cloak of blackness over the scene. We shall never know whether it was the hand of Providence which guided us, or if a kind-hearted German regiment withheld their fire; today, knowing what we do, we four are thankful that, for once, Fortune did smile in this death-ridden district; and if that poor, maimed lad we brought back is basking in the sunshine of some English hospital, perhaps he, too, is thankful.

Josef Schwärzler, a German casualty of the continuing battle to control the Oppy Gavrelle area.

I have said how well the trees of Oppy Wood looked on our arrival; they really looked beautiful and, with its chateau peeping through the branches, it was a picture of serenity to be admired. But on our fourth day in, the wood was reduced by a barrage of heavies, under our very eyes, to a mere, tangled mass of stumps, whilst the chateau (a treacherous machine-gun nest, we heard) was blown brick from brick. It was a wonderfully fearful sight to see the daylight gradually appear through the thickness of flying trees, all the more so as we could not hear the guns firing: they were so far behind us. The continuous whirring of those shells as they passed overhead, the crashes, crumps and crunches as they burst, flinging trees and branches skywards, was absolutely awe-inspiring. I do not know how many shells were used to destroy that wood; the bombardment lasted about an hour, during which time shells simply poured in. When it all stopped, we stood on the newly made fire-steps and were able to look right through the smouldering debris into part of Oppy village: a remarkable sight.

That night we moved out to the Railway Cutting; news got round that one of the other Brigades was to hold the line whilst *we were to act as carrying party to the rest of our Division who were going over the top to attack for Oppy Wood and village. (The 2nd and 63 Divisions* (sic) *had been unsuccessful and we knew what losses they had sustained: what a hope, we thought, for one Division where two good, fighting Divisions had failed! Still, those were the orders: it was just after midnight on the morning of May 3rd when we started to leave the line for the Railway Cutting.*

Private W Scott of 11 East Yorkshire survived the war.

(Before I continue my description of the past few days.... and I must say I feel a bit more cheerful after the decent rest we have had and with a few francs' pay to spend...I have just been told a big, Staff car containing several brass-hats and some French officers has just whizzed past our billet. Have been told it contained F.M. Haig and a French General but I was too late to see them; wish I had dashed out a bit sooner!)

There seems an awful lot to say about that Oppy stunt. I am told it was an absolute wash-out, even allowing for the inaccuracies and elaborations of our information, but the details as far as we were concerned are stamped so indelibly on my mind, I doubt if I shall ever forget any of it.

When the East Lancs took over from us about midnight, we filed out of the bits of trench as noiselessly as possible. All had been ominously quiet; perhaps five minutes elapsed, then Jerry started shelling the approaches to the line and everything seemed to me to be in a hopeless mix-up, nigh to pandemonium. Part of the relieving battalion had not reached the trenches; the other three battalions of our Brigade were coming in and moving forward to the freshly dug 'taking-off' trenches. We, the relieved, were moving out to the Railway Cutting. All on the same overland track; all inter-mingled, all tired and nervy. A nasty mess: huddled figures could be seen in every available shell-hole; dozens lay in the mud along the track. Flares kept going up and I could see how still each man stood as a flare cast its sickly glow over the ground, for movement might mean swift and deadly shelling. As the flare died out, the mass seethed forward in the blackness. In long, Indian file, our C.O. at the head, we gradually wormed our way towards the now heavily shelled

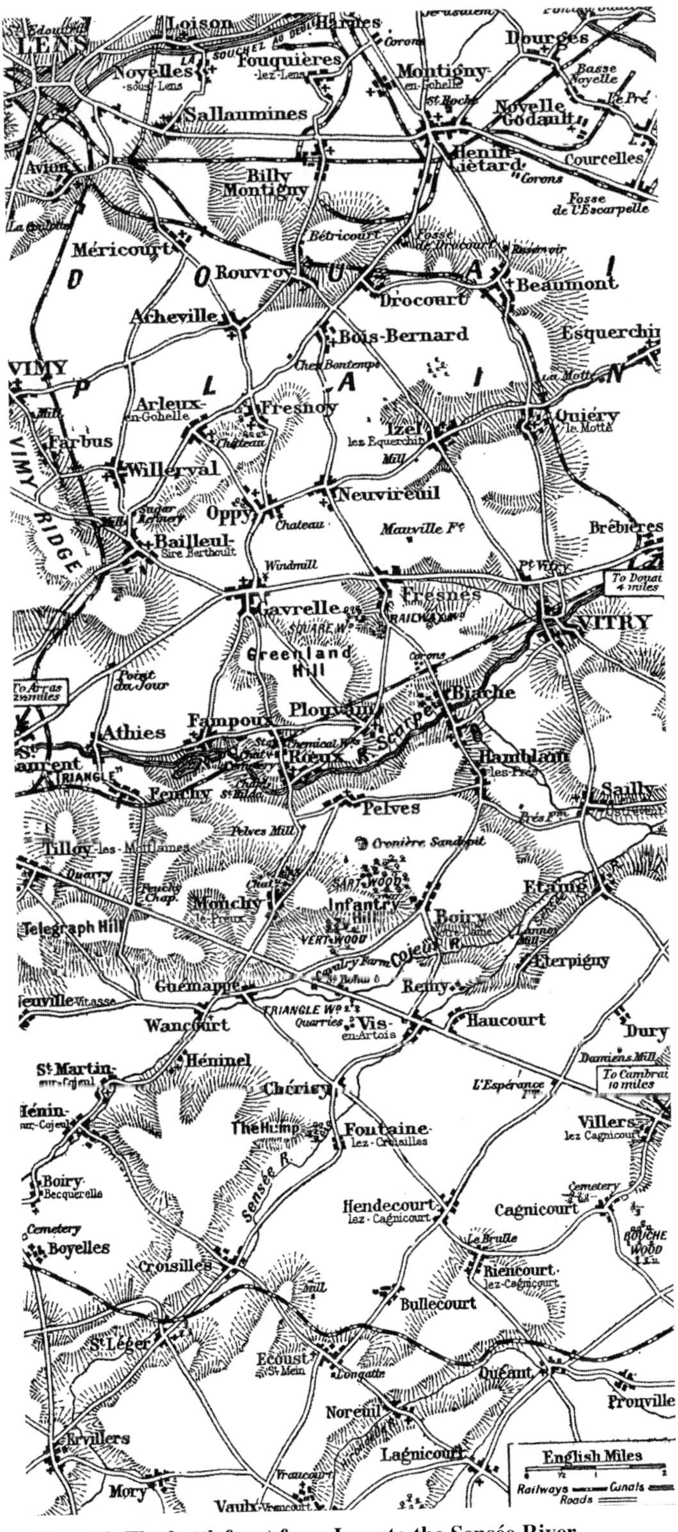

Map 16: The battlefront from Lens to the Sensée River.

Railway Embankment. Faint whispers and muttered imprecations came as from nowhere; blasphemous words mingled with unspoken prayers. We cursed and grumbled at the tedious approach to that danger zone: we wanted to get it over. (But what had <u>*we*</u> *to grouse about: there were others who went forward to the attack and to the unknown; theirs was a far worse job than ours and, God knows, ours was nothing to become envious about.)*

The last half-mile, the critical point, was reached. The C.O. ordered the file to break into little parties and, one party at a time, to hurry past this danger zone. There was a whistle and a shriek, a crash, a rending of stones, sleepers and metal railway lines...a momentary halt whilst the débris fell; then we dashed forward over the reeking permanent way...(how foolishly these engineers name their works!)...As we wiped the sweat from our brows with muddy hands, we breathed again and our hearts resumed their normal throb. We had passed the danger zone and got into the Railway Cutting. A prayer of thankfulness came to our lips; we hoped our pals behind us would be as lucky, but there were some whose movements coincided with that awful rending and crash and other names were added to the casualty-list.

We were pretty well done-in when we got inside the Cutting and were glad to find, as the rest of the Battalion came in, our casualties had not been as heavy as feared. A short rest (we got in about two and were up again at five-thirty that morning) and we assembled to carry bombs, ammunition and rations to the boys who had just gone over the top. After a quick breakfast, we set off, after some annoyance and not a little amusement caused by an argument between the officer in charge of our party (a new-comer to this sort of life) and Charlie Gold. The officer wanted to take us right through the middle of Bailleul which was being shelled continuously: the obvious way was the overland track and Gold told him so! Anyway, we eventually got our own way, skirted Bailleul (now a mass of flames and still being shelled vigorously) and reached the front-line to learn the attack had been a failure. There were some dreadful stories going round, but we were told to dump our loads and return for more. There was prolific shelling to our right and left but, apart from a few shrapnels and the odd H.E., very little came our way and the job was hardly as "windy" as we had expected. We repeated the journey, the armless and legless body of some poor chap

Working parties often came across the enemy as they attempted to consolidate positions.

killed during these last few terrible days serving as a guide-point; surely the most gruesome land-mark on record? Then we returned to the Cutting and heard that the rest of the Brigade had had a hell of a time and this has since been confirmed. I am worried about several of my pals in one of the other battalions; three or four are missing and we know quite a lot were taken prisoner though no definite news has come to hand as to my pals' fate. I can only hope they, too, are prisoners. I met Alf H. in Saint Catherine this morning and he is very worried about his brother who was with a bombing section.

We rested during that day; a few shells landed in the Cutting and, once again, Captain Lawn was wounded by a splinter! Ye Gods! That must be seven or eight times! (The gold braid people at home will be paying a dividend!) Also, our dinner dixie was riddled with shrapnel. We went out at night on a stretcher-bearing party: quite the most efficient and well organised affair I have been on. We first of all got in all the wounded we could find and scoured the whole area. I think it is creditable that every wounded man was brought in: a different tale to that of previous attacks on this seemingly impregnable wood, and far easier than that on that unforgettable November 13th, when mud and shelling made the task almost impossible. There were dozens of dead bodies about; we collected all we could and stacked them

While the British Army took care to try and identify the dead, mass burials in a heroes grave (heldengrab) were common in the German Army.

in piles ready for removal to a decent burial further back. I am still amazed at the casual way we piled those bodies, like so many huge logs, without any sense of horror at such a gruesome task; which again goes to show we must be getting hardened.

An anonymous corporal from 4 East Yorkshire serving with 10 East Yorkshire recorded a brief impression of his experiences that probably encapsulate the whole episode:

We took up position in shell-hole about fifteen yards in front of wood about 1 a.m.; German sentry shouted 'Halte!' For five hours lay in shell-holes, subjected to severe bombardment; Verey (sic) *lights dropping in holes and burning us. Then attack...Germans wired heavily on parapet, wire found mostly uncut. We took frontline but fell back later, finding Germans had support line connected to front line underground. Remainder of day spent in shell-holes from ten to twenty yards in front of German front line.*

Our commander killed on reaching my shell-hole; sniper blew his steel helmet ten feet high as he was standing to speak to me. Sniper occupied position in front tree, centre of wood; kept us down all day, assisted by his artillery. Saw large party on left being taken prisoners by Germans during day. On night approaching, commenced joining up shell-holes. At roll-call two mornings after, about forty men remained out of over one thousand.

The Times History of the Great War summed up the reasons for the attack and for its failure.

> *While the enemy retained Oppy and Roeux it was impossible to advance on a wide front north of the Scarpe against this part of the German line. Of the two villages Oppy was the more exposed, because it was menaced by the British in Arleux to its north and in Gavrelle to its south. Roeux, on the other hand, was protected on the south by the Scarpe and by the Germans between the river and the Sart Wood. To the defence of Oppy, Prince Rupprecht sent forward the Prussian 2nd and 1st Guard Reserve Divisions. The 2nd was disposed round Oppy; the 1st confronted the British in the vicinity of Gavrelle. Before daybreak on May 3, English troops, after the guns had thinned the trees and demolished the entanglements in Oppy Wood, burst into it, and entered the street leading to Neuvireuil. They penetrated as far as the south-eastern end of Oppy, but were forced back by vigorous counter-attacks. The Prussian Guards had not been entirely cleared out of the wood. Many from platforms in the trees poured jets of bullets from their machine guns; the wrecked chateau in the wood had not been reduced. Attacked in flank from the south and south-east by masses of Prussian Guards our men slowly evacuated the village and wood.*

A similar sort of story was happening to the other division in the attack. On their left flank 2 Division was so weak that a composite brigade was formed with 'A' Battalion from 5 Brigade, 'B' Battalion from 6 Brigade and 'C' and 'D' Battalions coming from 99 Brigade. The attacking force was under the command of Brigadier General Kellett, commanding officer of 99 Brigade, and had a total strength of about 1800 men. Its 'first objective was the rearward line of the "Arleux Loop" from the wood south of Fresnoy southwards; the second, the Fresnoy – Oppy road'. On the left flank was 'B' Battalion with 'C' Battalion on the right; 'D' Battalion was in close support. Artillery support was to be provided by one brigade from 31 Division and two independent artillery brigades.

Second Lieutenant F Walker of 11 East Yorkshire won the Military Cross during an attack on Fresnoy later in the year.

The Commanding Officer of 1 Berkshires compiled a report on his battalion's part in the attack two days later.

At about 1am 3rd May companies got into line along road... At 2am companies went out to the taped line, the first wave going about 100 yards in front. This was done to avoid the worst of the hostile barrage which came on. The barrage consisted of heavies on the road...and lighter guns on the ground nearer the German line. Barrage seemed to be controlled from OPPY village & wood. Our troops must have been seen moving into position, as the night was bright – moon behind them.

Our two companies, Royal Berks, were in position lying down in two waves of four platoons each with two special parties for strong points behind...troops on the right and left did not seem to be quite ready at 3.45am when our barrage commenced but then they all moved forward together. There was a tendency to converge from both sides as the advance was made. Direction was difficult to keep.

The hostile barrage commenced at once and is believed to have caused a considerable number of casualties to the left company and two (at least) Lewis Guns were damaged. There was no rifle or machine gun fire. The wire was well cut and the enemy offered little resistance, though the trench was fairly strongly held. Some made off across the open and through communication trenches. A good many were shot.

For about an hour the captured trench was consolidated but no block was made, the companies having joined hands with units to right and left. Bombs were called for and passed to the left where the bombing died down. To the right a severe bombing fight arose and bombs were called for. These were sent along together with what German bombs had been collected.

Between 5 and 5.30am

...after a sharp fight some little distance to the right men were seen to be getting out behind and running along apparently looking for room in the trench but finding it congested they dropped into shell craters. The companies were at this time without bombs of any sort and only 3 Lewis Guns when a hostile counter-attack commenced from the front over the top and along communication trenches. The hostile bombing attack from the right had reached the right of the companies.

By 6.10am

...considerable casualties were caused to the enemy's frontal attack which however came on and the companies were driven out, but mainly by the bombing attack from the right.

The village prior to the bombardment.

> *The men remained in the shell craters all day and were withdrawn at dark.*
>
> *The majority of the casualties occurred whilst getting back from the German front line and were caused chiefly by machine guns and snipers near OPPY.*
>
> *8 officers and 210 N.C.Os & men went into action of which 2 officers (both slightly wounded) and 94 ORs are now with the Battalion.*

Only the left of B Battalion had made any progress, and it was driven back by a strong counter-attack from Oppy. C Battalion, in touch with the Canadians, reached its final objective on the left and on the right captured the trench that constituted its first objective. The counter-attack from Oppy was checked by fire, but the enemy, after driving out B Battalion, entered the trench and bombed his way northward.

The situation was critical for a time, but with the use of both British and Canadian reserves a block was formed 400 yards south of 2 Division boundary; this secured the Canadian right flank and in turn their ability to hold the newly-captured village of Fresnoy.

This attack had been expected by the Germans who 'tried to fend it off by smothering the Canadians' forming-up areas with high explosive and gas. The Canadians swept forward regardless. Within a minute of zero hour the Germans had placed a blocking barrage across No Man's Land, causing heavy losses in the rear waves; but still the Canadians advanced, with 1 Canadian Brigade on the right and 6 Brigade on the

Garrison troops before the battle.

left pressing steadily on towards Fresnoy.

> *Alarmed at this unstoppable advance, the defenders of Fresnoy – from the 15th and 25th Reserve Divisions – turned their machine-guns on the ever-approaching Canadians; and the 6th Brigade, held up by uncut wire, suffered the inevitable casualties. The enraged survivors now swarmed into the village, determined to avenge their comrades' deaths, and in the heat of the moment many of the Canadians allowed their rage free rein.*
>
> *One young German machine-gunner, Gefreiter Harm Frerichs, 25th Machine Gun Company, had left the gun position to use a rifle instead, a chance decision that may have saved his life: 'I fired into the advancing enemy until I was surrounded and had to surrender. Later, walking past our gun position, I noticed that my pals had been battered to death. The Canadian guard told me that they will kill any machine-gunners that they can find or recognize by their uniforms. But it was my lucky day and I went unnoticed'.*

The *Official History* recorded that,

> *...the fighting in the zone of attack of the XIII. Corps had been both fierce and stubborn.*

However,

> *...weary as they were, the two British divisions had striven magnificently. The enemy's counter-attacks, too, both across the open and along the trenches, had been made with bravery and*

determination, particularly by the troops of the 1st Guard Reserve Division, which held the front from south of Gavrelle to just north of Oppy. The volume of artillery fire had been tremendous, especially in the bombardments of Oppy by the British and of Gavrelle by the Germans, but intense all along the front. The German fire had been particularly accurate and effective; in fact, most of the British stores of bombs and small arms ammunition were blown up and the supplies of water spilt prior to the 99th Brigade's attack on the 29th April—to the very serious prejudice of that operation. Though in the two days' fighting only about 600 prisoners had been captured by the XIII. Corps, both the 1st Guard Reserve Division and the 111th north of it had obviously suffered serious losses, their battalions having been frequently caught in the open by the British heavy artillery. That, however, was the best that could be said so far as the XIII. Corps was concerned. Otherwise, despite the gallantry and self-sacrifice of the troops, their effort had only just sufficed to support the local gains of the Canadians at Arleux.

To the north of Fresnoy, 27 Canadian Battalion, after only a two hundred yard advance, were heavily bombarded by German artillery resulting in many casualties. On their left flank 31 Canadian Battalion was held up by wire leaving 27 Canadian Battalion unprotected. The advance was halted.

In the right company of the 27th Battalion, Lt. Robert Combe was soon the only surviving officer. Signalling to the small number of men who were still with him, he continued through the German barrage. However, he found that if his small party were to reach the German line, they would also have to run the

The German cemetery at Fresnes, a nearby village. The dead from Oppy and Gavrelle were buried here.

gauntlet of the British guns as well. He steadied his men, but in the end only five men survived to reach the enemy line. When they entered the German trench they were accompanied by a few men from another company (from the 1st Battalion) whom they had picked up along the way.

The mixed group began to bomb along the trench, using German bombs as their own supply had dried up some time before. In all, eighty Germans were captured and 250 yards of trench line taken. Combe's men charged the enemy several times with great courage. Combe was always the first man round the traverse and into dug-outs until a German sniper killed him, just as a party of reinforcements arrived to assist him.

Map 17. The Battles of Arras, 1917.

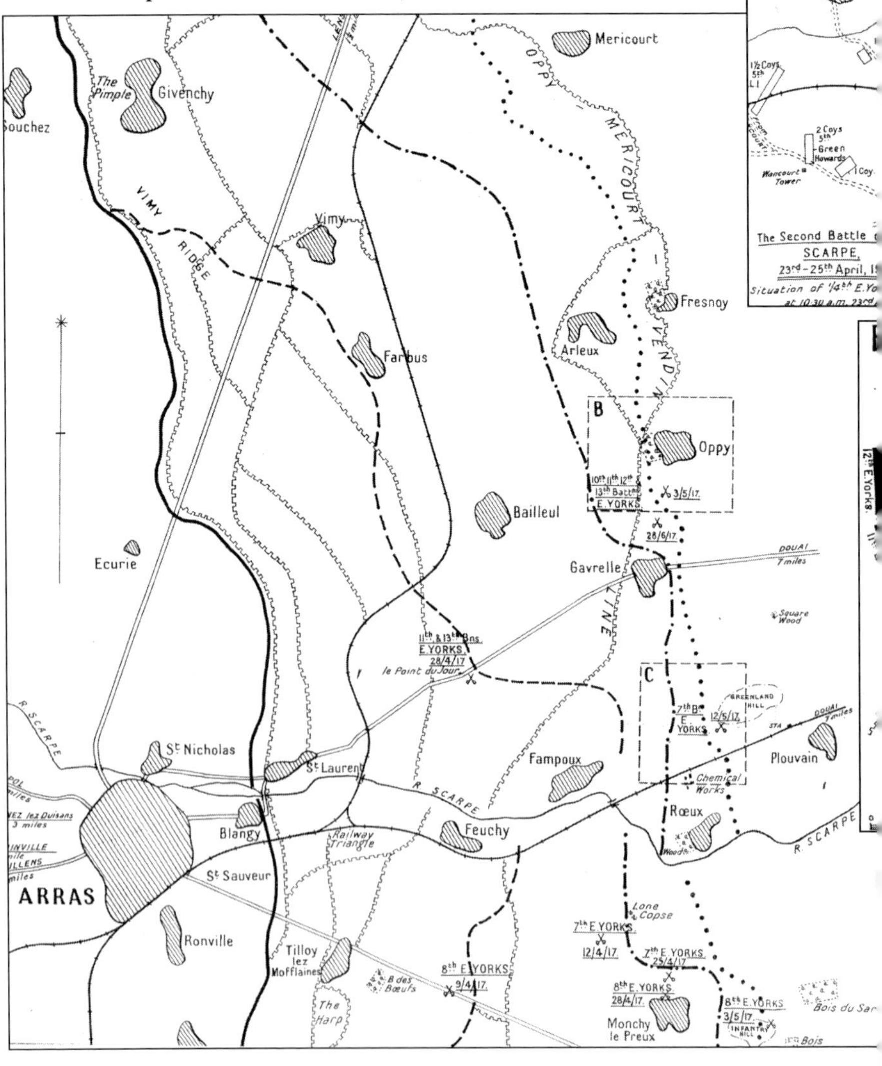

His Victoria Cross was gazetted on 27 June 1917.

The capture of Fresnoy was the only success of the day and the culmination of the Canadian successes on the Arras front. At the end of the battle all the attacking divisions were worn out, but 2 Division had been bled white.

> *By the morning of the 5th May the 5th Division had relieved the 2nd Division and the 1st Canadian Division, and the front from north-west of Oppy to north of Fresnoy was taken over by XIII from the Canadian Corps. It was not an easy position to hold, because Fresnoy was in a sharp salient and more than half the Oppy – Méricourt line between it and Oppy was still in the enemy's hands.*

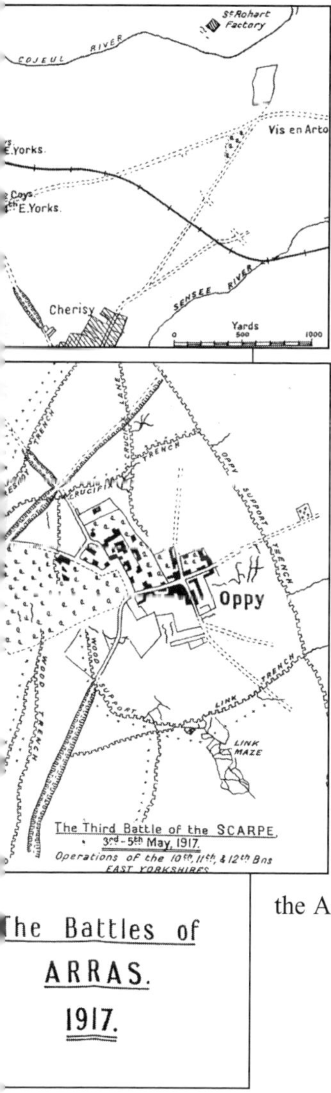

A counter-attack was inevitable.

After a heavy bombardment on the night of 7 May the Germans attacked at about 3.45 am on 8 May, catching the Canadian battalions during their relief; two battalions of 95 Brigade beat off the assault. Just two hours later, a fresh German division, 5 Bavarian, launched the real attack and quickly broke through, destroying 12 Gloucestershire Regiment and the right flank of 19 Canadian Battalion. The British artillery response was weak due to guns with broken recoil springs, guns damaged by fire and personnel suffering from gas shells. More importantly was the rôle of the mist; this was so dense that the infantry rocket signals could not be seen.

> *The line of 1/East Surrey was rolled up by the enemy. The battalion abandoned Fresnoy, but was almost annihilated in attempting to retire. The whole front in the Fresnoy salient fell back to the eastern outskirts of Arleux*

with only 13 Brigade on the right of 2 Canadian Division holding the attack on the Arleux to Neuvireuil road. A counterattack on 9 May by 5 Division failed. Similarly the final action on the Oppy front also failed when on 18 May, 18 Durham Light Infantry failed to capture the German front line on the right of Gavrelle.

The total casualties for 2 Division were 209 officers and men killed, missing and wounded while 31 Division suffered 3211 all ranks casualties. Casualties for the Canadian divisions were: 1 Division 2311 and 2 Division 2613.

Even though the second battle for Oppy was over, it was still not a pleasant place to be, as Private Surfleet noted:

> *We took over the line again from the East Lancs for a few more days and had a nasty job putting out telephone cables to the front line. There were no communication trenches; we set off in two parties over the top at dusk: Cpl. Whole, Nobby Clarke and the Signal Officer took one reel; Charlie Gold and I took the other. We went straight for the ridge just behind the front-line, aiming as near as possible in the blackness for where we hoped Company H.Q. would be. Circumstances made this far more difficult than it sounds. When about half way across our reel ran out; we returned for more, using the line, trailed in our hands, as a guide. Then Fritz started to shell that ridge heavily, as he always seemed to do. We found Whole's line had been cut by shellfire, the two ends being blown apart. In searching for them, we dumped our reel in a shell-hole and, after finding and mending their line, we could not find our reel, though we searched in dozens of shell-holes all around. Fortunately, Charlie had brought an extra one so, as the crumps got nearer and nearer, we decided to push on with that reel. At one halt we made, each of us stretched out in a shell-hole. Gold found a chap alongside him with his tin-hat cocked at a rakish angle and his hand on his rifle pointing towards the enemy. On getting no reply to his enquiries, Gold found the poor kid was dead; both his legs were off. We hurried away from that dreadful scene, only to stumble over the bodies of his comrades at intervals. (Quite evidently we had not got all the dead in on our night on the top, though I had thought all in the area we scoured were recovered.) There were far too many bodies out there to be healthy and we were surprised that these, which were just behind our front line, had been left. At that time we could not do anything about it; we had to look after the living and wounded and, after much ducking and dodging shell splinters, we eventually reached the front line. Just before we got there, I saw what looked like streaks*

The result of British counter-battery work.

of fire spurting from the bosche (sic) *machine-guns; they were horribly near, so near that conversation above a whisper was dangerous. I suppose it was the bullets we saw, or maybe tracer bullets; it was a strange sight.*

At the front-line, we met our other party, but the trench was so shallow and narrow and so crowded there that we were not able to take cover in it, which in view of the damned proximity of Jerry's line, was far from comfortable. I expected to get a bullet every minute, though, quite honestly, I felt less afraid there than I have done in many a place less exposed. (Perhaps my nervousness is going; though the sight of the orderly-sergeant who has just gone past with a list in his hand has given me that sinking feeling I always get when it looks like a working-party... so I am afraid it hasn't!)

We had to lay there, just behind the front-line, flat on our stomachs on the muddy top. Flare after flare shot upwards, lighting the surrounding parts up brilliantly and some of the remnants of the burning flares fell within a yard or so of our prostrate bodies. We watched them fall... almost felt them fall... with a feeling of awe. In the intervals of darkness, we reported our progress to the S.O. [Signals Officer] *and were ordered to return with what remained of our reel and repair both lines which had been cut by shellfire. We waited until a flare gutted itself and then, snatching up our reel, one holding each end of a rod on which it unwound itself, we sprinted back in the direction*

All that remained of the Château gates after the May battle.

of our first line, tearing, falling, headlong in our endeavour to make distance while a kindly blackness cloaked our movements before the next flare. Once we failed to stop quickly enough; a burst of machine-gun fire showed we had been seen and reminded us how near the two front lines were at this point. We fell flat; the bullets, fortunately high, flew overhead. This 'up and down business' was continued when the darkness covered us; each time a flare went up we remained motionless and it was a very weird scene which looked even uglier in the peculiar light. A dull 'plop' could be heard as the flare was fired, followed by a 'sizzling' sound as it tore upwards, until, its force spent, it burst with a crack into a brilliancy which put all Guy Fawkes' efforts in the shade: that was how a flare close up to the line impressed me and, on that occasion, the burning flares revealed some shocking sights. It was devastation and destruction in every direction; corpses lay all around, the bodies of those poor lads of the Divisions who attacked for this damned wood and village before us; how many, I wondered, already counted amongst the missing?...while rusty wire, broken equipment, rifles, ammunition and the like mingled with the churned up earth in such confusion, the scene was something very like a nightmare. We saw all this horror each time a flare went up; little wonder we cursed as we tore at that reel, little wonder we failed to notice or to heed the barbed wire. One thing I regretted (and still feel rather sorry about) during that night. Our reel became unmanageable, so we had to find some other stick on which to carry it as it unwound itself; we took the first thing we came across: the thin round upright of a cross of some unknown, nameless soldier. The cross-piece bore no name or inscription; shells fell with awful regularity all around so that the cross and the body it marked stood little chance of survival; yet it seemed a sacrilege. Even as we took it, I had a queer feeling that it was not right, but necessity made us do it: the lives of the lads holding that front-line were at stake; we could, only trust that the souls of the dead were in the hands of God, a thought which gave me some little consolation, for a cross out there in the forward areas is a sort of sacred thing. I hated doing what we did and still feel sorry, though sentimental feelings here in Arras are certainly out of place.

We found the other end of our line, joined up the ends, tapped in, heard voices from each end and hurried on towards the trench at Supports, thankful we had completed the job. When we got back, both lines were O.K. and Lieutenant Tonbridge gave us a bumper rum-ration (as, it seemed to me, a token of some little esteem!) and we tried to get some sleep in the already overcrowded dugout. Ten minutes later the other linesmen were turned out: both lines had been broken by shellfire. Gold and I were undisturbed until daybreak when we heard that, in spite of valiant efforts by Cpl. Tubb from C Company, both lines were still 'diss'. We got orders to prepare for a repairing stunt at night.

The day was fairly quiet, we got the lines ready for the night job and did a bit of trench repairing. Cpl. Whole's line was

The German cemetery in Oppy Wood was destroyed by shell fire before the assault.

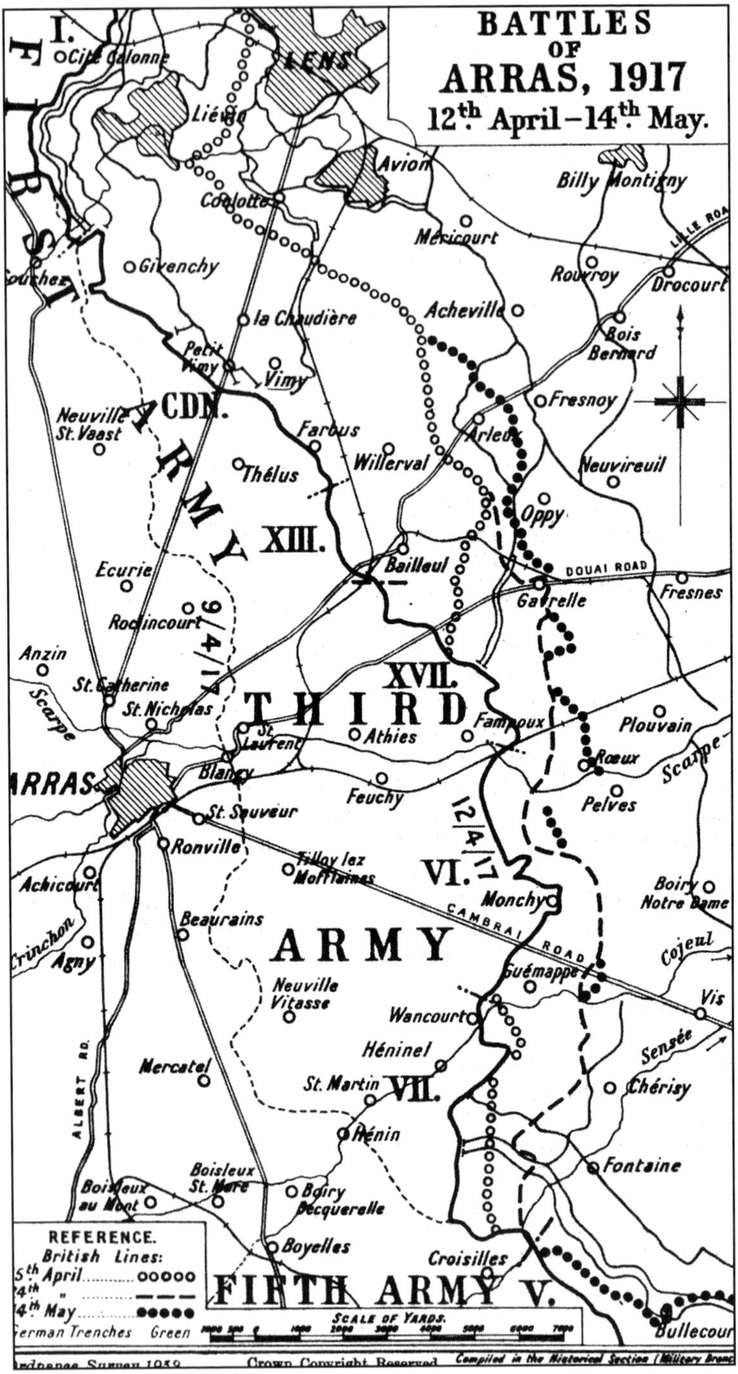

Map 18: British positions from 12 April to 14 May 1917.

beyond repair, so, at dusk, Charlie Gold and I set out with a new line, meaning to use what was left of Cpl. Whole's to mend our previous effort. We had got about half-way across on to the ridge which had been the previous front-line on one occasion and which, consequently, came in for a good deal of strafing, when Fritz opened out with one of his lightning barrages. Charlie had just finished making the joint and I was insulating it (happy that we had found the break so easily) when it started. I had the queerest feeling such as I could imagine a poor swimmer might get,

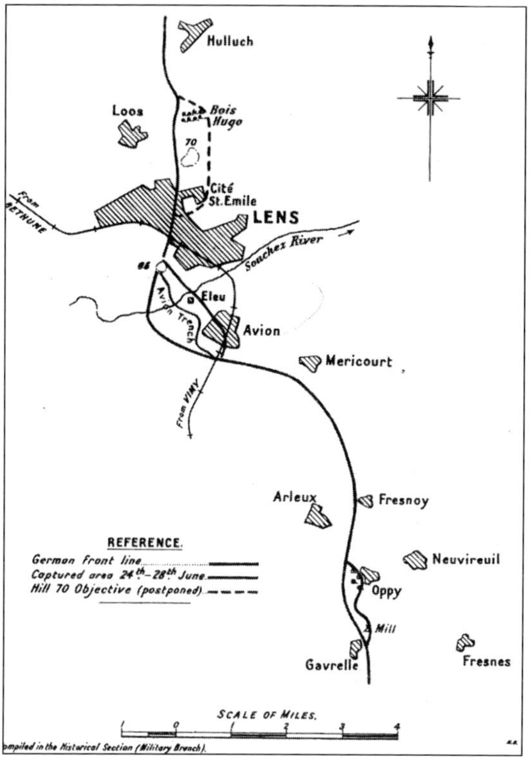

Map 19: Attacks on Avion and Oppy, 24-28 June 1917.

alone in mid-channel with a storm blowing up! Things came nearer and nearer to us: horribly near, and one shell I shall never forget, try as I may (and I am trying very hard these days). There was a frightening shriek and swish, a thud and then an appalling burst. We were covered with mud and earth; Gold had flung himself flat, simultaneously flattening my face into the mud. Splinters...great, horrible chunks of red-hot iron...flew in all directions, leaving us at first uncertain if it was earth or iron which hit us. After a breathless: "Are you alright?", we quickly made up our minds. Snatching up our pliers and insulating tape, we raced back to our starting-point, quite regardless of all the shells bursting around us. We were just about too windy for words and only stopped once in our flight, when we fell into a disused trench. Of course, it was madness to run like that; why we weren't killed remains a mystery. How safe our little trench seemed after that inferno on top! I am quite sure that was our nearest shave so far, for even amidst the din which was going on, it was quite easy to pick out that particular shell; it simply screamed towards us and I am sure we were so near to the burst that the flying pieces missed us. God only knows how.

The rest of the time in this sector needs little comment. Ration and water fatigues every night over the top to that hopeless bit of front-line were no sinecure, but, despite his nightly strafes, casualties were few and we are here to tell the tale. That is something, though who will stick this lot out if it goes on like this, goodness only knows. One bright spot in this black outlook: have just heard my pals in the attacking battalion are captured and alive.

During the day three Victoria Crosses were won, all of them posthumous; Lieutenant Robert Combe and Lieutenant Harrison have already been detailed. The third was won in unusual circumstances by Corporal George Jarratt of 8 Royal Fusiliers, who had been taken prisoner in the early stages of the attack near the village of Pelves south of Oppy. He and other POWs were in a dug-out when an attacking Sussex Regiment soldier, thinking it was inhabited by Germans, threw in a grenade. Jarratt responded immediately and placed both of his feet on the bomb in order to limit the explosion and save his comrades' lives. The explosion blew both his legs off and he died before stretcher-bearers could reach him.

Even with the shelling going on, life continued as normal.

2

Pen & Sword Books Limited
FREEPOST SF5
47 Church Street
BARNSLEY
South Yorkshire
S70 2BR

Chapter Four

The Indirect Approach
28 June 1917

The remainder of May and most of June were relatively quiet for the division, with life following the usual pattern: trench tours followed by company and battalion training. During this period certain platoons of each battalion in 31 Division were designated 'Storming Troops'. Out of the line there were the usual activities, such as a swimming competition and a horse show. When not in the line, sleeping arrangements were little better – bivouacs often consisted of a tarpaulin over a shell hole.

Quiet is comparative, as 11 East Lancashire found out when they returned to the trenches on the night of 11/12 May. Within hours of their arrival in the front line just south of the wood, they drove back an enemy raid. Two nights later Second Lieutenant J Lott led a bombing party north up Oppy Trench under cover of a Stokes mortar and rifle grenade barrage. After several attempts to break into a strongly wired German strongpoint fifty yards north of the junction of Bird Alley they retired; at each attempt the Germans had successfully repelled them.

On the night of 14/15 May, Second Lieutenant Lott and Second Lieutenant C McKenzie led bombing attacks up Oppy Trench and Wood Trench towards Oppy Wood in an attempt to capture Bird Alley, only to find that the trench was full of wire and progress was impossible. After a twenty-minute bombing duel the parties withdrew.

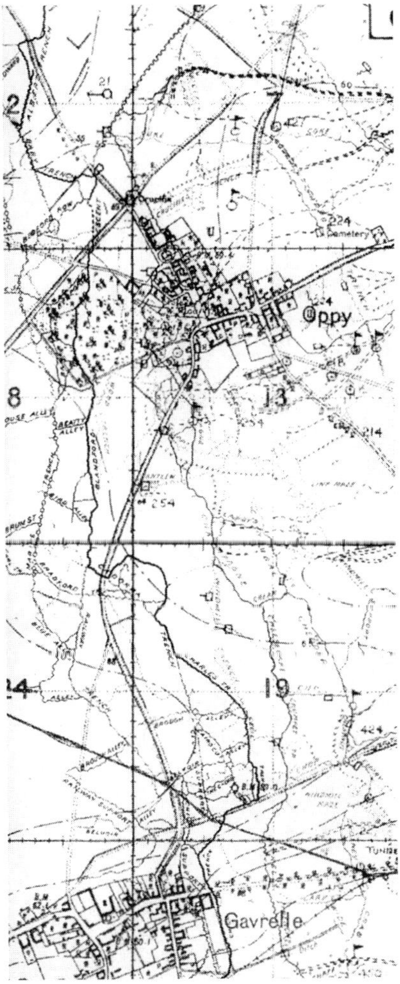

Map 20: Trench map showing positions in early April 1917.

An artist's impression of a trench raid.

Shortly after their arrival in British trenches, an enemy counter-attack was driven back.

For the third consecutive night, after the enemy strongpoint in Oppy Trench had been shelled by heavy artillery, Second Lieutenant Lott led a bombing party against it. Coming under a heavy bombing attack immediately, it was obvious that there would be no advance along the trench. To go over the top into mud, darkness and machine gun bullets would have been suicidal, so once again the party withdrew to their own lines.

As part of the Arras Battle, larger scale trench raiding was re-introduced. A raid was scheduled for 22 June while 28 June was to be the date for the next attack on Oppy Wood.

The strategic purpose of the whole attack was to focus German attention on the British front around Arras and was part of a feint towards Lens and Lille, over the period 26 to 30 June, which was to be carried out by I, XIII and the Canadian Corps. It would also divert attention from the problems the French were experiencing and the troop movements to the Ypres Salient for the July battle – 3rd Ypres.

While XIII Corps attacked around the Oppy area,

> *...the inner divisions of the Canadian Corps and I Corps were to attack on a frontage of 4-800 yards astride the Souchez river to cut out the German salient between Avion and the western suburbs of Lens, and to capture Reservoir Hill (Hill 65), overlooking the town.*

I Corps was also to capture Hill 70 to the north of Lens.

The tactical purpose of the assault was to advance XIII Corps line by between two to five hundred yards along a frontage of just 2300 yards. Originally scheduled for July, it had to be brought forward because some of the XIII Corps heavy artillery was to be transferred to Flanders for the forthcoming Third Battle of Ypres. Because it had to be brought forward, the attack on the area around the Souchez River, that was to be made in conjunction with it, had to be reduced in its scope – the attack on Hill 70 was postponed and only the German front defences west of Avion were to be captured.

92 Brigade relieved 94 Brigade in the Oppy-Gavrelle sector on 19 June. In order to gain information for the forthcoming attack, a brigade raiding party was planned for the night of the 22 June. Each of the four Hull Battalions were to provide two officers and fifty men for a raid on Cadorna trench. The object of this was detailed in Operational Order No. 1:

> *To kill Germans, secure identifications, and bring back MGs, also to reconnoitre the enemy's defences and note hostile MG emplacements.*

At zero hour, in order to disguise the real attack, the whole of 93 Brigade front would open fire with rifles, Lewis guns and machine guns and if they could be obtained, the brigade would also fire white German rockets, in an attempt to further confuse the enemy. There would be no artillery on 92 Brigade front until zero hour, when a barrage would open up just fifty yards from Cadorna Trench. At zero plus 1 (minute) the barrage would lift to Cadorna trench, and at zero plus 3, in order to allow the raiding party to enter the trench, the barrage would advance a further 100 yards. It would then lift again at zero plus 4 to Windmill trench; after a further forty minutes the barrage would then gradually die down. In an attempt to further confuse the enemy, the divisions on both sides of the attack would also put down an artillery barrage.

Zero hour was fixed for 10.20 pm. The raiders experienced only slight hostile machine-gun fire from Oppy Wood as they advanced across No Man's Land but before the raiding parties entered Cadorna Trench small parties of the enemy were encountered by all the battalion groups except those of the 13th; these were eliminated and prisoners taken.

Lieutenant Colonel Ferrand (11 East Yorkshire Regiment), officer commanding 92 Brigade Enterprise, wrote an account detailing what happened when they reached Cadorna trench:

> *CADORNA TRENCH was found to be obliterated and the*

front line advanced over it and beyond without knowing it. The right battalions found CADORNA TRENCH to be a series of shell holes connected by shallow trenches; and in rear of this were several empty MG emplacements. Several hostile posts were found in the rear of CADORNA TRENCH and these men ran away as we approached. Our men followed them up almost to WINDMILL TRENCH where the Germans ran into our barrage. A few prisoners were taken on the E side of CADORNA TRENCH and several casualties were inflicted on the Germans.

The raiders having gone close to our barrage on WINDMILL TRENCH were then ordered to withdraw and, during the withdrawal, a hostile machine-gun was found 30 yards East of the Gavrelle-Oppy road about c.l9.a.00.30, chained and pegged to the ground.

A great effort was made to bring it in but it was impossible to move it, so it was damaged with knobkerries [wooden truncheons with very unpleasant spikes sticking out from the enlarged end].

During the raid the Germans from WOOD ALLEY tried to get round our left flank but the flank guard which consisted of 1 Lewis Gun Section and ten men drove them off and inflicted severe casualties on them.

Lieutenant Colonel Ferrand, officer in command of the attach on Cadorna trench.

The raid was most successful, a considerable number of casualties were inflicted on the enemy and seven unwounded prisoners were brought in.

Our casualties were: 1 O.R. Killed. 1 Offr. & 31 O.R's Wounded (mostly slight) 11 O.R. Missing.

The real cost was higher: four soldiers were killed – Private W. Homan and Private P. Martindale (10 East Yorkshire), Private A. Cook (11 East Yorkshire) and Private A. Bull (12 East Yorkshire) with a small number of men dying of wounds in the days following.

The officers reported to Raiding Party HQ for a debriefing after the raid, prisoners were escorted to Divisional HQ – the Commercials alone brought in seven – and the men returned to Railway Trench for a mug of tea and a ration of rum. When the next battle for Oppy Wood started, 10 East Yorkshire formed the Brigade Reserve, 11 East Yorkshire held the front line and 13 East Yorkshire provided carrying parties for the attacking forces.

> *The 28th was dull and close, and in the late afternoon, black thunderclouds piled up on the southern horizon. At 7 p.m. an intense bombardment opened from the whole 14-mile front of the three corps from Gavrelle to Hulluch, to give the Germans the impression of a large-scale offensive against Lens; artillery on the way north from the Third Army to Flanders had been side-tracked to participate and increase the intensity of the bombardment. Whilst it was in progress, a violent thunderstorm broke over the battle area; forked lightning and claps of thunder joined with the flashes and roar of the guns, and the rain came down in torrents when, at 7.10 p.m., the infantry moved forward to the assault.*
>
> *On the XIII Corps front, the 94th Brigade of the 31st Division, north of Gavrelle, and the 15th Brigade of the 5th Division, opposite Oppy, assaulted on a frontage of a thousand and thirteen hundred yards respectively. The Germans were expecting* (an) *attack, and at 5.30 p.m., when the jumping-off trenches were full of troops, laid a barrage on them for ten minutes. It speaks well for the discipline of the two brigades that, despite two hundred casualties during this shelling, the order and drive of the assault was in no way affected. So rapid was the advance that when the German barrage fell on No Man's Land, three minutes after the start, it was already clear of troops. In the actual assault, few casualties were incurred, and, besides two*

The present day view of the area that was attacked on the night of 22 June.

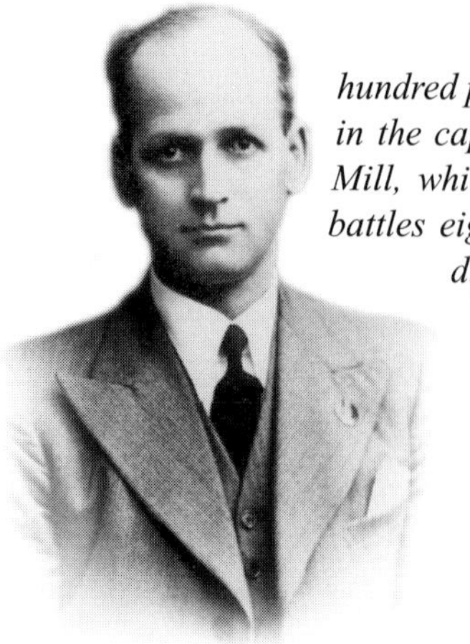

Thomas Southworth who won the DCM during an attack by 11 Lancashire in June.

hundred prisoners taken, 280 German dead were counted in the captured area. The objectives, including Gavrelle Mill, which had been so hotly contested in the Scarpe battles eight weeks previously, were occupied with little difficulty; but the heavy rain interfered with the work of consolidation. The new line gave good observation to the north-east and east, towards Neuvireuil and Fresnes, and to the south-east beyond Greenland Hill.

A successful advance was made by 46 Division and by 4 Canadian Division during the evening of 28 June, capturing the village of Avion and about 100 prisoners. This operation was undertaken in conjunction with 5 Division near Oppy on the right of the Canadians. Advancing on a two brigade front, 15 and 95 Brigades, in a sudden rush, cleared more than a mile of German trenches.

The engagement in front of Oppy was vividly described in *Twenty Years After* by a private in 1 Bedfordshire Regiment:

Our Company, 'B,' met with little if any opposition, and it was not long before we reached our objective. 'A' Company on our left, was held up for a time by a body of machine-gunners, who were determined to hold out at all costs. Here the Company Sergt.-Major issued orders that his men should lie down until reserves came up, and then with a determined charge they cleared the trench at the point of the bayonet.

As I rushed across the open, a German suddenly emerged from a deserted trench, and, on catching sight of me, immediately threw up his hands and shouted 'Mercy, Kamerad!' I never saw such terror depicted on a man's countenance. After being satisfied that he was completely disarmed, I sent him back to our rear.

The sight which met our eyes as we neared the German lines beggars description. Trenches were battered beyond recognition, while trench stores, equipment, rifles, etc., lay scattered and torn in all directions. The trenches of which we now took possession were about forty or fifty yards in front of Oppy Wood, just outside the village. Here we halted for a rest, and consolidated, remaining until the evening, when we again advanced and entered the Wood itself. Soon after our arrival it commenced to rain in torrents, turning the newly-ploughed-up earth into a thick, sticky mud, and making the work of entrenching much more difficult.

It is generally thought that by the end of 1914 the original BEF had

Map 21: Final British positions at end of the offensive, 24 May 1917.

ceased to exist. While the original battalions could never be the same, there were still a number of "Old Contemptibles" in the trenches. One such soldier, who was to die that day, was Private William Hyde of 1 Bedfordshire Regiment. At the age of twenty-four, he was a veteran of the retreat from Mons, La Bassée, Festubert, the Somme and Arras. His body was never found and he is commemorated on the Arras memorial.

Post June 1917

After 31 Division came the Canadians, who arrived in the form of 54 Battalion on 11 July, moving into the front line on 17 July. Immediately they started to annoy the enemy by active patrolling that was carried out by day and night; on several occasions the enemy was found and destroyed but without the prize of a prisoner. However, a raid on 22 July did receive messages of congratulation from both brigade and divisional commanders. Working together with 102 Battalion, a party of the enemy was encircled. Unfortunately owing to a misunderstanding they managed to slip away and the Canadians were forced to return, having inflicted many casualties on the enemy without a prisoner but with greatcoats and tunics for identification purposes.

Walter Busby, killed in action on 28 June.

After the battles had subsided and moved on to the Ypres Salient, the area around Oppy became relatively peaceful, as the 47 Division History noted when it arrived on that front,

> *...up till a short time previously the XIIIth Corps had been an uncommonly active one, but at the end of September, 1917, all was quiet.*

One unit that was stationed there during the period September to November 1917 was the Post Office Rifles. Two members of the battalion left their impressions of the area, E. De Caux MM (French interpreter for the battalion) and Captain (later Sir) George Clark:

> *...the Oppy-Gavrelle Divisional Sector consisted of a double brigade front on the limits reached by the Arras offensive of the spring, running from South to North in front of Gavrelle village, over a rise where the remains of the Mill once stood, to Oppy Wood, continuing through and beyond the wood for a couple of hundred yards to the North. The tall, stout trees, that had once composed Oppy were torn and shattered by the bombardment, but many still stood; great, gaunt skeletons, while those felled by shell-fire lay in every direction. The remains of Oppy village, on the east edge of the wood, lay within the Boche lines. The trenches over the whole front were deep and narrow...*

and unfortunately, as they were to learn later, that as they had been dug in dry weather there had been no need for them to have been revetted.

An officer of the Drake Battalion recorded what the wood looked like at this time in a letter to a wounded officer from the battalion:

Private Hurst with two of the Canadians who replaced British troops for a short while.

> *...we were entrenched in a semicircle round the wood and when I speak of the wood you will probably think of green tress, of mossy ground and wild undergrowth, of Oak, Pine, Elm and Fir, but then you haven't seen a shell-swept wood, and God grant you never may. It is a hideous thing. Scorched, blistered, torn, all its glory departed. Huge trunks lying on the ground, branches and twigs stripped of green strewn all over the ground. At night 'the deadly silence of the beaten and battered trees with not a rustle of leaf or a breath of wind' was broken only by an occasional burst of a machine-gun or the 'ping' of a sniper's bullet, accompanied now and then by the whine of a passing shell. The darkness was relieved every now and again by the flare of a German Very's* (sic) *light dropping well inside the wood and while the light lasted the silence seemed to be intensified whilst all eyes eagerly scanned their front.*
>
> *There was excellent dug-out accommodation. Long communication trenches led back up the slopes and over the crest on which the Hun had sat so long in front of Arras. Broad, wire-net-covered duckboard tracks led to the edge of the narrow-gauge railway that fed the battery positions up from St Catherine, a suburb of Arras. Thus reliefs were carried out in comfort, and carrying reduced to a minimum unknown in any other sector... battalions in reserve found excellent cover in numerous saps and galleries dug into the sides of a deep railway cutting.*

To Captain Clark 'it was a tame and "cushy" neighbourhood' and its

German troops in the front line just south of Oppy.

only defect was the poor quality facilities for the troops when out of the line.

Although the area was now relatively quiet, the areas around the wood and in the wood were not necessarily pleasant places to be. In the wood

> *...you were surrounded by limbless trees, broken branches and thick undergrowth and every now and then the nostrils were offended by the smell of unknown, unburied humanity lying round about.*

More than one soldier has recorded how much darker this section of the line was than the others, making movement at night very difficult. Lieutenant Pound of Drake Battalion recalled one particularly dark night when he was moving from one outpost to another. The night was as 'black as the pit from pole to pole' and finding a direction was very difficult.

> *We groped our way about and suddenly came up against a big tree trunk lying on the ground against which I banged my shins, negotiated the tree trunk and immediately got caught in some half hidden barbed wire, extricated myself from that, then my orderly disappeared in a shell hole breaking the silence of the night with muttered awful curses.*

He realised that they were completely lost. Expecting the noise to have awakened the Germans, who would respond with a patrol, and, standing motionless, they listened intently. They could hear and see nothing but 'a few headless tree trunks all of which in the darkness looked exactly alike'. But their luck was in. Moving off they again groped their way slowly along, 'slipping into shell holes, tripping over barbed wire, scrambling across large tree trunks strewn across' their path. Suddenly they heard a welcome sound, an English voice shouting 'Halt – hands up'. Pound recorded: 'It was a great moment! Thank God we had struck our lines!'

The area around Oppy and Gavrelle seemed to be a graveyard for aircraft. Whilst there was little infantry action, the artillery and Royal Flying Corps were both very busy.

> *Large patrols of both British and Boche 'planes sailed up and down the lines like cruising fleets, but without engaging each other. The Germans seemed to be keeping a good lookout and their pilots made several victims whose craft were sent down to join the half-dozen pitiful wrecks dotting the fields near Gavrelle. In the space of an hour one Sunday morning, two British aeroplanes were thus 'crashed' nearly atop of the helpless Riflemen who could only fire an impotent round or so from a Lewis Gun, supply a guard over the dead and salve the serviceable débris.*

Marine Trench provided, on a good day, a magnificent view of the Douai plain, where, with a telescope, 'the hour could be read on the Clock Tower in the afternoon.' Other observations included a fat Hun who was watched learning to ride a bicycle on the Izel road while on another day an arrogant officer was observed stepping from his motor-car and throwing off his greatcoat before striding off towards the trenches. On another afternoon, for two whole hours, observers watched German battalions marching unmolested, in columns of four, in the distance behind the village of Roeux.

Even the enemy artillery was subdued by this time. However, the arrival of 47 Division's own artillery that had stayed on in the Ypres Salient after the infantry had left, soon changed things. As soon as they arrived they began to strafe the enemy on every possible occasion in order 'to make the war as unpleasant as possible for the enemy, even though the penalty of retaliation (prompt or deferred) was the inevitable consequence', mostly for the infantry.

Watching the aerial combat.

The divisional history continued:

There was never any intention, however, on the part of the Division to give the enemy a rest, and as soon as our own artillery took over they started wire-cutting, to enable a series of raids to be carried out in conjunction with similar or larger enterprises on other fronts. The enemy was well wired in; the artillery gave necessary attention to that matter. The British lines were also well wired in, so much so, indeed, that in some sub-sectors infantry battalions were under the necessity of cutting lanes through their own wire during their first tour in the line so as to furnish an exit to their patrols. A novelty at this time was the supply of smoke and incendiary shells to field-guns. The former gave promise of most useful results, but the latter, though wonderful to look at on a dark night and warranted 'to set fire to a trench-board under a foot of water', were of more doubtful effect, and were later little used.

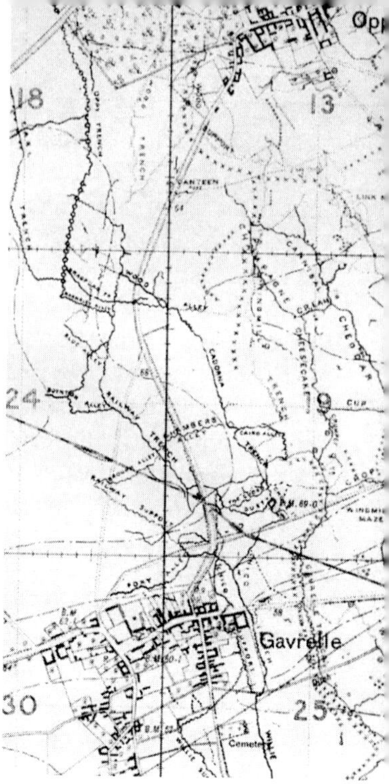

Map 22: Trench map showing positions after the battles of 1917.

On 10 October the battalion returned to the front and this time occupied the trenches opposite Oppy Wood described by their French interpreter as 'one of the most desolate spots on the whole front'. On the night of their arrival, a gas attack had been planned.

700 cylinders filled with a very deadly gas were projected into the Boche lines in Oppy village by a party of specialists who, having done their worst, rapidly departed. A burst of artillery fire was timed to cover the crack of the discharge of the projectors.

The gas killed friend and foe:

one rifleman of the Eighth was killed accidentally... and several poisoned.

While it may have been a relatively quiet period, the front was not inactive. The day after the gas casualties, a German wandered into A Company's lines whilst on a ration-carrying fatigue, having lost his way. The same night an enemy patrol rushed a post held by B Company, at a point where a path through the wood crossed the line, carrying off a Lewis gun and an identification after wounding the NCO in charge and killing one man. The battalion believed that the troops opposing them were Polish and erected a sign that read 'PRZYCTA DO NAS BYNDZIETA MIELIDORBZE' which the soldiers in the battalion believed meant 'Come over and have a tot of rum'. In spite of this benevolent message the vicinity of the board became very unhealthy, drawing much enemy fire [The message should have read *Choć I napy się kieliszka rumu*].

Revenge is sweet and, during a period out of the line, a party from B Company trained for a reprisal raid that would take place on 25 October at 1.40am. The raid was to be led by Second Lieutenant Fryer and Sergeant Fryer with thirty men; its target was Crucifix Corner on the northern edge of Oppy Wood. At this point

> *...the German trenches were three hundred yards away and the ground was difficult. A gale of wind was blowing and at 1.30 a.m. came a heavy squall of rain. At zero a sudden burst from howitzers and eighteen pounders in Bailleul village brought no response from the enemy, not even a shower of lights.*

The night was of inky darkness but as they moved over No Man's Land grenades were thrown at them.

> *They threw some back and at once rushed the trench. A Boche in it fled. Fired on, he shrieked, but got off. No prisoner was secured. Eight green lights spluttering in the falling rain recalled the raiders after an absence lasting forty minutes.*

After a rest the battalion returned to the front. The weather had now broken and their main enemy seemed to be the trenches they were in; un-revetted as they were, the parapets constantly fell in.

Private Surfleet experienced the trenches in January and, having served on the Somme during the winter of 1916, recorded that although the trenches were relatively quiet, 'they were about the wettest set of trenches' he had ever been in.

Death was always present but it did not always come from the enemy. Private Surfleet recalled one such tragedy on 31 January 1918 on the day they were due to be relieved from the trenches between Oppy and Gavrelle:

> *...one of our sergeants and a few men went out on a patrol just in front of our line. They had done the job and were coming in when, owing to a misunderstanding over the pass-word, our company Lewis gunners*

Two German grenades found in the Oppy area.

How the Germans viewed British troops in the trenches.

opened fire, killing the sergeant and two men. They had got no reply to their challenge; raids by the enemy were very frequent then so, fearing an attack, they thought to do their duty by opening fire on the supposed raiders. The dreadful pity of it all is that this darned good soldier, the sergeant in charge (who had been out here since 1914) was somewhat hard of hearing and it seems certain he failed to hear the challenge.

Later that day, as they were preparing to leave the trenches:

> *...there was a German raid on the section held by D Company. Again, the Lewis gunners opened fire and the bosche* (sic) *were repulsed with heavy losses, leaving four prisoners behind.*

Chapter Five

The Final Battles
March to October 1918

The offensive launched on the Western Front on 21 March by the German army was an attempt to force the course of the war in the favour of the Germans before the American armies arrived in ever-increasing numbers. Initially successful, it soon ran out of steam and also out of any useful direction.

Defending the Arras region was XIII Corps, consisting of 3 Canadian and 31 and 56 British Divisions. Intelligence gathered by First Army showed that with the arrival of a great train of heavy artillery, after the start of the general German offensive, there was to be an attack in the Arras region. First Army predicted that the attack would not extend further north than just past Oppy Wood. The proof that the enemy were about to attack came at 5.30 p.m. on 23 March, when they

> *...exploded a land mine under the wire in front of Towy Post, and appeared to be manning the line opposite the divisional front thicker than usual. Harassing fire was turned on the German trenches, and the reserve brigade was ordered to stand to at 5 a.m. in future.*

A wounded prisoner, taken during a raid on 23 March, confirmed the attack and gave the date as 25 March (actually 28 March). Sergeant Udall, MM and two bars, recalled what happened during the raid to take a prisoner. The raid was led by Lieutenant Capley who got into trouble as soon as he entered the German trench:

> *...he went to fire his revolver and it wouldn't work, so he had a stand-up fight with the Jerry. He got a punch in the jaw and his teeth were all bashed in, but he got back, and they got a prisoner.*

All that remained of the Gavrelle windmill by 1918.

A German trench mortar *(Minenwerfer)* in a carefully prepared emplacement.

The prisoner told his interrogators

> *...that the 101st Reserve and 102nd Reserve Regiments, belonging to the 219th and 23rd (Reserve) Divisions, had occupied the Wotan Stellung, behind the front line, on the night of the 24th. These divisions had come from Riga, and would attack on the 26th together with the 240th and 5th Bavarian Reserve Divisions. They were to advance to a depth of four kilometres with the right flank on Oppy, and then swing round towards Vimy. The battalion section of the 471st Regt. had already 60 trench mortars in position, and 8 more trench mortar companies were to arrive on the night of the 25th. The ammunition was already in the line.*

The intelligence report added that this agreed with statements by other prisoners about an attack on La Bassée on 26 March.

Although securely entrenched, the area in front of Oppy Wood and Gavrelle was a terrible part of the line, recalled Private Harry Goodby:

> *...the Royal Naval Division had attacked there the year before, and their bodies were still hanging on the wire where they'd been caught up. The trench that was now our support line was called Naval Trench. That was their jumping-off point. It was most depressing to see these bodies everywhere.*

Not only were there bodies visible above ground but, as Corporal Pankhurst observed, when they dug pits for their Stokes mortars there 'were bones and parts of bodies everywhere'.

Knowing exactly where and when, it was no surprise when, at 3am, a violent bombardment fell on the whole front being held by VI, XVII and XIII Corps. In further confirmation, a few minutes before the assault, the defending troops saw a glistening line of bayonets rising out of the morning mist. On XIII Corps front the main thrust fell on 56 Division who were facing the troops of 167, 168, and 169 Regiments.

The bombardment lasted four and a half hours, obliterating most of the front line posts; fortunately most had been evacuated because of the probability of such an attack, but where this had not happened the troops occupying them were lost; the pathetic last message from one post was, 'The Germans are on the wire. We'll do our best'.

On the night the only two fully-garrisoned posts were Towy Post (behind the support line), south of Gavrelle, and the new Wood Post (the original Wood Post had been obliterated on 21 March) that was nearby, in the front line, immediately west of Oppy. These were probably not located by the enemy, and escaped destruction.

> *Their garrisons of the 1/6th London* (Queen's Westminster Rifles) *and 1/4th London* (Royal Fusiliers) *offered a firm resistance until surrounded; and even then the survivors, four officers and forty men, cut their way out.*

The divisional history describes this last stand:

> *...the glorious little band of Queen's Westminsters knew what was happening, but kept cool. Gradually they were forced into a small and cramped area; Lewis guns and rifles dealt with the Germans in the open, clearing the ground round about and forcing the enemy to seek the safety of the battered trench; but the store of bombs was getting low. Capt. Lowndes, ably supported by Second Lieutenants L.W. Friend and J.C.B. Price, after hanging on to the last moment, directed his dwindling company to fight through the Germans in the rear, using the remaining bombs, and swiftly, desperately, they broke through and reached Naval Trench and joined the rest of the battalion around headquarters.*

One of the survivors was Sergeant Frank Udall, MM and two bars, of 4 Royal Fusiliers who was eighty yards behind a front line post; behind him were two or three Vickers machine-guns. He recalled what happened:

> *Jerry starts his bombardment with big trench mortars. Awful things they are! You think every one's going to hit you! But our artillery's opening up, I can tell you! Anyway, Jerry comes over.*

Map 23: German plans in preparation for 1918.

Well, there was nothing I could do but what I had done. I'd taken a load of bandoliers, and these bandoliers are divided into sections with about fifty rounds of ammo in them, five in each section, so I'd been taking the bullets out from every other section and laid them on the bandoliers on the fire-step ready for the men to man the trench. I also saw that all the grenades were fused up and ready. Jerry didn't do much when he came over. He came on a bit, but he didn't do much. Of course the forward post went and we had to go back a bit, but only so as we could fight. The idea was to get at least eighty yards back from the line we were in, so that he can't reach that far with his own grenades.

Moving back to a straight line of trench, he gathered a couple of snipers who he got to lie down on the top of the trench to cover himself and a survivor from the over-run post. His good fortune continued when he saw two Germans getting into the trench and taking aim at them. 'How they missed us, God Almighty knows! I supposed they must have been just as bloody scared as we were.' Both of them dived back into a box structure in the trench and started throwing their grenades at the two Germans. The next threat was from a German officer who was directing his machine gun team at them. These were quickly despatched by the snipers but the threat was still there; they now had Germans in front and back.

Realising they were cut off they set off to find the rest of their unit. Heavy fire forced them to take cover in a shell-hole where they found a badly-wounded officer, Captain Duffey. Also in the shell-hole was a Sergeant-Major James who wanted help in getting the Captain back to

German reserves in Willerval, a village close to Oppy.

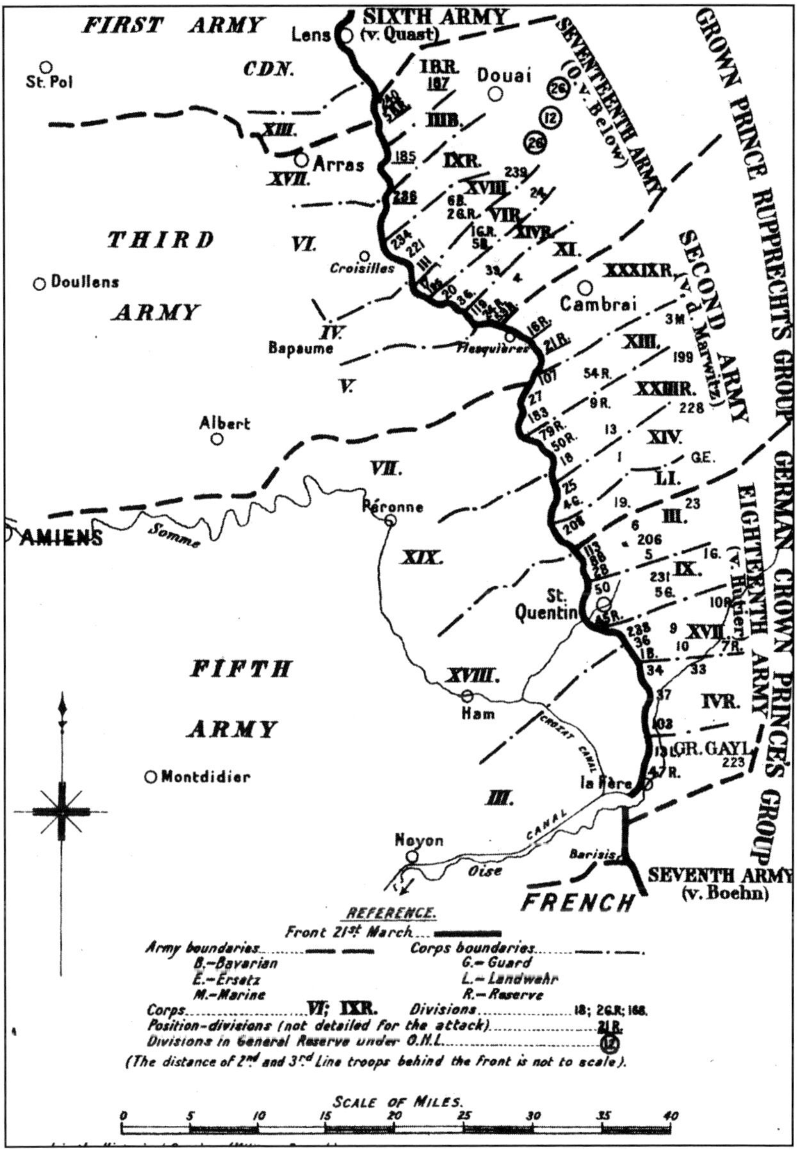

Map 24: Distribution of German Forces on the front of attack.

British lines. Somehow between them they managed to find another sergeant, four men and a duckboard upon which to place the officer. Setting off, Sergeant Udall looked back and saw a German who looked like an officer approaching the sergeant and the four men carrying the officer. Shortly after he got back to the British lines, the carrying party arrived and the officer was sent off to an aid post. Questioning the sergeant, he found out that the German officer spoke English and had

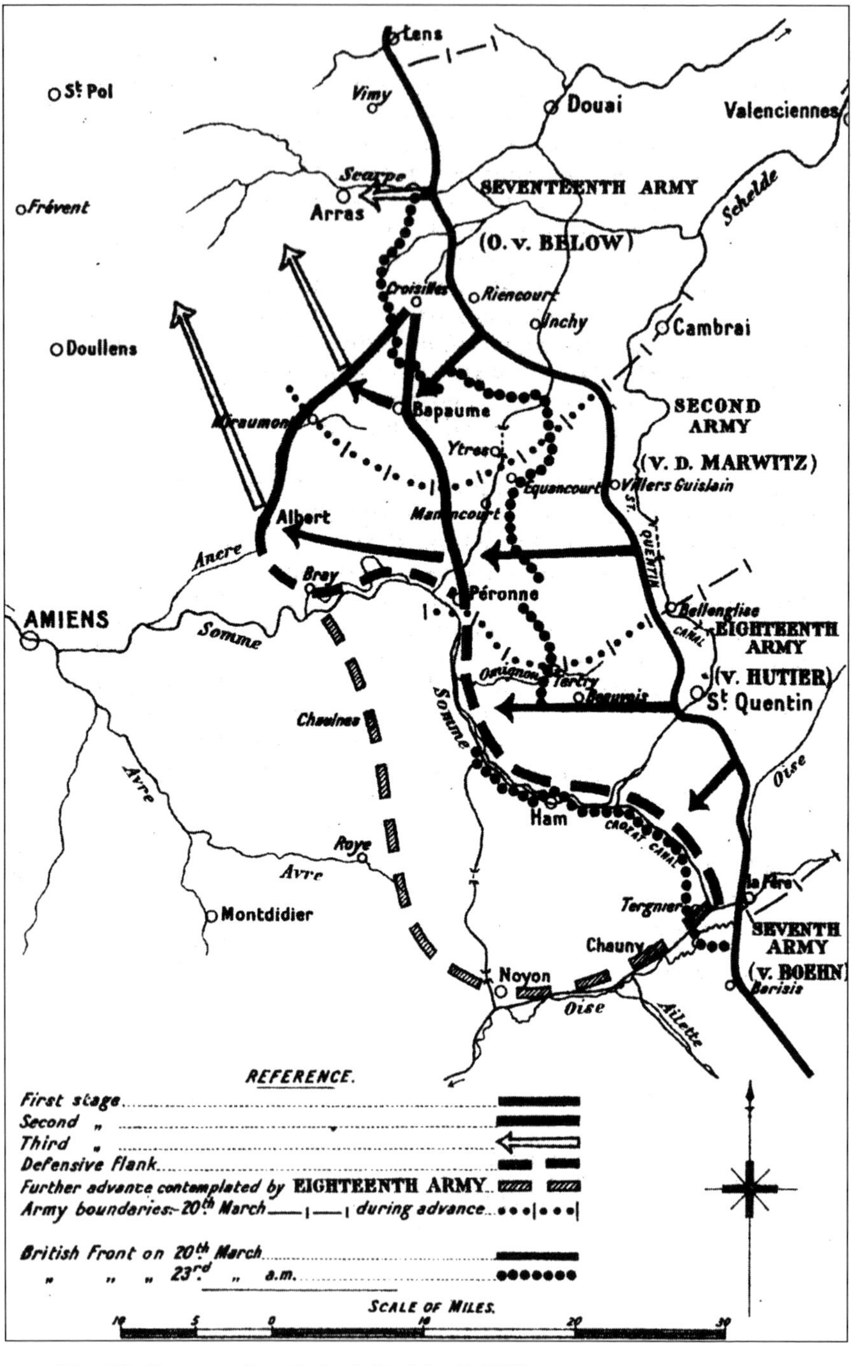

Map 25: German plan of attack for March 1918.

asked them what they were doing; upon seeing the DSO ribbon he had commented that he was a brave officer, and gave them permission to continue, and promised not to fire at them.

The spot chosen for the attack by the Germans was the junction of 4 and 56 Divisions' fronts, an overlooked shallow valley with swampy ground, lacking in trenches. Although guarded on either side by strong points and support trenches, the heavy bombardment allowed the attackers to use the valley to turn the flanks of both divisions. As a result 169 Brigade of 56 Division was quickly forced to move back to the reserve line of the Forward Zone where 1/16 London Regiment took a heavy toll of the Germans who were advancing shoulder to shoulder through Gavrelle to be met by fire from fourteen machine-guns.

The divisional history records one strange way of advancing during the opening stages of the attack on 169 Brigade front. When attacks by low flying aircraft and shelling from field guns dragged out into No Man's Land had failed, the advancing enemy infantry stood up, threw their rifles into a shell-hole in front of them, held up their hands, and advanced, only to drop by the side of their rifles and resume the battle.

Generally the German attack made limited progress and as the assault did not extend north of Oppy, 56 Division was able to muster up a strategic reserve of two battalions and a Field Company of Royal Engineers. However, Oppy Post was smothered by artillery and trench mortars, and was eventually overwhelmed; of the two officers and 48 soldiers in the garrison, only one officer and five men escaped.

Changing tactics, the Germans, with strong artillery support, started working up communication trenches with the result that the right flank

Inspecting a 'stormtroop' in late spring.

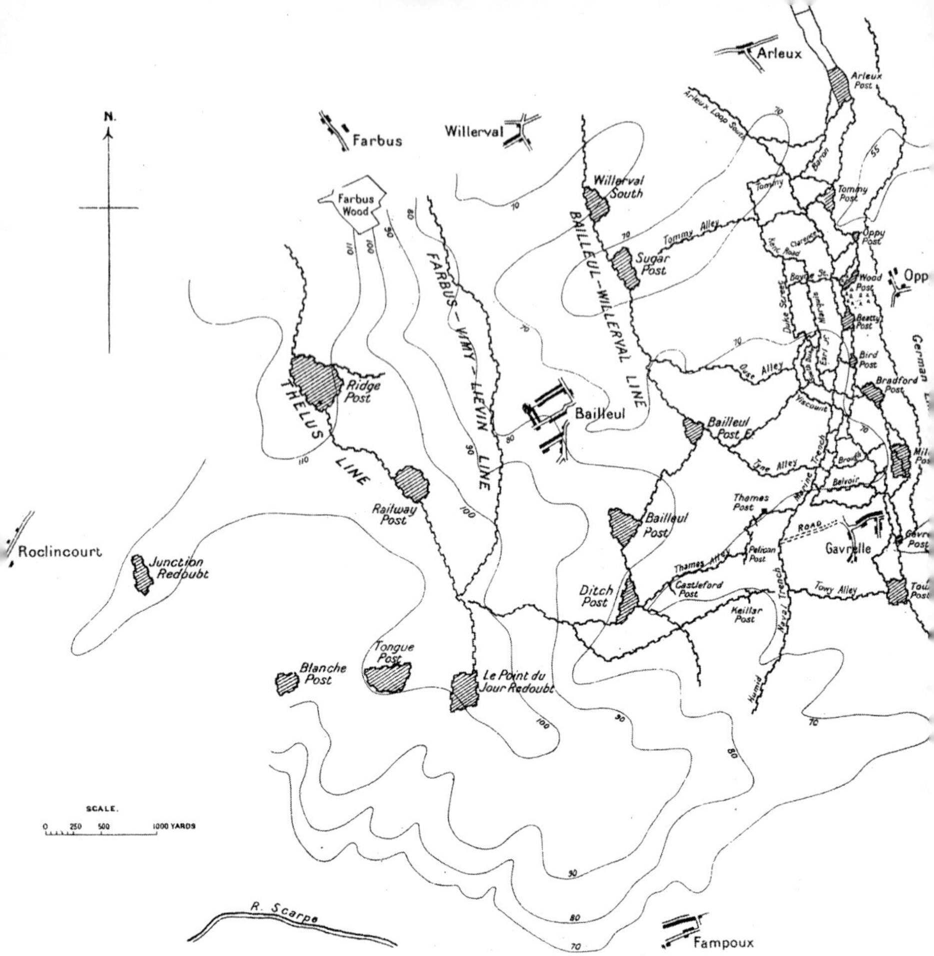

Map 26: 56 Division defence lines at 28 March 1918.

of 169 Brigade was endangered. At 10.30 am Major General Dudgeon ordered 169 Brigade to retire to the Battle Zone.

By 11.30am the position of 168 Brigade was similarly critical. From Oppy Wood the Germans were firing their rifles into the brigade lines. The Germans worked

> *...past its right flank, in spite of the severe losses inflicted on them by the field artillery barrage, as well as by the heavy guns which were shelling those attempting to attack frontally from Oppy.*

Upon receipt of orders from Corps Headquarters, the divisional commander directed 168 Brigade to move back to the Battle Zone to allow contact to be made with the Canadians on their left.

An unusual sight noted that afternoon by Corporal Pankhurst were

Map 27: Trench map to show positions of posts at the time of the German attack.

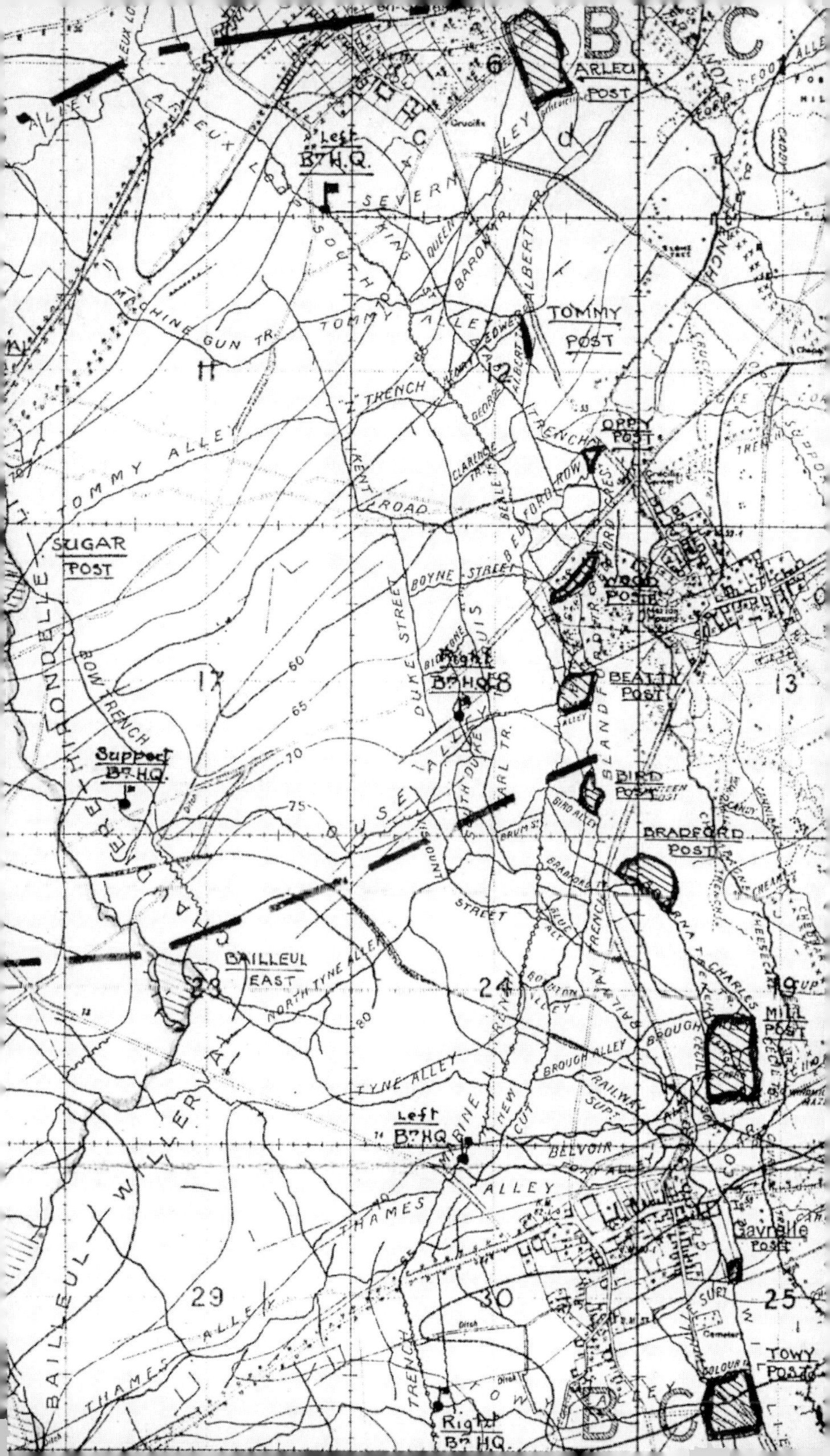
ARLEUX POST
Left Bn. H.Q.
SEVERN
MACHINE GUN TR.
TOMMY ALLEY
TOMMY POST
TRENCH
KENT ROAD
OPPY POST
BEDFORD ROW
SUGAR POST
BOYNE STREET
WOOD POST
DUKE STREET
Right Bn. H.Q.
BEATTY POST
BOW TRENCH
Support Bn. H.Q.
BIRD POST
BIRD ALLEY
OUSE ALLEY
BRADFORD POST
BAILLEUL EAST
NORTH TYNE ALLEY
STREET
MILL POST
TYNE ALLEY
BROUGH ALLEY
Left Bn. H.Q.
BELVOIR
THAMES ALLEY
Gavrelle Post
TOWY POST
Right Bn. H.Q.
BAILLEUL WILLERVAL
THAMES ALLEY
5
6
11
12
17
13
24
19
29
30
25

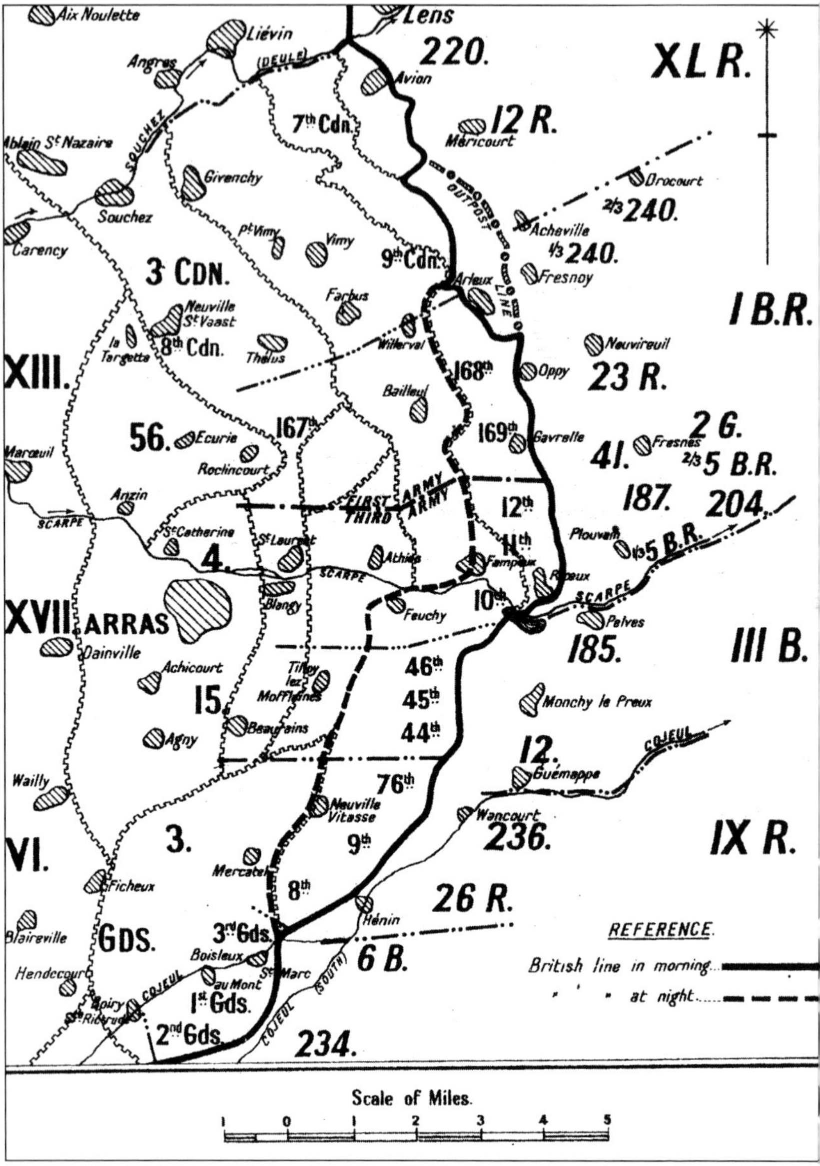

Map 28: Allied front line after the assaults of 28 March.

the men of the London Scottish. They were

> *...advancing in open order with fixed bayonets, just as if they were going for a country walk. They were dropping and dropping as they went, the guns were firing, the shells were bursting, the machine-guns were going, and they just went on.*

With this withdrawal, the front line on the north of the River Scarpe was continuous and firmly established in the front trench of the Battle

Zone. German attacks continued but 'the enemy, disheartened by the resistance which he had encountered and the casualties which he had sustained, began to relax his efforts'. By the last attack on 56 Division at 5 pm which was 'repelled by the concentrated barrage of guns, machine guns and rifles "Mars North", like "Mars South", had failed.' Even so the official German communiqué reported that 56 Division had been annihilated! That evening Ludendorff issued orders for the Mars attacks to be stopped; 'It was an established fact', he recorded later, 'that the enemy's resistance was beyond our strength.'

When 56 Division was withdrawn into reserve it had suffered 2824 casualties; of these 4 London Regiment had two officers killed, three wounded, one wounded and missing and four missing, while other ranks' casualties amounted to fifteen killed, forty three wounded, twelve wounded and missing and 156 missing, a total of 236 casualties in less than a day's action.

Summing up the day, an unknown sergeant of 5 London Regiment told Rifleman Smith that it had been

> *...the finest day in the history of the regiment...there's not many of 'em left, but we've killed simply thousands with bombs and rifle fire and Lewis-guns. Fritz hasn't got a kick left in him.*

The Final Phase
August to October 1918

The success of the Allied offensive on 8 August and its continuing success meant that the war would return to Oppy; it was not long before the British arrived at the Oppy line of defences. Even though the Germans were now retreating it did not mean that they had lost the will to fight, as the 2 Northants War Diary entry for 20/21 August shows: 'large enemy raid on Bn. Front…1 killed, 1 missing & 1 missing & wounded; raid unsuccessful & beat hasty retreat. Pte Broderick MM for gallantry during enemy raid' and again on 24 August: 'front line trenches still untenable owing to previous night's gas shell bombardment'. Such discharges were common from both sides and were aimed at keeping the other side on the alert.

However, in general, 8 Division History regarded the area as 'a quiet one in which the enemy's infantry, well sheltered in deep-dug trenches behind strong belts of wire, showed little enterprise' and even when it took over the Oppy sector to relieve 52 Division the only concern on such a 'relatively quiet front' was the length of the line they

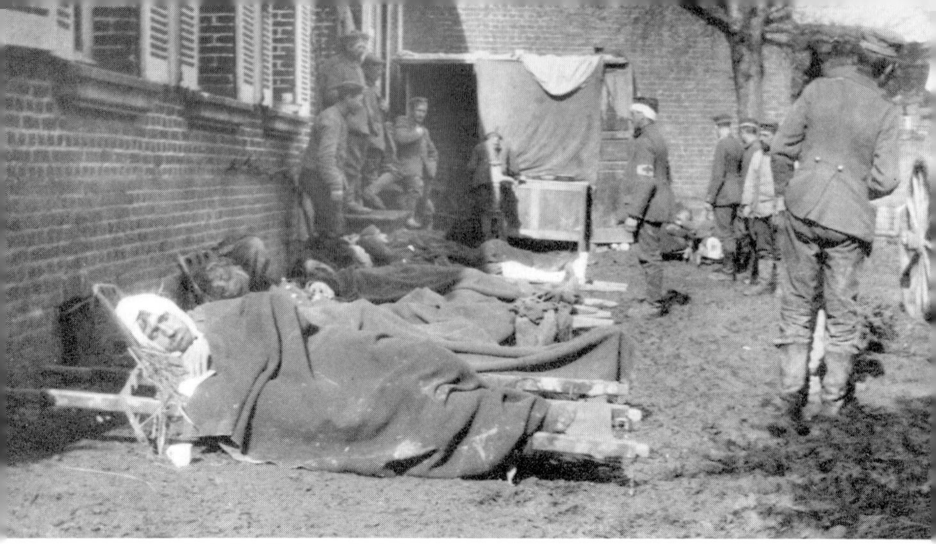

German wounded on the road at Fresnoy.

were holding and that the division was not fully trained. 'However, as the front was so quiet a one, it was found possible to have one battalion of each brigade right back for training.'

The final battle of the Scarpe began on 26 August. That evening 8 Division sent out patrols from each brigade

> *...to test and, if possible, to occupy the German front line opposite them. By 6 a.m. next morning this was done, and in some places the forward movement had been carried to the support line.*

However, as has been seen previously, this was not the case with Oppy Wood, where considerable opposition was met with. Further south it was discovered that Gavrelle had been evacuated, allowing troops to move into the area south of Oppy.

On 28 August 24 Brigade (8 Division) pushed forward to Albert Trench.

> *Between 5 and 9.30pm enemy delivered three counter-attacks, all beaten off on 25th and 24th Brigade front. At 9.45 pm enemy again attacked 24th Brigade heavily with the result that the Right Battalion* [1st Sherwood] *were driven out of Oppy Wood and portion of Blandford Trench south of the wood but held the enemy on the line of Marquis Trench.*

The National Archives have a detailed report of the part played by 1 Sherwoods in the actions between 26 to 29 August that resulted in a letter of commendation from General Heneker. B Coy was detailed for this task. The report clearly shows the fluidity of such attacks. Lieutenant Colonel Mitchell wrote that:

...on 26 August 1918 the Battn. received orders at 8pm to occupy part of the enemy trench position after dusk.

They went over at 1am. At 3am as no report had come in I told 2/Lt A F GERRARD to proceed to the forward areas (to) *ascertain the position and report. At 5am I moved my Bn HQrs forward to OUSE ALLEY at B17C1.2.*

At 6.15 am I commenced to receive reports from 2/Lt GERRARD to the effect that progress was being made S of OPPY WOOD, little opposition.

No news came to hand regarding the position N of the wood so I ordered 2/Lt. H GREAVES MC to take C Coy forward and occupy KENT ROAD - DUKE ST. This he did.

The Bosche (sic) *was no doubt taken by surprise and thus the early stages of the advance encountered little opposition. When the enemy had had time to recover himself and estimate the strength of our attacking force he sent parties of bombers supported by MG fire from OPPY WOOD to work their way up the C.Ts* [communication trenches] *and counter attack us.*

This was difficult to cope with as the enemy knew every inch of the ground. At this time we had very few bombs ourselves, we slowly evacuated the most advanced positions and formed a line in MARQUIS TR. I then ordered C Coy to move up from DUKE ST – KENT ROAD to MARQUIS & link up with B Coy. This was done, considerable opposition being encountered on the way.

At this stage casualties were coming down with several officers, amongst them Second Lieutenants KING & GERRARD

Map 29: Trench map at the time of the British attack.

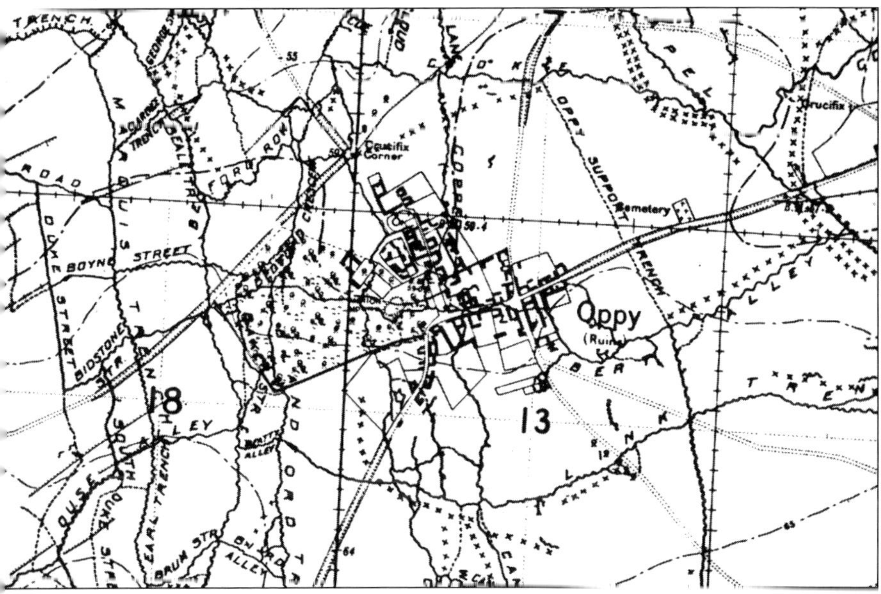

German machine gunners were often the last troops to vacate a trench.

and the liaison officer of the RFA.

I therefore sent word to CAPT PEARSE who had up to look around (sic) *and size up the situation to assume command of the forward Companies and reorganise. On his request I attained artillery situation on OPPY WOOD which relieved the pressure.*

Taking advantage of this PEARSE got the men to resume the offensive, and supplies of bombs having meanwhile been sent up the enemy was bombed back traverse by traverse.

By this means we were able to occupy the line BEALE TR.

My object was to establish a line BLANDFORD TR from BRADFORD TR on my right N. of BEDFORD CRES as far as BEDFORD ROW.

One Vickers gun was placed in OUSE ALLEY at the point where it could bring indirect fire on to OPPY WOOD.

Keeping touch with the flanks was very difficult – on the right the A&SH [Argyll and Sutherland Highlanders] *of the 51st Div were in N. TYNE ALLEY – VISCOUNT ST. but did not push up further. We kept in touch with them by constant patrols.*

On the left our flank reached as far as TOMMY ALLEY – 'Z' TR thence by CLARENCE TR BEALE TR – BEDFORD ROW. Touch was kept with Worcesters by frequent patrols. We were holding 1500x of front. I sent up 2 platoons of D Coy to be kept in support. The late afternoon & enemy were quiet so I pushed up A Coy to relieve B Coy and put the latter in BOW SUPPORT to get a night's rest.

The next day, 28 August,

...the 2/R. BERKS relieved A&SH during the night 27/28th and took over position VISCOUNT ST – BLUE ALLEY.

I asked them to occupy RAILWAY TR so as to keep in touch.

The line BLANDFORD through OPPY WOOD to BEDFORD CRES was carefully reconnoitred but being an old British trench which had been almost shelled out of existence we decided to stick to our line BEALE TR – BAKER ST BEDFORD CRESCENT at the same time holding posts at the Eastern end of all CTs running with BLANDFORD.

While making a tour of the lines about 11.30am the Bosche started shelling our lines heavily. I noticed with what accuracy he placed his shells at intervals all along the line of MARQUIS TR.

At 12 noon I discussed the situation with PEARSE, as the shelling still continued (I) *went to B HQ to ask for retaliation.*

Unfortunately a new Brigade of RFA (Royal Field Artillery) *from an Army Group was now covering us. This liaison officer was with me but explained that part of his guns were behind THELUS RIDGE and the other were moving up to new positions.*

The response to an appeal for support was therefore disappointing and a few 4.5 hows [howitzers] *pitched in MARQUIS TR, some of them even* (fell) *behind the forward H.Qrs at junction of OUSE ALLEY and SOUTH DUKE ST.*

During this time the post established by C Coy in OPPY WOOD was subjected to continual attention from the direction of

Fresnoy Wood from the road into Oppy; this wood was also full of troops.

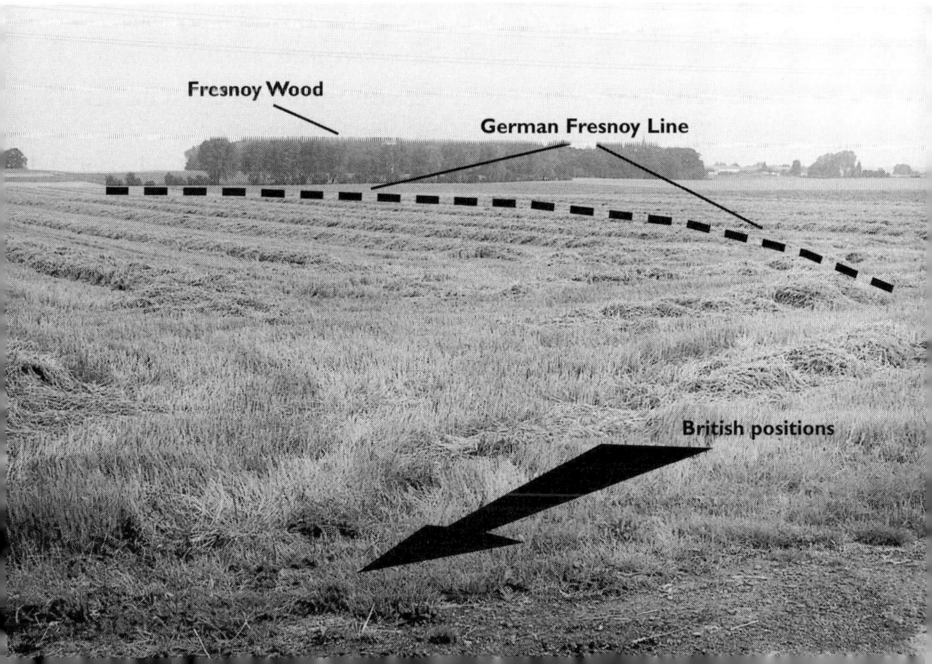

the mound [chateau remains], *the Bosche* (sic) *at the same time making persistent efforts to outflank the post, the overgrown trenches & much grass around providing excellent facilities for him to do so.*

Permission was given to C Coy to withdraw this post to BEALE TR.

Remaining 2 platoons of D Coy having been sent forward Captain PEARSE attached one of these to C Coy to meet any attack from the direction of the wood.

At about 1.50pm an intense barrage was opened on our lines lasting for 10 minutes. On its lifting the Bosche was seen to be coming on both on the right and left. S.O.S was put up but brought no immediate response. The whole of our line was now attacked, those on the right advancing over the top and those in the centre & on our left, bombing up the CTs. Enemy was carrying full equipment, clearly evidence of his intention to turn us out & re-occupy his old positions.

A series of fights at close quarters ensued under pressure of which our line was slowly withdrawn to MARQUIS – EARLE, a better defensive line, fighting every inch of the way. Here there being a continuous and fairly good line with good field of fire the enemy was held up and all subsequent attacks repulsed.

A Coy on the right bombed the Bosche (sic) *back & re-occupied their positions in BEALE TR. In order however to form a continuous line straight through, these were afterwards evacuated and the Coy front established in EARL TR & BLUE ALLEY. This also afforded the Artillery a good line to shoot on if requested re BLANDFORD. During the hand-to-hand fighting which took place, our fellows gave more than they took & many*

Some of the guns captured as the Germans pulled back across the rest of the front. In the Oppy area the troops stayed dug in.

Map 30: The operations of the British Army from 8 August to the Armistice.

deeds of great gallantry were done. Second Lieutenant Spatcher in particular fought for hours on end bombing, working a L. GUN using his revolver also rifle & bayonet. He personally accounted for several Bosche, his great gallantry raised the spirit of his men to a pitch of enthusiasm.

Before evening there were two more separate periods in which our line was heavily shelled but the artillery support was still not working in the way we could have wished.

The night passed quickly & at 4am – 5.30am the forward positions were taken over by the 2/NORTHAMPTONSHIRE REGT. & the positions in rear BOW TRENCH – BOW SUPPORT were relieved by 7am 29/8/18. During the afternoon 28th at least 3000 bombs were thrown by us, 1000 of which were German stick bombs salved by us in their lines.

Our casualties amounted to nearly 100, most of which were from shell fire. In the individual fighting the known enemy casualties inflicted by different individuals enable us to state that more enemy were killed than of ours. The sense of proportion in which one looks at a battle like this changes according to the particular phase of the war.

In the early days an engagement causing 100 casualties would have been considered an event, now it is mere detail. Nevertheless for the Battn it was a very stiff battle, the enemy was driven off repeatedly with loss & the grit & bravery of all ranks was worthy of the highest praise.

At 3.30pm on 29 August, 2 Berkshire advanced and occupied the line from Cecil Support to Charles and Cadorna trenches, while 2 Northants re-occupied the whole line of Blandford Trench, including the western portion of Oppy Wood and pushed on into Champagne Trench.

After the battle had moved on.

A German trench after the battle.

For their stiff resistance on 28 August the Commanding Officer of 1 Sherwoods received a thank you from the Commanding Officer of 8 Division, Major General Heneker.

> *My Dear Mitchell, I wish you would convey to all your officers and men who were in the line when the Boche attacked you so heavily and persistently on the 28th inst., my thanks for the gallant fight they put up. I can always rely upon the 1/Sherwood Foresters to do the right thing. Tell your fellows what I say.*

The area then became comparatively quiet but busy until a German deserter (an Alsatian) from 17RIR (Reserve Infantry Regiment) of 15 Reserve Division, stated that there would be a raid, probably on the night of 3/4 September. To counter this threat British artillery soaked the area with gas. Undeterred, an enemy party about 25 strong attempted to raid a post of 23 Brigade at Arleux crucifix on the night of 4 September; they were driven off by rifle fire. During the night a further three raids were made, all of them unsuccessful, against Baron Trench, Crucifix Trench and Cadorna Trench. German casualties are unknown although they did leave behind one dead soldier of 69 IR in Crucifix Trench. British casualties amounted to six other ranks.

Arrangements for a raid by three platoons of 1 Sherwoods were completed on 6 September; these included a smoke barrage and a rehearsal over a taped course at Mont St Eloi. At dawn the next day they raided Oppy village, capturing eight prisoners from 17 RIR. Their

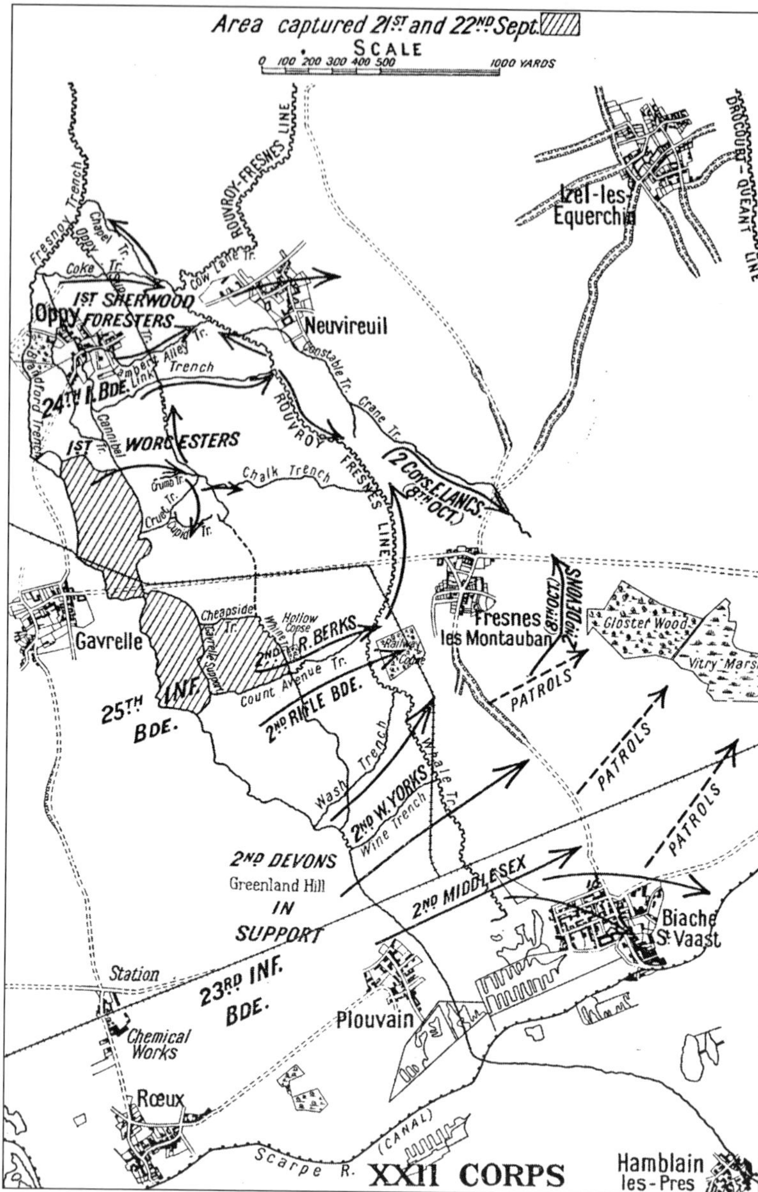

Map 31: Attack on the Rouvroy-Fresnes Line from Oppy.

casualties amounted to one other rank slightly wounded.

A further enemy raid was carried out on 16 September, this time successfully. Advancing under a barrage, on a post of 2 Berkshire, they killed one soldier, wounded another and took five prisoners. That same night 1 Worcesters raided German trenches southeast of Oppy; only four Germans were seen and these ran away when they saw the British troops.

The German retreat through Luxembourg; by October the whole front was moving.

As a result the British soldiers established two advance posts in the area.

The pressure continued with a raid on 20 September by an officer and twenty men from 2 Northants north of Oppy Wood; 'objective reached, enemy seen in trench; no casualties'. On 26 September C and D Companies advanced in conjunction with units on their right and left, taking five prisoners. Later in the day the battalion mounted a further raid with one officer and twelve men but in the three trenches that were raided there was no sign of the enemy.

At midnight on 26 September, 24 Brigade attacked under a barrage and advanced slightly by seizing posts in Oppy Wood and to the left. 1 Sherwoods reinforced the southern corner of Oppy Wood without casualties but by 12.04am the Germans were ready to retaliate and put down a barrage on the forward positions, killing two men and wounding three of a wiring and consolidating party. Sergeant Russon, DCM, displayed courage and promptitude under heavy shellfire in bringing in the wounded and in reorganising the remainder of the party for work.

On 27 September Third Army started its offensive south of the Arras sector. At the same time 20 Division of VIII Corps (First Army) on the Arras front made a successful diversionary attack against the Fresnoy sector north of Oppy. However, in the Oppy area only small advances were made into Whine Trench and Gavrelle Support but the area was not quiet. There was intermittent hostile shelling and ordinary harassing fire by British heavies, day and night, with British field guns and machine guns joining in at night.

On 2 October it was discovered that the Germans in the northern sector of VIII Corps had retired. 58 Division pushed forward, finding little opposition, except for the area around Cité St. Auguste. The next day Lens was found to be clear of Germans. Further south, resistance was stiffer between Méricourt and Acheville but 20 Division made progress and reached the northern branch of the loop on the Méricourt to Lens railway on 3 October.

South of 20 Division, on 8 Division's front, the enemy were not retreating; patrols sent out by the division on both 2 and 3 October found the Germans firmly entrenched. The war diary for VIII Corps recorded that on 3 October

> *...three prisoners* [1 Sergeant Major and two other ranks] *and one machine gun captured as result of successful raid by 1st Sherwood, S.E. of Oppy, belonging to 187th Division which relieved the 15th Reserve Division last night.*

However, the next day a short length of the German front line immediately north of Oppy was taken and held, linking 8 and 20 Division's flanks. VIII Corps War Diary recorded the event:

> *Several posts established by the 8th and 20th Divisions in the enemy's front and support lines between Gavrelle and Méricourt in face of opposition. 17 prisoners and 1 machine gun captured during the day. Before his withdrawal the enemy mined his roads*

A destroyed factory southeast of Oppy.

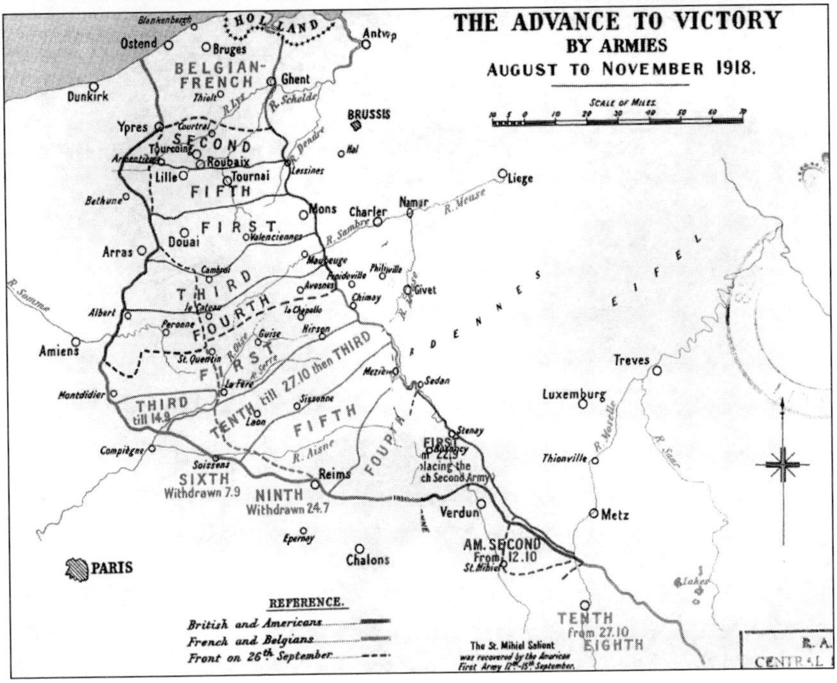

Map 32: The Advance to Victory.

> *in places and destroyed a number of dugouts. Several dugouts were baited with 'booby' traps and the remainder he had no time to destroy as our patrols forced him to withdraw quicker than was his intention.*

On 4 October, 'as a result of patrolling, the enemy were located in Oppy Support, Whale Trench, Hollow Copse and Oppy Village in fair strength'. Advancing on Oppy, with orders to hold any ground they took and not retire, 1 Sherwoods captured a sergeant and two men. The next day they bombed their way up Coke Trench and established a post at the junction with Oppy Support, killing two of the enemy and capturing three. They then pushed out along Link Trench and established another post, this time at the junction of Link and Oppy Support.

Later on the same day, 20 Division linked up with 58 Division and managed to 'establish posts in the enemy's front line on the western side of Fresnoy and Acheville'; 20 Division then went into Corps reserve and was replaced by 12 Division, that had been fighting at Vendhuile. By 7 October 12 Division had taken over a front of 11,000 yards from Oppy to Eleu dit Leauvette on the Canal de Lens with all three brigades in the line.

The division was quick to take the offensive as a private of 9 Royal Fusiliers, 12 Division, (formerly a police constable) recalled in what *Twenty Years After* considered one of the most unusual actions of the

Having cleared Oppy the Allied armies capture the last German in Gavrelle.

war. This took place in Scabbard Trench, near Oppy Wood.

We – the 8th and 9th – went to attack, but when we arrived Jerry attacked and got in first, so we had to get him out before zero and go after him when he had got home; but we couldn't get him out in time, and when the barrage came down there was utter confusion. Some went over, some were engaged with Germans in No Man's Land, while others were clearing the remnants out of our trench.

While some of our men were fighting in the German trenches, Germans were fighting in ours. We carried our objectives in the end and, after we were relieved, we assembled in the 'Triangle' near Arras for Roll Call. There were only a few to tell the tale, and our C.O., Col. Overton, burst into tears when he saw what was left of the battalion.

There were further German counter attacks on 5 October which 8 Division's War Diary noted were made against the Sherwood Foresters without any real dash. One attack was beaten off without difficulty and again in the afternoon they were easily beaten off on two occasions; four of the enemy were captured, along with a number of maps.

It was now time for the final battle for Oppy and on 6 October the attack began; at the time the area was defended by 189 IR of 187 Division. By bombing along trenches, 24 Brigade cut off Oppy and captured its garrison. The War Diary of VIII Corps makes the operation sound very simple:

the 1st Battalion Sherwood captured Oppy with 2 officers and 22 ors. [other ranks] *Fresnoy taken by 12 Division.*

Before the final assault, a patrol was sent out to gauge the enemy's strength. They worked up Lambert Alley with orders to capture the strong point in the village centre. However, the trench was blocked and had camouflaged rabbit wire netting on top that stopped the soldiers from throwing bombs into the trench. The patrol was then fired on by two machine guns but managed to get onto Marion mound in the wood from where they were able to fire upon the enemy, drawing trench mortar fire down on themselves in reply. The conclusion reached was that in the centre of Oppy village there was a strong and well-concealed enemy post.

The attacking troops also established new defensive posts southeast of Oppy.

> *1st Sherwoods carried out a well executed operation. One platoon came down from the north of Oppy while another advanced northwards along Oppy Support and joining hands encircled the town. They seized the junction of Oppy Support and Lambert Alley and occupied the sunken road running east from Oppy. Captured 2 officers and 34 or* [other ranks], *six MG and totally cleared Oppy.*

The prisoners taken in Oppy were from 5, 8, 9 and 10 Companies of 189 Regiment from 187 Division. The Worcesters captured Oppy Support trench taking thirty-eight Germans and fourteen machine-guns.

At 5am on 7 October 8 Division attacked the Fresnes – Rouvroy line on a front of two miles immediately north of the Scarpe. Very rapidly the two attacking brigades (23 and 24 Brigades) carried Biache-St. Vaast and the whole of the powerful line of defences as far north as the Fresnes-Gavrelle road. Following the success of their attack to the south of Oppy, 23 and 24 Brigades turned north and worked up the

1940 – the British Army march towards Oppy once again.

trenches as far as Oppy. 'By the evening the greater part of the system between Oppy and the Scarpe was in the hands' of 8 Division 'with the exception of a small portion in Gloster Wood and near Fresnes.' During the day over 130 Germans and eighteen machine guns were captured. The day's fighting showed, according to *VIII Corps Journal,* that 8 Division 'had found the enemy in sufficient strength to prove that he had no immediate intention of evacuating this line'.

For bravery during the attack on Oppy village and the surrounding area, four men of 1 Worcestershire Regiment received the DCM: Private Batchelor, from Glasgow, who during the whole day,

> *...showed marked gallantry and the maximum of eagerness to keep in touch with the enemy. At a critical moment in the attack he crawled ahead along the parados under heavy machine gun and rifle fire, and inflicted heavy casualties by Lewis gun fire upon the enemy. His skilful firing of rifle grenades on several occasions enabled his section to advance and make ground good with no casualties.*

Private Brown from Poole was the 'leading bayonet man of a bombing party' who 'showed great courage and resolution in pressing forward to his objective in spite of strong opposition and heavy enemy bombing and machine gun fire'. Private King from Birmingham showed

> *...great initiative in an attack on a strongly held machine gun position. With one other man he pushed to an exposed flank to cover the position, personally capturing thirteen prisoners and greatly helping to secure the ground won.*

Fourthly, there was Sergeant Seale from Birmingham, who took over as platoon commander when the officer and platoon sergeant became casualties.

> *He rushed forward and took charge of the platoon, and, both by his work and excellent example under heavy machine gun fire and bombing, undoubtedly enabled the resistance to be overcome and the very strongly fortified line to be entered. He killed, both by rifle fire and bombing, many of the enemy.*

With Oppy gone, 23 Brigade were able to take the Fresnes-Rouvroy position between Biache St. Vaast and Fresnes-lès-Montauban and by the end of 7 October were outside Vitry-en-Artois. Further north the division moved up as far as Neuvireuil, joining up with 12 Division south of Fresnoy; 12 Division had arrived from service further south and occupied 11,000 yards between Oppy and Lens. By 9 October the battle had moved to the Drocourt-Quéant line. In the three days of fighting 8 Division had captured 218 prisoners, 43 machine guns and a trench Mortar. The war was over for Oppy until the next time – 1940 and the Battle of Arras and finally September 1944.

Cemeteries in the Area

German war dead were originally buried in the churchyard at Oppy and later in the wood. However, as a result of the intense British shelling of the area, these graves had all but disappeared by the end of the war. Any that survived were moved after the war to concentration cemeteries like Blangy. For more information about German cemeteries see *Gavrelle* in the Battleground Europe series.

British war dead were removed from the battle area as soon as was practical and moved to cemeteries in the vicinity. Consequently there are no war graves to be seen in the immediate area. Burials in small local cemeteries were moved after the war to bigger cemeteries. However, the most relevant cemetery to the battles for Oppy is Orchard Dump in Arleux-en-Gohelle where many of the dead were taken straight after the battles. It also contains a large number of unknown soldiers who were exhumed from battlefield graves in the area after the war. It is probable that it contains the remains of Second Lieutenant Jack Harrison who, according to a deposition in his file at the National Archive, was found only to be unceremoniously dumped on a pile of corpses that had been cleared from the area in front of Oppy the next day.

One only has to look at the cemetery registers to see how serious

The original German cemetery at Oppy was in the churchyard. Here German troops pay their respects to Oberst v. Reitzenstein who died on 18 February 1914.

German cemetery at Arleux.

was the fighting for Arras in 1917; it is also interesting that much of this section of the Arras battlefield is very much Canadian. Much has been written about the quality of the Canadian soldier; in fact many of them were actually English, Irish, Scottish or Welsh; they were Canadian soldiers only because they happened to be living in Canada when the war broke out. In the same way, the cemetery registers show that many Americans were keen to fight well before their government was. We find, but to a much lesser extent, the same is true in the British battalions who included in their number Americans, Australians, Canadians, West Indians and representatives of most other countries of the Empire.

In a number of cases the soldier served under an alias that was discovered probably on his death. This inevitably leads to the question: why? It is especially puzzling when they were over the legal age to join the army and therefore did not need parental consent. Why would they isolate themselves in this way? Such incidences make interesting pieces of research.

Many of the entries give the age of the soldier, a not inconsiderable number of them being aged eighteen or nineteen. Further research in many cases would reveal fraudulent under-age enlistment by many who subsequently experienced much active service.

'Gone but not forgotten, from dear wife & children' – poigna inscription on the gravestone o twenty-seven year old Gunner Edward Williams of 276 Briga RFA, from Makerfield in Lancashire.

Visiting cemeteries and looking at the dates inscribed on the headstones provides, in most cases, a tiny cameo of what happened in the area and what units passed through, in some cases during a short period of time; other cemeteries however encompass the whole war. In this section I have provided basic information about the cemetery and its whereabouts as well as further details of some of the casualties. I have not tried to provide the reader with a detailed picture of the action that resulted in the creation of the cemetery. It is interesting to look and wonder and then research: so I will leave this to the reader.

I have concentrated on cemeteries in a northerly direction to Gavrelle because these are more likely to contain casualties from the Oppy battles – although not all of them will. I have included some because of their close proximity and their general interest. Cemeteries to the south of Oppy are thoroughly covered in *Battleground Europe: Gavrelle.*

Cemeteries covered by this book:

Albuera, Bailleul-sire-Berthoult
Arras Memorial
Arras Road, Roclincourt
Arleux Communal
Bailleul-sire-Berthoult Public
Bailleul Road East, St Laurent-Blangy
Bailleul Road West, St Laurent-Blangy
Beehive Cemetery, Willerval
Bois-Carré, Thélus
Chili Trench Cemetery, Gavrelle
Gavrelle Public
Highland, Roclincourt
La Targette
Lichfield Crater, Thélus
Naval Trench, Gavrelle
Nine Elms, Thélus
Orchard Dump, Arleux-en-Gohelle
Point-du-Jour, Athies-lès-Arras
Roclincourt Military
Roclincourt Valley
Thélus Communal
Thélus Military
Zivy Crater, Thélus

Albuera Cemetery, Bailleul-sire-Berthoult

The village of Bailleul-sire-Berthoult is eight kilometres northeast of Arras and the Cemetery is west of the village. Wheelchair access is possible only with difficulty. For further information regarding wheelchair access, contact the CWGC Enquiries Section on telephone number 01628 634221.

Bailleul-sire-Berthoult was occupied by 2 Division on 13 April 1917 and Albuera Cemetery was made in April-November 1917 by fighting units; the origin of its current name is not known and it was often called Bailleul Military Cemetery. The cemetery was enlarged after the Armistice when graves were brought in from the battlefields of Arras. It is divided into two plots, called (exceptionally) North and South. Albuera Cemetery contains 253 Commonwealth burials and commemorations of the First World War. 110 of the burials are unidentified but there are special memorials to fifteen casualties known to be buried among them. The cemetery also contains one German war grave.

Among those buried in the cemetery are J E Anderson, an American serving with the Royal Field Artillery; Private J Langtry, DCM, who served as Private Ford; Airman 2nd Class R Hickman (13 Squadron), observer/gunner who died when his BE2c was shot down over Fresnoy, and W Garling, a German soldier of 6 Battalion, 60 Field Artillery Regiment, who died as a PoW, probably while clearing the local battlefields.

Albuera Cemetery.

Arras Memorial and Faubourg d'Amiens cemetery.

Arras Memorial & Faubourg d'Amiens Cemetery

Faubourg d'Amiens Cemetery and the Arras memorial are in the western part of the town of Arras in the Boulevard du General de Gaulle, near the Citadel, approximately two kilometres due west of the railway station.

The Panel Numbers quoted at the end of each entry for the memorial relate to the panels dedicated to the Regiment with which the soldier served. In some instances, where a casualty is recorded as attached to another regiment, his name may alternatively appear within their Regimental Panels. Refer to the on-site Memorial Register introduction to determine the alternative panel numbers if you do not find the name within the quoted Panels. Wheelchair access to the cemetery is possible, but may be by alternative entrance. Contact the CWGC on 01628 507200.

The French handed over Arras to Commonwealth forces in the spring of 1916 and the system of tunnels upon which the town is built was used and developed in preparation for the major offensive planned for April 1917. The Commonwealth section of the Faubourg d'Amiens Cemetery was begun in March 1916, behind the French military cemetery established earlier. It continued to be used by field ambulances and fighting units until November 1918. The cemetery was enlarged after the Armistice when graves were brought in from the battlefields and from two smaller cemeteries in the vicinity. The cemetery contains 2650 Commonwealth burials of the First World War. There are ten Commonwealth burials of the Second World War. In addition, there are thirty war graves of other nationalities, most of them German. The graves in the French military cemetery were removed after the war to other burial grounds and the land they had occupied was used for the construction of the Arras Memorial and Arras Flying Services Memorial. The Arras Memorial commemorates almost 35,000 servicemen from the United Kingdom, South Africa and New

An unexploded shell by a cemetery wall.

Zealand who died in the Arras sector between the spring of 1916 and 7 August 1918, the eve of the Advance to Victory, and have no known grave. The most conspicuous events of this period were the Arras offensive of April-May 1917 and the German attack in the spring of 1918; Canadian and Australian servicemen killed in these operations are commemorated by memorials at Vimy and Villers-Bretonneux. A separate memorial remembers those killed in the Battle of Cambrai in 1917. The Arras Flying Services Memorial commemorates more than 1000 airmen of the Royal Naval Air Service, the Royal Flying Corps, and the Royal Air Force, either by attachment from other arms of the forces of the Commonwealth or by original enlistment, who were killed on the whole Western Front and who have no known grave. During the Second World War, Arras was occupied by British Forces Headquarters until the town was evacuated on 23 May 1940. Arras then remained in German hands until retaken by Commonwealth and Free French forces on 1 September 1944. Both cemetery and memorial were designed by Sir Edwin Lutyens, with sculpture by Sir William Reid Dick. Located between the two special memorials of the 1914-1918 War is an individual memorial commemorating an officer of the United States Army Air Force, who died during the 1939-1945 War. This Type B memorial, is inscribed with the words "Believed to be buried in this cemetery".

Among the burials are Second Lieutenant J D Aiken, a Canadian, born in South Africa, who served in the British Army; Allah Baksh of the Supply and Transport Corps; Private A G Allan, a miner, who had served in the Militia and the territorials, and who had re-enlisted in September 1914, was wounded at Neuve Chapelle and the Somme; Sowar Arjun Singh of 6 King Edward's Own Cavalry; Private Ballam who served as Private Harris; Major A E Barton, MID, who had served in the South African War; Second Lieutenant G F Barton, aged eighteen; Airman 2nd Class J H Bolton (13 Squadron); Private Brock, a 1914 volunteer who had served at Gallipoli and was accidentally killed; Private E J and Lance Corporal L F Bromwich, 15 Royal Warwickshire Regiment, two brothers killed on the same day; Corporal F Brown, 28 Kite Balloon Section; Corporal J A Brown, MM, a Fellow of the Institute of Chemistry and member of the gas section of the Royal Engineers; Lance Corporal F Buttress, born in Birmingham, lived in America and who died serving with the Tyneside Irish; Sapper W Carroll, who died of heart failure at the age of forty; Gunner A S Castell, who died from the effects of gas; Sapper R Chatt, who died of accidental injuries on 11 November 1918; Private S Clinch, Private R L Cockburn and Private K J MacLeod, who died aged seventeen; Privates F Cowcill, J Evans, G Gilbert and C W F C Gluck, all of whom were aged eighteen; Private A Cunningham, who died in 1917 aged forty-nine; Sapper G E Davies from New Zealand who served as Davis; Second Lieutenant H Daws, who returned from Brazil in 1914 to enlist in the Artists' Rifles; Captain (Brevet Major) J L Dent, DSO, MC, who went to France in 1914; Chaplain 4th Class The Revd. E F Duncan, MC, who was attached to 103 Indian Civil Service Regiment; Sergeant H H Figg of the Army Gymnastics Staff; Major F Graham, DSO, MC, aged twenty-three; Gunner A G Grist, a constable with the Port of London Authority who had been called up from the Reserve in August 1914; Private Hoare who served as Private Healy; Bombadier E G Humphris, Headmaster of Englishcombe School, Bath; Lieutenant T W Jones, MD, ChB, DPH of the RAMC; Private F J Labbett, a member of the Institute of Chartered Accountants; Driver Lal Khan, who died of influenza on 8 December 1918; Private Byford who served as Private Lewis; Lieutenant A G Mackay of the RFC; Gunners M and W McIsaac, brothers killed on the same day; Major W B McTaggart, DSO, aged twenty-five; Chaplain 4th Class, The Rev. Charles Wand attached to 4 East Yorkshire Regiment; Conductor D Murray, DCM; Sowar Nawaz Khan of 19 Lancers from the Northwest frontier of India; Lieutenant Colonel H N Packard, DSO; Gunner Ram Charand from India who died of influenza on 28 February 1919; Private Barclay who served under the name of Smith; Lieutenant A C Strachan, MC and Bar; Second Lieutenant B Strachan (12 Squadron); Captain A Y G Thomson, MC and Bar, attached to the General Staff; Lieutenant Colonel H E Trevor, whose father was the Surgeon General; Private Trotskey of the RAMC; Corporal W T Uloth, MM, who accidentally drowned in the Arras canal on 12 November 1918; Sapper P G Ward, drowned on 21 May 1917; Private Wilkinson, an American serving with the Machine Gun Corps; Private R S Williams, from Montego Bay, Jamaica; Captain H H Wilson, DSO, who had served in the South African Campaign where he was twice mentioned in despatches.

Arras Road Cemetery, Roclincourt

Roclincourt is a village a little east of the road from Arras to Lens and Lille. Arras Road Cemetery is on the west side of the main N17 road from Arras to Lens, about 6 kilometres north of Arras, and north of the village of Roclincourt.

Roclincourt was just within the British lines before the Battles of Arras, 1917; 51 (Highland) and 34 Divisions advanced from the village on 9 April 1917 and 1 Canadian Division attacked on their left, across the Lens road. Arras Road Cemetery was begun by 2 Canadian Infantry Brigade soon after 9 April 1917 and, until the Armistice, it contained only the graves (now at the back of the cemetery) of seventy-one officers and men of 7 Canadian Infantry Battalion (British Columbia Regiment) who fell in April, May and June 1917; but in 1926-29 it was enlarged by the concentration of 993 graves from a wide area mainly north and east of Arras. There are now over 1000 1914-18 war casualties commemorated in this site. The cemetery covers an area of 4084 square metres. It is enclosed on three sides by a stone rubble wall, and against the road by a retaining wall. Old dugouts exist under the northeast corner and on the southwest boundary. The following are brief particulars of the burial grounds from which British graves were moved to Arras Road Cemetery:

Baisieux Churchyard (Nord): six, October 1918.
Bellaing Churchyard (Nord): two Canadian, October 1918.
Bourlon Communal Cemetery (Pas-de-Calais): one, September 1916, and one Canadian, September 1918.
Comines Communal Cemetery (Nord): five (including one Canadian), 1914-1917. The permanent German Extension on the West side contains 2257 identified and 1903 unidentified German graves.
Ecaillon churchyard (Nord): one, January 1919.
Givenchy-lès-La-Bassée Churchyard (Pas-de-Calais): Givenchy is associated with (among other episodes) the stand made by 55 (West Lancashire) Division in April 1918, and it has been 'adopted' by the City of Liverpool.
Mairieux Churchyard (Nord): one, November 1918.
Mouchin Churchyard (Nord): two, October 1918.
Penin Churchyard (Pas-de-Calais): one, November 1916.
Peronne-en-Melantois Churchyard (Nord): four, October 1918.
Rumegies Churchyard (Nord): ten, October and November 1918.
Sainghin-en-Melantois Churchyard (Nord): three, March 1917 - October 1918.

Sin Churchyard, Baisieux (Nord): three, April - November 1918.
Tincques Churchyard (Pas-de-Calais): one, May 1916.
Vendin-le-Vieil Communal Cemetery (Pas-de-Calais): one, September 1915.
Wannehain Churchyard (Nord): two, October and November 1918.

Burials in the cemetery range from shortly after the start of the war and go through until the end, with the youngest being eighteen and the oldest forty-five. Among those buried in the cemetery are an Irish doctor, Captain J M C Gaston, MC; CSM R Holt, a veteran of the South African War; two aviators, Second Lieutenant F W Ferguson (87 Squadron) and Lieutenant H Welch (1 Squadron); Captain A F G Kilby, VC, MC, 2 Battalion, South Staffordshire Regiment.

Arleux Communal Cemetery

At the T-junction on the D50 turn right and then left. This contains five graves from 1940.

Bailleul-sire-Berthoult Public Cemetery

Bailleul-sire-Berthoult is a village eight kilometres northeast of Arras on the road to Hénin-Lietard. The communal cemetery is southeast of the village on the road to Gavrelle.

The communal cemetery contains the graves of nine British soldiers, in two plots, who died in the vicinity during the fighting in May 1940; all were regular or territorial soldiers from 5 or 50 Division. The youngest was nineteen and the oldest thirty-three; four served with the Green Howards, three with the East Yorks, one with the Middlesex Regiment and one with the Signal Corps. All three East Yorkshire soldiers were fathers and their headstones have poignant inscriptions. Two soldiers, whose graves could not be located precisely, are commemorated by special memorials inscribed 'Buried near this spot'.

Bailleul Road East Cemetery.

Bailleul Road East Cemetery, St. Laurent-Blangy

Leave St. Laurent-Blangy on the D919 towards Bailleul-sire-Berthoult for about two and a half kilometres. Bailleul Road East Cemetery is about two kilometres northeast of the village on the south side (right) of the road.

A greater part of the village was included in the front taken over by British troops in March 1916 and the remainder fell into British hands on the first day of the Battles of Arras, 9 April 1917. Bailleul Road East Cemetery was begun by 34 Division in April 1917 and carried on by fighting units until the following November; Plot I, Row R, was added in August 1918. Plots II, III, IV and V were made after the Armistice by the concentration of isolated graves from a very wide area north, east and south of Arras and from two other burial grounds. There are now over 1000 1914-18 war casualties commemorated in this site. Of these, over half are unidentified, and seven special memorials record the names of soldiers from the United Kingdom buried in Northumberland Cemetery, Fampoux, whose graves could not be found on concentration; and a number of graves in Plot V, identified as a whole but not individually, are marked by headstones bearing the additional words, 'Buried near this spot'. Every year of the war is represented in the cemetery, but more particularly the last nine months of 1917. The cemetery covers an area of 4486 square metres and is enclosed by a rubble wall. There were two burial grounds from which British graves were brought to this cemetery: firstly, Northumberland Cemetery, Fampoux, that was on the west side of the road from Fampoux to Bailleul-sire-Berthoult. This road was called Northumberland Lane, and a neighbouring trench was called Northumberland Avenue. The cemetery was used by fighting units between April and July 1917 and one further burial was made in it during September 1918. It contained the graves of 69 soldiers from the

Mass grave in the German cemetery near Bailleul Road East.

The grave of a German casualty from 3 May 1917.

United Kingdom, and these (except seven which were not found) were concentrated into Plot V of Bailleul Road East Cemetery. Secondly, Lagnicourt 'Soldiers' Cemetery' (the German name) was near the southeast side of the village of Lagnicourt. It contained the grave of one RFC Officer who fell in October 1916.

Among the 1293 burials are the following: Able Seaman T R Anderson, whose parents were both doctors in China; Private D Collins, a Belfast man serving in the Black Watch; Private D Cronin, who was killed on 19 October 1914, aged seventeen, serving with 2 Royal Irish Regiment; Private J H N Graham, who served as Private Nixon; Lieutenant R C Guthrie-Smith, son of Major General Sir Herbert Guthrie-Smith, KCB; Lance Corporal A J Inkster, an Irishman who lived in America but served with the Black Watch; Second Lieutenant F M Lawledge (RFC), shot down flying a Sopwith Strutter, who had been the engineer in charge of the location survey for the Hudson's Bay Railway between 1912 and 1914; three DCM winners - CSM S O'Neill, Lance Corporal V F Pamment and Private W C Riggins; Lieutenant J W Pinckney, a New Zealander serving in King Edward's Horse; Private I Rosenberg, a war poet considered by some the greatest after Wilfred Owen; Second Lieutenant A C Shakerle, a Canadian serving in the Royal Field Artillery; Private R O von Stieglitz, an Australian with an aristocratic German name and Corporal P V Wrightson, a forty-six year-old Londoner serving with the South African Infantry.

Bailleul Road West Cemetery, St. Laurent-Blangy

St. Laurent-Blangy is a village adjoining the northeast side of Arras. Leave St. Laurent-Blangy on the D919 towards Bailleul-sire-Berthoult for approximately 1.5 kilometres. Bailleul Road West Cemetery lies on the north (left) side of this road. The entrance will be found by leaving the D919 onto the D60 towards Roclincourt and taking the first small track on the left. Wheelchair access is with some difficulty. Contact the CWGC on 01628 507200.

Part of the commune and the greater part of the village of St. Laurent-Blangy were included in the front taken over by British troops

Headstone of Private Isaac Rosenberg. Note pebbles on the top.

in March 1916 and the remainder fell into British hands on the first day of the Battles of Arras, 9 April 1917. Bailleul Road West Cemetery was constructed by 12 Battalion Royal Scots in May 1917. There are now nearly 100 1914-18 war casualties commemorated in this site. Of these, a small number are unidentified. The date of death was in all cases 9 April 1917. The cemetery covers an area of 359 square metres and is enclosed by a low flint wall on a rubble base.

The following are among the ninety-eight burials: Private F Emmingham, who was eighteen when he was killed in action on 9 April 1917; Sergeant H G Gary, MM, who served as Sergeant H G Foster; Corporal J Hamilton, MM, a Belfast man serving with the Royal Scots; Second Lieutenant M Hillier, who was born in China where his parents still lived and Captain T W Martin, MC, doctor to a battalion of the Royal Scots.

Beehive Cemetery, Willerval

Willerval is a village in the Department of the Pas-de-Calais, ten kilometres northeast of Arras. Beehive Cemetery is one kilometre north of the village and 600 metres by the footpath from the west side of the D50E road to Méricourt, in a place called Lorgette.

Beehive cemetery.

The cemetery owes its name to a German machine-gun emplacement known to the British troops as 'The Beehive'. It was made by fighting units after the occupation of Willerval in the Battles of Arras, 1917, and it was used as an advance cemetery until the following September; one grave was added in March, 1918. There are now nearly fifty 1914-18 war casualties commemorated in this site. Of these, a small number are unidentified and one, which cannot now be found, is represented by a special memorial. The cemetery covers an area of 360 square metres and is enclosed by a concrete curb.

Bois-Carré cemetery.

Bois-Carré British Cemetery, Thélus

Thélus is a village seven kilometres north of Arras and the cemetery is one kilometre east of the village on the south side of the D49 to Bailleul-sire-Berthoult.

Thélus village, which stands on the Vimy Ridge, was captured by the Canadian Corps on the 9 April 1917 and remained in British hands until the end of the War. The commune contains Battle Memorials to 1 Canadian Division and (at Les Tilleuls) to the Canadian Artillery. Bois-Carré British Cemetery was begun by units of 1 Canadian Division in April 1917 and used until the following June, and the 61 graves thus made are in Plot I. It was greatly enlarged after the Armistice by the concentration of graves from the surrounding battlefields, and a Canadian soldier, accidentally killed in 1919, was buried in Plot I, Row F. During the 1939-40 War, the cemetery was used in April 1940 by No. 8 Casualty Clearing Station. There are now over 500 1914-18 and a small number of 1939-45 war casualties commemorated in this site. Of these, nearly sixty from the 1914-18 War are unidentified and special memorials are erected to one soldier from the United Kingdom and one from Canada known to be buried among them. Other special memorials record the names of ten Canadian soldiers and three from the United Kingdom, buried in smaller cemeteries, whose graves were destroyed by shellfire. The cemetery covers an area of 1898 square metres and is enclosed by a brick wall. The following were the more considerable burial grounds from which graves were concentrated to this cemetery:

Bumble Trench Cemetery, Vimy (CC 186)* on the road from Vimy to Lens before the railway crossing. Here were buried, in May-August 1917, nineteen Canadian soldiers and five from the United Kingdom.

Canadian grave CD 27 Neuville-St. Vaast, 1828 metres west of Petit-

The special marker stone in Bois-Carré cemetery.

Vimy, in which forty-eight Canadian soldiers who fell on 9 April 1917 were buried; almost all belonged to either 54 or 102 Battalions.

Vimy Station Cemetery, where seventeen Canadian soldiers were buried in April and May 1917.

[*The numerous groups of graves made about this time by the Canadian Corps Burial Officer were, as a rule, not named but serially lettered and numbered.]

Among the 508 burials are: Privates C R Bow, J Feltner, R Morris and C R Storey, Americans serving with the Canadian Army; Second Lieutenant G Everingham (RFC); Second Lieutenant R A Fergusson, a New Zealander serving with the Royal Fusiliers; Driver T Horridge who enlisted under-age; Second Lieutenant K I MacKenzie aged eighteen in 1917; Lieutenant D J McRae (RFC); Private Metch, a Serbian serving with the Canadian Army; Private A N M Morrison, an Australian serving with the Canadian Army; Private C Mosseri, an Egyptian serving with the Canadian Infantry; Captain L L Richardson, MC (25 Squadron) and Second Lieutenant D C Wollen (25 Squadron). Three soldiers served under aliases: Private Monpetit as Private Anderson, Private Trodden as Private Burns and Private Springett as Private Forbes.

Chili Trench Cemetery, Gavrelle

Gavrelle is a village to the south of Oppy. The cemetery is 1.5 kilometres southeast on the northeast side of the minor road to Fampoux.

Gavrelle was captured by the Royal Naval Division on 23 April 1917, lost on 28 March 1918, and reoccupied by 51 (Highland) Division on the following 27 August. Chili Trench Cemetery was made in April and May 1917, mainly by units of 37 Division; it was also known as Gavrelle Road Cemetery, or Fampoux Cemetery. A further four Commonwealth graves from Monchecourt Communal Cemetery were removed to Chili Trench Cemetery in 1934. The cemetery contains 196 burials and commemorations of the First World War; nineteen of the burials are unidentified and eighty-six graves destroyed by shellfire are now represented by special memorials. The cemetery also contains the grave of one airman of the Second World War.

Among the 197 burials are three fliers, Lieutenant T H Broadley and Second Lieutenant R H Dilloway, both of 62 Squadron, who were shot down near Cambrai in September 1918, and Flying Officer D Bury of 111 Squadron, who was killed in 1940, when he flew his Hurricane into an electricity pylon while being chased by a Messerschmitt 109. His father, Captain Edmond Bury, died on 5 December 1915 and is buried in Rue-Petillion Military Cemetery. A further soldier serving under an assumed name was Sergeant D Johnston, who served as D Simpson.

Chili Trench cemetery.

Gavrelle Public Cemetery

Gavrelle is a village and commune eleven kilometres northeast of Arras, on the N50 road to Douai. The communal cemetery is southeast of the village on the road to Plouvain. There are seven British graves; they are in two plots which lie on each side of the main path from the entrance. All the graves are from the Second World War.

Highland Cemetery, Roclincourt

Roclincourt is a village a little east of the road from Arras to Lens. Take the N17 from Arras until the junction of this road and the D60. Travel along the D60 to Roclincourt village. The Cemetery is northeast of the village and is reached via a single-track farm lane which is

Highland cemetery.

signposted from the Thélus road. Wheelchair access is with some difficulty. Contact the CWGC on 01628 507200.

Roclincourt was just within the British lines before the Battles of Arras 1917 and it was from the village that 51 (Highland) and 34 Divisions advanced on 9 April 1917. Highland Cemetery was made (under the name of Roclincourt Forward Cemetery No. 1) when the battlefields were cleared after 9 April 1917, and Plot I, Rows A and C, and Plot II, Rows A and D, are almost exclusively occupied by the graves of 51 Division. Plot I, Row B and Plot II, Row C were made, after the Armistice, by the concentration of graves from the battlefields of Arras; Plot II, Row C contains graves of Canadian Field Artillery and Railway Troops brought from Fond-de-Vase British Cemetery, nearly 1.6 kilometres east of Maroeuil. There are now over 300 1914-18 war casualties commemorated in this site. Of these, nearly fifty are unidentified, and a special memorial is erected to a soldier from the United Kingdom who is known to be buried among them. The cemetery covers an area of 1159 square metres and is enclosed by a low flint wall.

Among the 322 burials in the cemetery are: Private J Cairns, an under-age Irish soldier serving with a Scottish Highland Regiment; Lance Corporal H Ferguson from the West Indies; Captain, The Reverend J S Grant, MC, a clergyman serving as a soldier; Gunner W E Holder, an under-age soldier serving in the Canadian Field Artillery; Captain G L Jackson, MID, son of Brigadier General G Jackson;

Second Lieutenant B H Last, killed in action in 1917, who had enlisted as a private in 1914; CSM J T Morrison, DCM; Private D McDougall, another under-age soldier; Lance Corporal F Swift, an Englishman serving with the South African Infantry; Private J B Walker, at forty, the oldest soldier in the cemetery and Private J Watson, yet another under-age soldier.

La Targette British Cemetery (Aux-Rietz)

Neuville-St. Vaast is a village 6.5 kilometres north of Arras, a little east of the road from Bethune to Arras. La Targette British Cemetery lies to the southwest of the village on the northwest side of the road to the village of Maroeuil (D55). Wheelchair access to this cemetery is possible but may be by an alternative entrance. For further information regarding wheelchair access contact the CWGC on 01628 507200.

La Targette British Cemetery, formerly known as Aux-Rietz Military Cemetery, was begun at the end of April 1917 and used by field ambulances and fighting units until September 1918. Nearly a third of the graves have an artillery connection; in March-April 1917, the artillery of 2 Canadian and 5 Divisions, and certain heavy artillery units, had their headquarters in a deep cave at Aux-Rietz. Sixteen graves were brought into the cemetery from the immediate neighbourhood after the Armistice.

The cemetery contains 638 First World War burials, forty-one of them unidentified. There are also three Second World War burials, two of which are unidentified. Sir Reginald Blomfield designed the cemetery.

Among those buried in the cemetery are: Sowar Babu Singh of the Alwar Lancers, Lance Daffadar Garaj Singh of Gardner's Horse; Gunner E S Blanchard, Sergeant H E Briscoe and Private C J Chapin, Americans serving with the Canadians; Private R H H Biddulph, a

La Targette British Cemetery.

science graduate of McGill University, Montreal; Lieutenant Col R H Britton, DSO; Air Mechanic 3rd Class D J Carpenter of No.1 Balloon Section, RAF; Major S H Doake, DSO, who landed in France in August 1914; Second Lieutenant W W Gibbs, who had returned from East Africa in 1917 to enlist; Private I C Howell from Jamaica; Second Lieutenant P McLeod Innes, head boy of Haileybury College, who gave up a history scholarship to Trinity College, Cambridge to enlist; Flight Sub-Lieutenant J N McAllister of the Royal Naval Air Service who was serving with 10 Wing RFC; forty-eight year-old Corporal E A McIntyre, another American who could not wait for his country to enter the war; Private A Mortenson from Denmark and Lieutenant N Sworder (5 Squadron).

Lichfield Crater, Thélus

Lichfield Crater is a small cemetery situated by the hedge of the motorway A26 (Paris-Calais) behind the village of Neuville-St Vaast. On entering Neuville-St. Vaast, follow the directions for the Vimy Canadian Memorial and take the third road on the right toward the wood, go over the motorway and take the first right towards the fields. The cemetery lies in a field approximately 450 metres from the crossroads. The design of this site makes wheelchair access impossible. For further information regarding wheelchair access contact the CWGC on 01628 634221.

Lichfield Crater was one of two mine craters (the other being Zivy Crater) that were used by the Canadian Corps Burial Officer in 1917 for the burial of bodies found on the Vimy battlefield. The original name for Lichfield Crater was CB 2 A. The crater is essentially a mass grave and contains fifty-seven First World War burials, fifteen of them unidentified. All of the men buried here died on 9 or 10 April 1917 with one exception, a soldier who died in April 1916, whose grave was found on the edge of the crater after the Armistice and is the only one marked by a headstone. The names of the rest of those buried in the crater are inscribed on panels fixed to the boundary wall. W H Cowlishaw designed the cemetery.

Among those buried in the cemetery are: Private E R Askew, an Englishman living in America who served with the Canadians; Private F Feindell, of 25 Canadian Infantry, who was born in America; Lance Corporal E W Sifton VC and also Sergeant P C Till, who in civilian life had been assistant wire chief of the New Brunswick Telephone Company.

Naval Trench Cemetery, Gavrelle

The cemetery is about 0.75 kilometres southwest of the village on the D42E down a one-kilometre track. Wheelchair access is with some difficulty. Contact the CWGC on 01628 634221 for further information.

Naval Trench Cemetery is named from a second-line trench made by 63 Division in the summer of 1917, occupied as headquarters by the Queen's Westminsters in March 1918 and retaken by 6 Black Watch on 26 August 1918. The cemetery was constructed by fighting units between April and November 1917. The cemetery contains fifty-nine First World War burials, two of them unidentified. The identified burials are from 30, 47 and 63 Divisions. There is one burial of the Second World War in the cemetery, that of Captain Millar of 2 Scottish Rifles, who died from small arms fire on 21 May 1940.

Nine Elms Military Cemetery, Thélus

Thélus is a village about six and a half kilometres north of Arras and one kilometre east of the main road from Arras to Lens. The cemetery is on the western side of the main road and about one and a half kilometres south of the village. Wheelchair access involves some difficulty. Contact the CWGC on 01628 507220 for further information.

Nine Elms was the name given by the Army to a group of trees 460 metres east of the Arras Lens main road, between Thélus and Roclincourt. The cemetery was begun, after the capture of Vimy Ridge, by the burial in what is now Plot I, Row A of eighty men of 14 Canadian Infantry Battalion, who fell on 9 April 1917; this and the next row were filled by June 1917. Three burials were made in Plot I, Row C, in July 1918. The rest of the cemetery was made after the Armistice by the concentration of British and French graves from the battlefields of Vimy and Neuville-St. Vaast and from certain small cemeteries. There are now nearly 700 1914-18 war casualties commemorated in this site. Of these, almost 150 are unidentified and a special memorial is erected to one Canadian soldier, believed to be buried among them. Other special memorials record the names of forty-four soldiers from Canada and ten from the United Kingdom, buried in other cemeteries, whose graves were destroyed by

Captain W Carroll buried in Albuera Cemetery – killed in action on 3 May.

shellfire. Four graves in Plot IV, identified as a whole but not individually, are marked by headstones bearing the additional words: 'Buried near this spot'. The great majority of the British graves are of April 1917; the French are of 1914 and 1915. 177 French graves have been removed to other cemeteries. The cemetery covers an area of 3355 square metres and is enclosed by a low brick wall.

The following were among the burial grounds from which British graves were moved to Nine Elms Military Cemetery:

Arras Road Cemetery, Thélus, on the roadside a little north of Nine Elms Cemetery. This graveyard, originally called CA 39, contained the graves of forty-six Canadian soldiers, thirty-nine of whom belonged to 15 Battalion, and most of whom fell on 9 April 1917.

Grave CA 26, Roclincourt, by the roadside a little south of Nine Elms Cemetery, in which were buried seventy-two Canadian soldiers of 5 Battalion who fell on 9 April 1917.

Grave CA 35, Neuville-St. Vaast, 914 metres west of Nine Elms Cemetery, in which were buried twenty-three Canadian soldiers of 15 Battalion who fell on 9 April 1917.

Grave CA 40, Thélus, 274 metres west of the main road, by the light railway track. Here were buried forty-four Canadian soldiers of 16 Battalion who fell on 9 April 1917.

Grave CB 10, Thélus, 274 metres southwest of the hamlet of Les Tilleuls, in which were buried fifty-two Canadian soldiers and two from the United Kingdom who fell in April and May 1917.

Grave CC 3, Vimy, just south of the highest point of the Ridge, in which were buried fifty-eight Canadian soldiers who fell on 9 and 10 April 1917.

Roclincourt Square Cemetery (or Roclincourt Forward Cemetery No. 5), one kilometre north of the village of Roclincourt, containing the graves of twenty-three soldiers of the 51 (Highland) Division who fell on 9 April 1917.

Seaforth Grave, Roclincourt (or Roclincourt Forward Cemetery No. 4), a little northwest of the Square Cemetery. Here were buried twelve NCOs and men of 1st/4th Battalion Seaforth Highlanders who fell on 9 April 1917.

Among the 742 burials are: Major S J Bothwell, DCM, killed in action aged 41; Privates J P Dalton, C Jones and C Kraft, all under-age soldiers; Lance Corporal C E Kingsley, an American serving with 14 Canadian Infantry; Sergeant R A Edmunds, DCM; Corporal C Elrick, an American serving with the Royal Scots; Lance Corporal F Fulton, who served as F Valley and Private W J W Sutherburg, an American who served under the alias of Private Wallace; Private I Kojima, who was born in Japan; Private H J McGray, Corporal W Purdy, Sergeant F Shipley, Private D Smithson and Sergeant W M Robinson, five Americans who could not wait for their country to join in the war; Sergeant T E Tysall, at forty-three the oldest soldier in the cemetery and R E Wallace, who at the age of twenty-four, had reached the rank of major.

Orchard Dump Cemetery, Arleux-en-Gohelle

Arleux-en-Gohelle is a village on the main Arras to Hénin-Lietard road, the D919. The Cemetery lies on the left side of this road approximately one kilometre from the village of Bailleul-sire-Berthoult. Wheelchair access is with some difficulty. Contact the CWGC on 01628 507200 for further information.

The cemetery was begun in April 1917, on the new front resulting from the Battles of Arras, and it was used by the units holding that front until the following November. These original burials are in Plot VI, Row K, and Plot I, Rows A to F, and are arranged in an irregular fashion. The cemetery was greatly enlarged after the Armistice by the concentration of graves from the neighbouring battlefields and from other burial grounds. During the 1939-45 War, No.2 Casualty Clearing Station was at Rouvroy, three kilometres northeast of Arleux, and the cemetery was used again. There are over 3000 1914-18 and twenty 1939-45 war casualties commemorated in this site; those from World War Two died during the phoney war, of illness or accident. More than four-fifths of the graves from the 1914-18 War are unidentified, and special memorials are erected to ten soldiers from the United Kingdom and four from Canada known or believed to be buried among them. Other special memorials record the names of thirty-eight Canadian soldiers and six from the United Kingdom, buried in other cemeteries, whose graves were destroyed by shellfire. Certain graves in Plots VII, VIII and IX, identified collectively but not individually, are marked by headstones bearing the additional words 'Buried near this spot'. The cemetery covers an area of 9,402 square metres and is enclosed by

Orchard Dump Cemetery.

rubble walls on three sides. A tablet in the cemetery records the fact that the site was given by the widow of a captain in the French 72 Infantry Regiment, killed in action in August 1914. The following were among the burial grounds from which British graves were removed to Orchard Dump Cemetery:

Fresnes-lès-Montauban Communal Cemetery, in which five soldiers from the United Kingdom were buried by 26 Field Ambulance in October 1918.

Fresnoy Churchyard, between Lens and Arras, where the enemy buried a Royal Flying Corps officer in March 1917.

Fusiliers Cemetery, Bailleul-sire-Berthoult, 800 metres southwest of the village beside the railway line, where eleven men of the Northumberland Fusiliers, four of the Royal Fusiliers and one Royal Marine were buried by 63 Division in April and May, 1917.

Ouse Alley Cemetery, Bailleul-sire-Berthoult, about one kilometre northeast of the village, where thirty-eight officers and men from the United Kingdom were buried by their comrades between June 1917 and February 1918.

Quiéry-la-Motte British Cemetery, 800 metres northwest of la Motte, where twenty-seven soldiers from the United Kingdom were buried by 2 East Lancs and other units in October 1918.

2 Canadian Division Cemetery, Willerval, midway between Vimy and Acheville, where sixteen Canadian soldiers were buried by 2 Canadian Division in May 1917.

East Yorkshire Regiment headstones in Orchard Dump Cemetery.

Farbus Comunal cemetery contains a number of Great War burials.

Willerval Canadian Cemetery (or Vancouver Road Cemetery) made by 2 Canadian Division in May 1917 and containing the graves of thirty-four Canadian soldiers. It stood about midway between Vimy and Fresnoy.

Willerval Churchyard, where four men of 3 Canadian Battalion were buried in April and May 1917.

Among the 3043 soldiers buried in the cemetery are: Privates W R Apt and T A Steer, and Corporal D F Tait, Americans serving with the Canadians; two Canadian privates from Eaton's Motor Machine Gun Battery; Lieutenant A J Jessop (56 Squadron); Private J T Kelly, who was killed in action at Oppy Wood on 29 August 1918; Gunner H G Kingsland, manager of the Co-operative Store in Gillingham, Kent; Private C Moncrieff who served as Private McAdam and Private C C Satchwill, a Canadian serving in the British Army. As evidence of how active the air war was over this small sector, we find the following are buried in the cemetery: Lieutenant G T Morris (59 Squadron); Airman 2nd Class G Pawley (25 Squadron); Second Lieutenant H S Pell (40 Squadron); Lieutenant D M F Sinclair (40 Squadron); Lieutenant J M Souter (59 Squadron); Lieutenant W S Spence (16 Squadron); Lance Corporal Francis, killed on his twenty-second birthday and Second Lieutenant M Simon, aged eighteen, whose body was only recently found near Oppy Wood.

It is possible that this cemetery contains the bodies of Second Lieutenant Harrison, VC, and Lieutenant R Combe, VC.

Point-du-Jour Military Cemetery, Athies-lès-Arras

Leave St-Laurent Blangy on the D42 (Athies to Biache-St.-Vaast) and drive into the village of Athies-lès-Arras. After 500 metres take a left turn onto the Rue du Chauffour. Continue for 1.2 kilometres down a small track and the cemetery will be seen on the right. Wheelchair access to the cemetery is possible, but may be by alternative entrance. Contact the CWGC on 01628 507200 for further information.

Athies was captured by 9 (Scottish) Division, which included the South African Brigade, on 9 April 1917. It remained in Allied hands until the end of the war. Point-du-Jour was a house on the road from St. Laurent-Blangy to Gavrelle, and by 1917 it had become a German redoubt, captured by 34 Division on 9 April. Two cemeteries were made on the right of the road from St. Laurent-Blangy to Point-du-Jour, No. 1 Cemetery becoming the present Point-du-Jour Military Cemetery. It was used from April to November 1917, and again in May 1918, and contained at the Armistice 82 graves (now part of Plot I). It was then enlarged when graves were brought in from the battlefields and from small cemeteries north, east and south of Arras. There are now 794 Commonwealth servicemen of the First World War buried or commemorated in this cemetery; 401 of the burials are unidentified but special memorials commemorate twenty-two casualties known or believed to be buried among them. Other special memorials record the names of six casualties buried in other cemeteries, whose graves were destroyed by shellfire. There are also three Second World War burials and six French war graves. Sir Reginald Blomfield designed the cemetery.

Among the 893 burials are the following: soldiers from the 1 Royal Guernsey Light Infantry, who died on 1 December 1917 during a German counter-attack at Cambrai; Lieutenant Colonel C J Burke, DSO, 2 Royal Irish Regiment attached 1 East Lancashire Regiment, who went to France in command of 2 Squadron RFC in August 1914; Second Lieutenant Coxe (6 Squadron) shot down near Cambrai while flying a BE2c; CSM D A Farrington, MC, a pre-war regular soldier; Second Lieutenant O C Godfrey (27 Squadron) killed while flying a Martinsyde G100 near Cambrai; Private Hawes from New Zealand, serving with the Northamptonshire Regiment; Lance Corporal T C Hook, MM, a South African from Norfolk; Private C M McGrew, a seventeen year-old American serving with the Canadians; Lieutenant Colonel F S N Savage-Nesbitt, DSO, of 1 Battalion South Staffordshire Regiment, who served in the Boer War and was a veteran of Ypres (1914), Neuve-Chapelle, Fromelles, Festubert and Arras and CQMS F E Shortland, an Australian serving with the North Lancashire Regiment.

The entrance to Roclincourt Military Cemetery.

Roclincourt Military Cemetery

Roclincourt is a village a little to the east of the road from Arras to Lens. Take the N17 from Arras until the junction of this road and the D60 (first CWGC sign here). Travel along the D60 into Roclincourt village, for approximately one kilometre, to a right turn (direction St Nicholas). Take this road for approximately 175 metres to a lane on the right. The cemetery lies 100 metres away at the foot of this lane.

The French troops who held this front before March 1916 made a military cemetery (now removed), on the southwest side of which the present Commonwealth cemetery was made. It was begun by 51 (Highland) and 34 Divisions in April 1917, and contains many graves of 9 April, the first day of the Battles of Arras. It continued in use as a front-line cemetery until October 1918, and after the Armistice, graves, mostly from the battlefield north of Roclincourt, were brought into Plot IV, Row F. Roclincourt Military Cemetery contains 916 Commonwealth burials of the First World War, thirty-two of them unidentified. There are also four German war graves. Sir Reginald Blomfield designed the cemetery.

Among the 920 burials are: Lieutenant P H Adams who was killed in action at Oppy Wood on 3 October 1918; Lieutenant A R D Bacon killed at Oppy Wood aged nineteen on 25 April 1917; Private J M

Barber, an adopted son; Airman 2nd Class T Brooke (5 Squadron); Private J C Clarey of the Tank Corps and Private R Fraser who were killed in an enemy air raid; Private W K Dornan, aged eighteen; Second Lieutenant W P Ferguson, aged twenty-one, who was killed in his ninth engagement in nine months; Major A J S Hammans, MC, *Chevalier of the Legion of Honour*, aged twenty-five; Private S C Hanson, an eighteen-year-old American serving with the Canadian Infantry; Lieutenant Colonel E W Hermon, DSO; Second Lieutenant H J James, who had served in the ranks before being commissioned; Captain D C P Kindersley, DSO, *Croix de Guerre*, at forty-five, the oldest soldier in the cemetery; Lance Corporal G W King, DCM; Lieutenant Colonel R H Leyland; Sergeant J Mandeville; DCM, MM; Second Lieutenant D H Mckie who had returned from Brazil to volunteer; Lance Sergeant R McLeish, DCM; Major A Plow, MC, MM, who at the age of twenty-eight had served as a soldier in the trenches, had been commissioned and had risen to second-in-command of a battalion – all in less than four years; Private A O Pryer, killed in action at Oppy Wood on 5 May 1917; Major C H R

The headstone of a DCM winner in Roclincourt Military cemetery.

Two of the headstones in Roclincourt Military Cemetery.

Scholefield, *Croix de Guerre* (with Palm), Chevalier of the *Order of the Crown* of Belgium, a twenty-two-year-old Irishman; Second Lieutenant E Smith (RAF); Second Lieutenant J W W Sutton, MC, aged nineteen; Second Lieutenant T R M Taylor who had also served in Palestine; Sergeant L L Turner, an Associate of the Royal College of Science in Ireland, who served in the gas warfare section of the Royal Engineers and died of wounds caused by gas; Chaplain 4th Class, The Reverend A T Veryard and Privates A Frey and H Meyer, two German soldiers.

Roclincourt Valley Cemetery

Roclincourt is a village a little to the east of the road from Arras to Lens. Roclincourt Valley Cemetery lies to the northeast of the village on a farm track signposted off the Thélus road. Wheelchair access is with some difficulty. Contact the CWGC on 01628 507200 for further information.

Roclincourt was just within the Allied lines before the Battle of Arras in 1917 and it was from here that 51 (Highland) and 34 Divisions advanced on 9 April 1917; 1 Canadian Division attacked further north across the Lens road. Roclincourt Valley Cemetery (originally called Roclincourt Forward Cemetery No. 2) was begun after 9 April 1917 by the units that fought on that day. It was used until the following August, when it contained the graves of ninety-four soldiers, of whom forty belonged to 51 Division. The cemetery was enlarged after the Armistice when graves, almost all of April 1917, and mostly from 34 and 51 Divisions, were brought in from smaller cemeteries and from the battlefields. The cemetery now contains 518 burials and commemorations of the First World War. Eighty-three of the burials are unidentified but there are special memorials to four casualties known or believed to be buried among them. Sir Reginald Blomfield designed the cemetery.

The more important of the smaller cemeteries concentrated into Roclincourt Valley Cemetery were the following:

King Crater Cemetery, Roclincourt: a mine crater, it contained ninety-nine burials in five big graves, made by 34 Division in the middle of April 1917, all dating from 9 April. All but two belonged to the Tyneside Brigades of the Northumberland Fusiliers.

Kite Crater Cemetery, St. Laurent-Blangy: containing fifty-three burials of 9 April 1917 in five big graves, mainly from 34 Division.

Rabs Road Cemetery, St. Laurent-Blangy: containing twenty burials of 9 or 13 April 1917, sixteen belonging to 15 or 16 Battalion Royal Scots.

Roclincourt Long Cemetery (called at one time Roclincourt Forward Cemetery No. 3): containing sixty-eight burials of 9 April 1917, all 51 Division.

Thélus Road Cemetery, Roclincourt: made by XVII Corps and containing forty-two burials of 9 April 1917, all again from 51 Division.

Among the 548 burials are the following: Lieutenant D Bennell, aged thirty-one, who enlisted in the Royal Horse Artillery in 1903, served for seven years in India and was commissioned in the field in 1915; Private F Crompton, from Widnes, who served in the South African Infantry; Private W Gage, a Scotsman who served in the South African Infantry; Corporal M Greenacre, an adopted son; Privates J Groom and H Hatt, two Londoners serving with the Royal Scots; Private V Heather, an only child from Surrey who served with the Northumberland Fusiliers; Private E Lourie, MM, at forty-one, the oldest soldier in the cemetery; Second Lieutenant W Manifold, an Australian serving with the Royal Field Artillery; Sapper McCallum, a Scotsman serving with the New Zealand Engineers and Major V Walrond, aged twenty-seven, twice Mentioned in Despatches.

Thélus Communal Cemetery

The village cemetery contains one military grave, that of Corporal C E Bowen of 5 Division Signals, Royal Corps of Signals, who died on 22 May 1940.

Thélus Military Cemetery

Thélus is a village in the Department of the Pas-de-Calais, 800 metres west of the N25 Arras-Lens main road, and 6.5 kilometres north of Arras. Thélus Military Cemetery is in the open country, 1.5 kilometres northwest of the village. Wheelchair access is with some difficulty. Contact the CWGC on 01628 634221 for further information.

The village, which stands on Vimy Ridge, was captured by the Canadian Corps on 9 April 1917, and it remained in British hands until the end of the War. The oldest part of Thélus Military Cemetery is a large grave, originally called CB 8 and now forming Plot II, which was made after the capture of the Ridge; the remaining Plots were made by fighting units from June, 1917 to September, 1918, except for Plot IV and part of Plot V, which were brought in from the battlefields of Vimy and Thélus after the Armistice. There are now nearly 300 1914-18 war casualties commemorated in this site. Of these, over thirty are unidentified.

The cemetery covers an area of 1459 square metres and the access

Thélus Military Cemetery from the RN17.

path an additional area of 357 square metres, and is enclosed by a red brick wall.

Among the 296 burials are: Lieutenant E A Abbey, an American serving with the Canadian Mounted Rifles; Lieutenant R W Biggar, the son of a King's Counsel; Lieutenant A C C Bloomfield who enlisted in 1 Canadian Mounted Rifles and became a Trumpet Sergeant Major in Lord Strathcona's Horse before being commissioned in his original regiment – he was killed in action on 8 April 1918 aged eighteen; Private J T Oram, another under-age soldier on enlistment; Privates T W Wiggins, O M Tulk, H L Goodin and Sergeant H Clark, four Americans who enlisted in the Canadian Army; Private A V Skinner, a married American serving as Private Vernon; Private G Malakonis, a Captain of Volunteers in Macedonia who originally came from Crete; Lance Corporal S O Rose, whose father lived in Denmark; Second Lieutenant U H Seguin (16 Squadron); Private Smith from Amsterdam; Private Llewellyn from Wales, serving in the Canadian Army as Private Thomas and Private Gottlieb Lanzen of the German Army.

Zivy Crater Cemetery, Thélus

The cemetery (originally called CB1) is on the south side of the road from Thélus to Neuville-St. Vaast, to the south of Lichfield Crater. The location or design of this site make wheelchair access impossible;

Zivy Crater Cemetery.

contact the CWGC on 01628 634221 for further information.

Zivy Crater was one of two mine craters (the other being Lichfield Crater) that were used by the Canadian Corps Burial Officer in 1917 for the burial of bodies found on the Vimy battlefield. The crater is a mass grave and contains fifty-three First World War burials, five of them unidentified. The names of the men buried in the crater, all of whom died in April or May 1917, are inscribed on panels fixed to the boundary wall. W H Cowlishaw designed the cemetery.

Among those buried are: Private J Noble, an under-age soldier; Sergeant H Lieb, MM, who served as Sergeant Leary and Private B Pantall, an Englishman who served as Private Symonds in the Canadian Infantry.

WALKING AROUND OPPY

For this and the two vehicular tours, a good quality map is essential. The French IGN Série Bleue with a scale of 1cm to 250m provide all the detail a traveller needs for a battlefield trip. The two maps needed for this area are **2506E** and **2406E**.

By the end of the war, Oppy was classified as a ruined village and was completely rebuilt; the position of the church was moved and the road system realigned. As a result there are no historical remains left to view except in the wood that, unfortunately, is closed to visitors. After ordnance clearance the wood was replanted without levelling the ground and it is possible to see some of the shell holes.

Park your vehicle near the Hull Memorial; behind this is the wood. **To the right** is the French memorial to the fallen of the village. **Follow the road past the church and take the first left into rue du Bois**. As you enter this road you can look into the wood and see shell holes. **Follow the road round until it rejoins the main road to Arleux**. Although this section of the

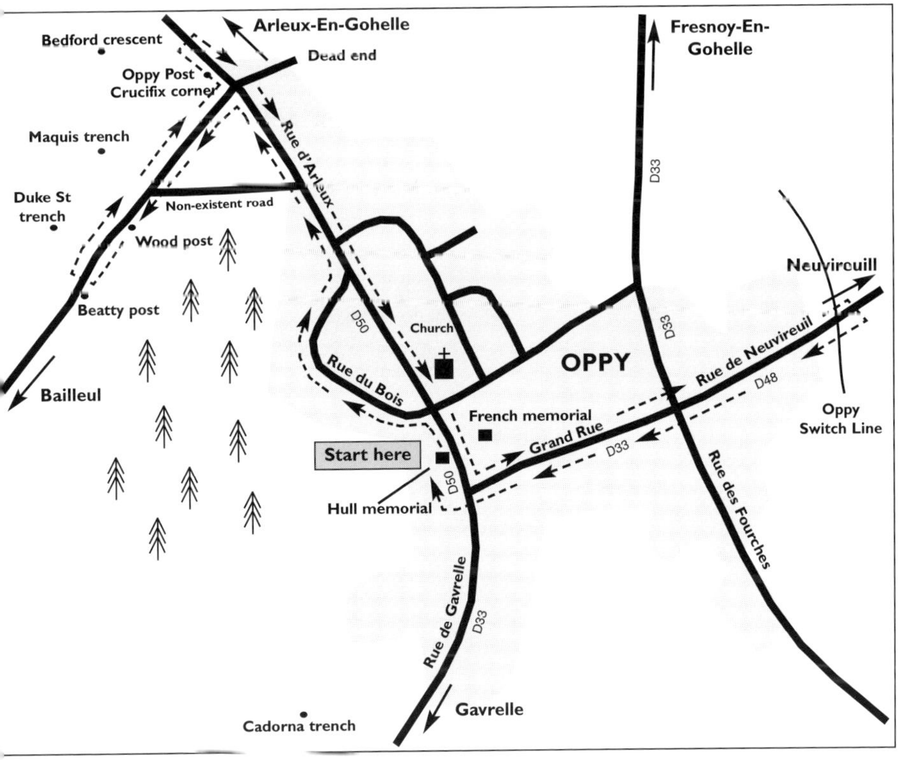

Map 33: Street map of Oppy.

The road to Neuvireuil after the village had been rebuilt.

village has been realigned, it is easy to envisage this area as a series of ruined houses peopled by snipers, and machine-guns firing through the remains of the wood. **Continue along the Arleux road** and just where the wood finishes on the left is the site of a now non-existent road that joined the main road to Bailleul-sire-Berthoult. In the wood at this point were the local château, the Town Hall and Marion Mound. **Walking in the**

The same road during the occupation.

The village achool before the war.

direction of Arleux along this road, you come to a crossroads to Bailleul and Arleux. **Down this road**, about 100 yards on the left, stood Oppy Post in March 1918. On the right is a dead-end road that was originally Crucifix Corner and a road that led to Fresnoy. This whole area was criss-crossed by trenches and was attacked by the Canadians and British on many occasions. **Turn left at the crossroads** and walk towards the wood. To the left, just in the wood, during March 1918 was Wood Post. On the right were the 1917 British positions for each of the attacks; flat ground with no cover and easily visible to the defender. At the point where the wood stops was a major German trench and in March 1918 this was the site of Beatty Post. **Turning directly away from the wood** and facing the pylons, you are in the position of the German defenders watching the attacking British troops. If you continue along the road, you are taken through Marquis Trench and Duke Street. On the left would have been Blandford and Cadorna Trenches. **Returning to the crossroads, turn left** and, after a short distance, you cross

The Hull memorial with Oppy Wood behind.

over the point where Bedford Crescent and Bedford Trench crossed. **Head back to the village square and at the junction turn left on to the D48 to Neuvireuil**. After about 400 yards the road crosses over the Oppy Switch Line.

The only remains of the battle that are likely to be found if you venture off the roads are shrapnel balls and unexploded shells; these are often left at the roadside by the farmers for collection by bomb disposal teams. Care must be exercised, as they are still potentially lethal. **Return back to Hull Memorial.**

Oppy Wood – Crucifix Corner was on the left of the picture.

EXPLORING THE OPPY AREA BY CAR

Car Tour 1: Gavrelle & Fresnes-lès-Montauban

Upon arriving at the village of Gavrelle, locate the memorial to 63 (Royal Naval) Division.

Royal Naval Division memorial at the entrance to Gavrelle.

Proceed through the village. On the right is the Town Hall with a plaque to the men of the Queen's Westminster Rifles who were killed in the area during the German attack of 28 March. **Turn right and follow the D33 to Roeux/Fampoux.** About 100 metres on the left is the place where the Germans constructed a Christmas tree from unexploded British shells in 1916. **Take the second right to Fampoux, the D42E**. Follow the Commonwealth War Grave signs and Naval Trench will be found on the right. **Turn right back in the direction of Fampoux**, and, after **crossing over the A26**, you find Chili Trench Cemetery on the right.

Map 34: Modern day map of the tour area.

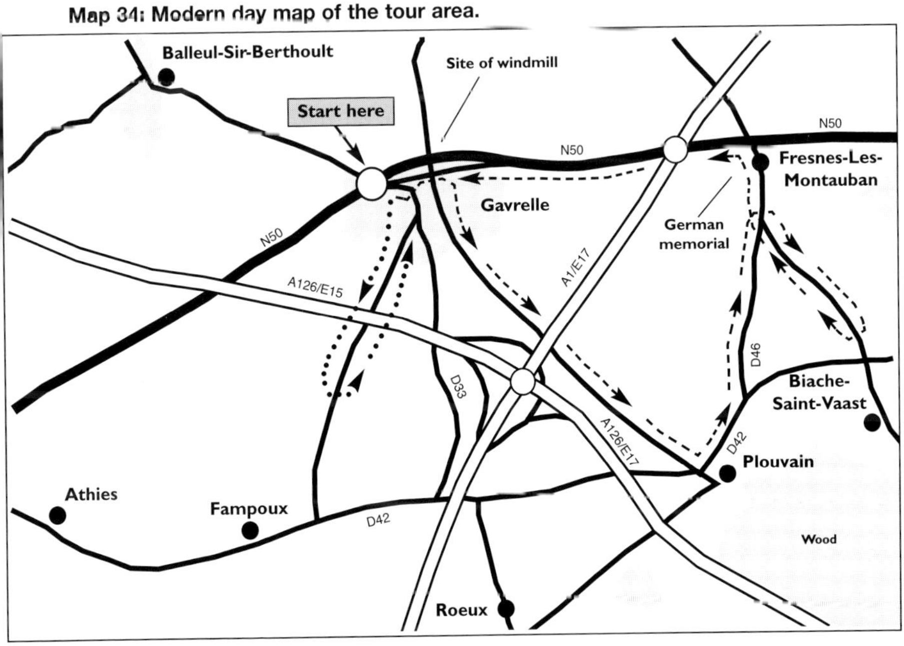

Hood Battalion Cross in Gavrelle church.

Return to Gavrelle on the same road and **turn right to the church.** Inside the church is the Hood Cross, commissioned and paid for by Arthur Asquith, the commanding officer of Hood Battalion, to commemorate the capture of Gavrelle by the Royal Naval Division. Also in the church are two plaques. The first is to those who were killed in the war, the second records the adoption of the village by the City of Westminster. On the east end of the church are traces of shell damage from 1940. Outside the church is the village war memorial with the names of the dead and a plaque to the French 34 Division.

Continuing in the direction of Fresnes, take the first right (road to the Stade). About 300 yards down this road is the local cemetery that contains seven war graves from 1940 and a memorial to a priest who was deported and executed in 1943 (the priest had created false documents to help airmen and soldiers evade capture; for the full story see *Gavrelle* in the *Battleground Europe Series*). The plot on the right of the cemetery was the German cemetery during the war.

Follow the road until a T-Junction is reached and turn left on to the D42. Follow this road through Plouvain and **at the railway line turn left onto the D46** to Fresnes. **At the junction, turn right and follow the D43 for approximately $1\frac{1}{2}$ miles.** On the right is the communal cemetery that contains a French war memorial with individual plaques. To the right of the memorial are British graves from the Second World War.

Return in the direction of Fresnes and, just as you reach the outskirts of the village, look for a farm track on the left. Walk down this track and about sixty yards on the left is a German cemetery memorial. The graves have gone but the memorial is too big to move. **Continue along the track** and you come to Railway Copse; like Oppy Wood, this too is private. In the wood can clearly be seen shell craters from British artillery shells; the wood was used as a forming-up area for German counter-attacks. In the line of the track in the distance is Hollow Copse.

Return to the road and turn left into Fresnes. At the junction is the French war memorial. **Continue on this road until the N50 is reached and then turn left to return to Gavrelle.**

Most of this area was a German back area where troops came to rest after frontline service, but with the Arras offensive it became part of the frontline. The whole area was criss-crossed with trenches and barbed wire belts. To fully appreciate what it looked like a trench map is essential. The Naval & Military Press have produced a CD-Rom containing trench maps that cover the whole of the Western Front, including the Oppy area. For more detailed information on this area of the battlefield at the extreme southern end of the Oppy area, see *Gavrelle* in the *Battleground Europe Series.*

Marker stone showing the extent of the German advance in 1918.

Car Tour 2: Oppy, Bailleul, Fresnoy & Willerval.

From Gavrelle church drive towards Fresnes-lès-Montauban, but almost immediately turn left onto the D33 to Oppy. About 75 yards on the right is a dead-end road that used to be the main road to Oppy before the N50 was re-aligned. At the end of this road, on the left, is a memorial to twelve cavalrymen of the French 23 Dragoons who were killed near this spot, on the Gavrelle-Izel Lane (no longer in existence), by German machine-gun fire from the windmill. The original memorial was built on the site of a chapel that was destroyed during the fighting in 1917. When the memorial became unsafe it was replaced by the present structure.

Return to the main road and turn right along the road to Oppy, taking the second right after going under the N50. Drive up the spoil heap. The area straight ahead is where Gavrelle windmill stood (by March 1918 this area had become Mill Post) and to the left was Cadorna Trench. The electricity station on the left is built over the site of Railway Trench and Brough Alley. Behind the site of the electricity station is the site of two Victoria Cross actions on

Unexploded ordnance left by the village sign.

Bois de Fresnoy from the Oppy to Arleux road.

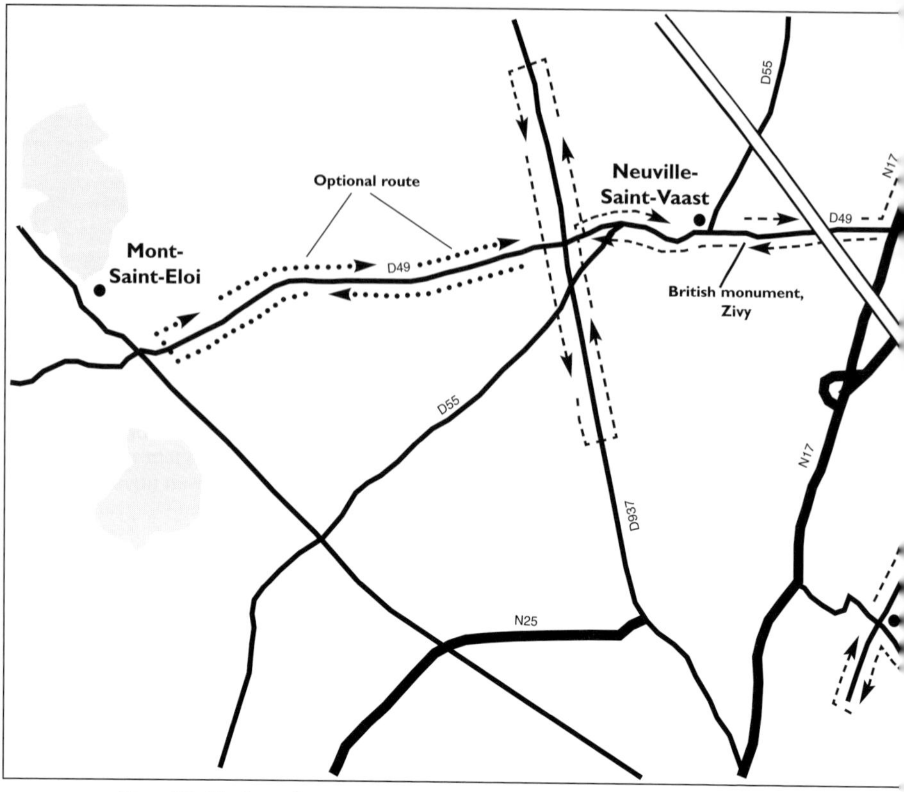

Map 35: Modern day map of the area.

29 April 1917 (2/Lt R L Haine, VC, MC and bar and 2/Lt A O Pollard, VC, MC and bar, DCM). Oppy Wood can be seen to the left. **Drive along the D33** and, as it bends to the right, note the fields on the right; this was the site of Bradford Post and 100 yards further on, in the fields to the left, was Bird Post. About 150 yards further on the traveller crosses the 1918 German front line.

In the village, turn left on the D50 to Bailleul. Fifty yards on the left stands the Hull Memorial and behind this is the wood. On the right is the French war memorial. Take the first left alongside the wood. If you get out of the car and look into the wood at the closest point, it is possible to see what appear to be shell holes and traces of trenches. Along this road was the entrance to the château. **Continue on this road and turn left onto the D50 again. At the intersection, take the left to Bailleul**. On the right of this crossroads was Crucifix Trench. As you drive along the edge of the wood, you pass the positions where the British troops would have been attacking to the right over the flat ground. At the corner of the wood was Oppy

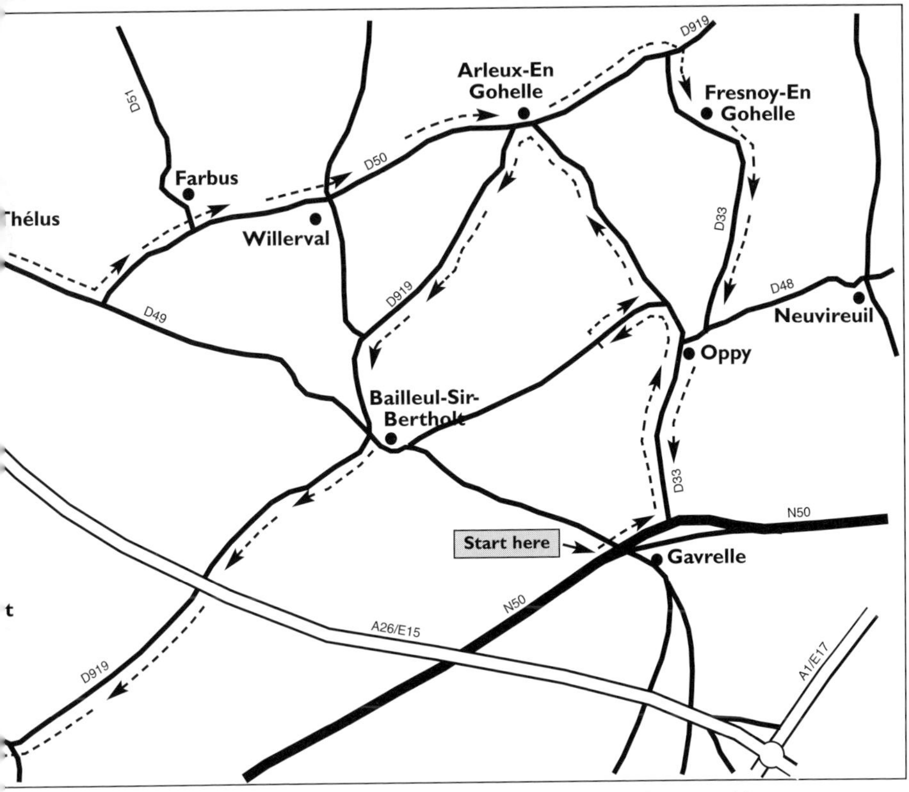

Trench and behind that Oppy Support. Further on is a parking area that lies over the sites of Marquis and Earl trenches. The pylons on the right roughly follow the attack positions for the 3 May battle. If you look towards the electricity station, you get a view of the area for the 28 June attack. **Return along the road to the junction. Turn left on to the D50**. A short distance down this road on the left was Oppy Post and Bedford Row; Fresnoy Trench was on the right. The road passes over the Vendin-Méricourt line with Fresnoy Wood on the right in the distance.

The site of Crucifix Corner.

Plaque commemorating the defence of the area by the Queen's Westminsters during the German offensive in 1918.

The Fresnes war memorial.

Plouvain communal cemetery memorial.

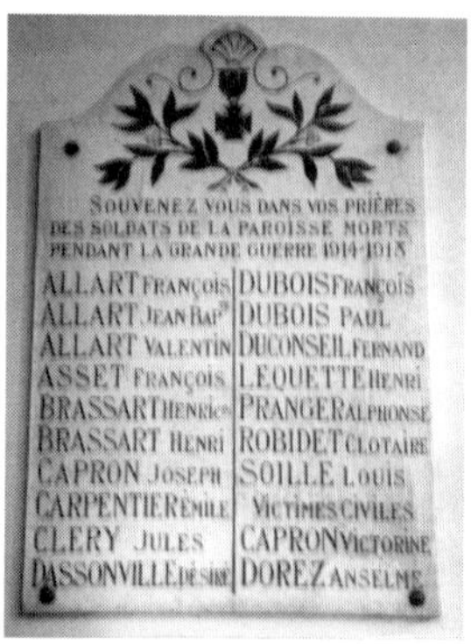

Plaque detailing the inhabitants of Gavrelle who were killed during the war.

34th French division memorial outside Gavrelle church.

In Arleux, turn left at the T-junction, after the church, onto **the D919 to Willerval** (turn right and then left for the communal cemetery with five second war graves). On the left is the French war memorial. **Proceed along the D919 to Bailleul** and, about half a mile after leaving the village, Orchard Dump Cemetery is on the right. **Proceed to Bailleul** and, on the left, just after the gas pumping station, are the remains of a sugar factory destroyed during the war but used as a headquarters structure. The local cemetery along the D49 to Gavrelle has a small number of 1940 burials.

Arleux war memorial.

In the town, follow the D919 to Roclincourt; Albuera Cemetery is signposted on the right. The tarmac road turns into a cobbled track and just under the railway line there is a small piece of land to park a car. The cemetery is a short walk along a grass track. **Back at the main road, turn right along the D919 heading for St. Laurent.** About 1000 yards after the A26, Bailleul Road East is on the left. **Fork left to leave the main road** and fifty yards after the British cemetery, you find a German concentration cemetery. In it are buried the dead from the Oppy area. Out of a total 31,939 burials, 22,000 are in a mass grave. With two such cemeteries close to one another, it is easy to compare the two styles of remembrance. Behind the cemetery is a railway embankment that was used as a Divisional HQ for troops in the Gavrelle area.

Continuing south along the D919, take the right turn on the D60 to Roclincourt. From 1917 on, this,

Roclincourt war memorial.

Memorial for those who fought in the Roclincourt area during 1915 and 1916.

together with Ecurie and Neuville-St. Vaast, were rest and training areas for troops in the Arleux, Oppy and Gavrelle trenches. On the right, about 200 yards along the road, is a French memorial on top of the remains of a German pillbox. This marks the start of the German frontline.

In the centre of Roclincourt, turn left and follow the sign to Roclincourt Military Cemetery. After 300 yards, turn right, to find the cemetery at the end of small road where parking is quite tight. Some of the Oppy dead are buried here. **Return to the centre**, **and at the roundabout go straight over in the direction of Thélus.** Fifty yards on the right is the local war memorial and on the left is a memorial to the troops who fought in the area:

View towards Oppy looking towards Bird and Bradford Posts.

Gavrelle Memorial to the French Dragoons who were killed near the spot in 1914.

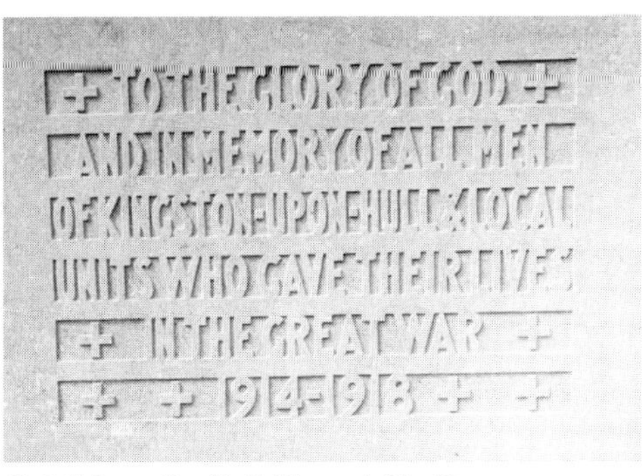

Detail from the Hull Memorial in Oppy.

The French Memorial in front of the church.

To the memory of all the brave men of the 88th Infantry Regiment who fought heroically in this place (9 May 1915–4 March 1916). Remembering the officers, non-commissioned officers and men of the 88th and 288th Infantry Regiments and the 135th Territorial Infantry Regiment. Died on the field of honour 1914-1918.

Thélus war memorial.

Continue along the road to Thélus and on the right, just before leaving the town, **is a small road called Rue du Douai**. **Proceed along this unclassified road for 800 yards and turn left to Highland Cemetery**. The road down to the cemetery is a cart track but is navigable by car. **On returning to the unclassified road, turn left and, after 150 yards, turn left again** down a badly pot-holed cart track (more suitable for 4x4 – but navigable if done slowly) to find Roclincourt Valley Cemetery. The view down to the main road is over the 1915 battlefield from the German perspective. **Returning to the main road (C101), turn right**. 800 yards after leaving the town is a French memorial on the left. This commemorates Lieutenant Henry Labesse who died on 16 June 1915; it also commemorates all the troops who fought in front of Roclincourt and marks the 1915 frontline.

Memorial to Lieutenant Labesse that also indicates the 1915 front line.

At the church junction in the centre of Thélus, turn right to Bois Carré Cemetery, which is on the right at the end of the town. Also on the right, about 300 yards further on, is the 1 Canadian Division monument. This was erected at Christmas 1917 in memory of their several engagements between March and July 1917.

Turn back into the town and on the left, in the centre, is the French war memorial. **Continue along the D49** and, on the right, at the junction with the N17, is the Canadian Artillery monument. This was built and unveiled a year to the day after the capture of Vimy Ridge. General Byng performed the ceremony on 9 April 1918. The South African Heavy Artillery Battery, who also participated, are remembered on the plaque. The memorial stands directly over a dugout, the entrance to which was under the steps in front.

Canadian artillery memorial during the 1930s.

Straight over, on the D49, just after the A26, on the left there is Zivy Crater. It is better to reverse the car to the cemetery using the cart track just before it. Lichfield Crater Cemetery is about 600 yards north of Zivy Crater but can only be approached through Vimy Ridge.

Return to the main road to Neuville-St. Vaast and turn left. After 300 yards, turn left onto an unclassified road and follow it

Neuville-St. Vaast Town Hall showing the commemorative plaques, with (inset) plaque commemorating the taking of the village in 1915.

for just over 1½ miles. At the T-junction, follow the signs to Arras Road Cemetery. Return to the unclassified road and follow it for a further 800 yards to Nine Elms Cemetery.

Proceed back to the D49 and turn left to Neuville-St. Vaast. In the centre of the town, on the left in a small square, is the French war memorial. On the right is the Town Hall to which are affixed two commemorative plaques. One is to the memory of Jean Tison, a member of the French Forces of the Interior who was shot by the Germans in May 1944. The other is to the memory of Lieutenant Henri Lievin, Medal of Honour winner, who was arrested on 21 June 1944; nothing further is known about what happened to him after that date.

Follow the road straight on (signposted Autres Directions) and turn right on to the D49, Autres Directions and ND Lorrette. At the crossroads, on the right is a memorial commemorating the destruction of the village in mining operations by the French on 9 May 1915. (There are caverns and subways underneath this whole region.) On the other side of the road, on the D49 to Mont St. Eloi, is a private war museum that has much to see. It is also well worth following the road to Mont St. Eloi to view the outstanding ruins and to

The Canadian Artillery monument at the present time.

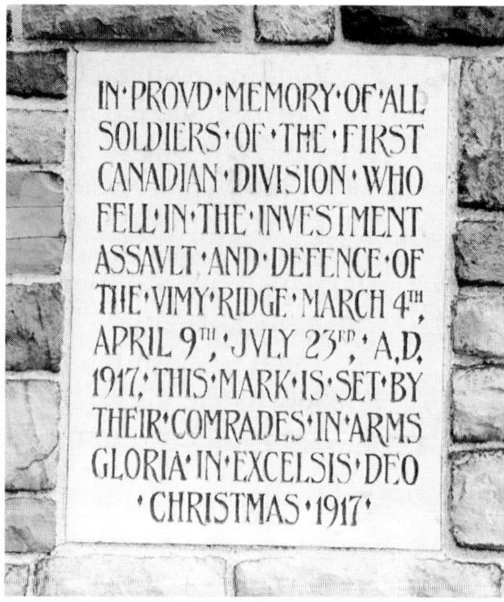

Memorial and detail to the fallen of 1 Canadian Division

Entrance to Zivy Crater.

appreciate its strategic importance, with its commanding views over the Arras area. Mont St. Eloi was the site of an Augustinan abbey in the seventh century but the famous ruined towers are from the eighteenth century, when during the Revolution the abbey was secularised, sold and then pulled down, leaving only the gate and towers. These were all but destroyed by German artillery fire in 1914 and later used by Foch's army in 1915 as an observation post. In the valley below the village was a Royal Flying Corps airfield.

Turn right at the memorial, on to the D937 (direction of Souchez) and, on the right, after a mile, stands the Polish memorial to the 1915 fighting. On the other side of the road is the Czech cemetery and memorial for the dead of two wars.

Return down the D937 and continue past the memorial and museum to the German cemetery near Maison Blanche. This cemetery, is one of the biggest German cemeteries in France and holds the remains of nearly 45,000 Germans. In the summer a volunteer maintenance team of students and German soldiers work there. **Turn right from the cemetery and then left at the D55 to Maroeuil** for La Targette British and French cemeteries.

Head back to the junction of the D937 and the D49 and follow this to the N17. Turn left onto this road and, shortly after leaving the town, Thélus Military Cemetery can be seen on the left. This can be a very dangerous road: it is easier to park on the large grass verge on the right before walking across the road to the cemetery, a few hundred yards further away from the road.

Driving towards Vimy Ridge, take the first right to Thélus. If you turn back, you can see the commanding view of the ridge that gave it its importance to both sides. **Follow the road into Thélus,** and, on the left, is the town cemetery that contains a number of war graves: four French soldiers killed (1914, 1915, 1916 and 1918), an unknown soldier, two Belgian civilian victims from May 1940 (Louis Dubois and Rémy Honore) and two British soldiers (one unknown artillery man and Corporal C E Bowen of the Royal Signal Corps – both from 1940).

Continue along the D49 and turn left onto the D50 to Farbus. Turn left at the cemetery on the D51 to Centre Ville where, outside the church, is the local war memorial, and a few yards further on, another memorial to the soldiers who fell at

The Czechoslovak memorial.

The French war memorial at Neuville-St. Vaast.

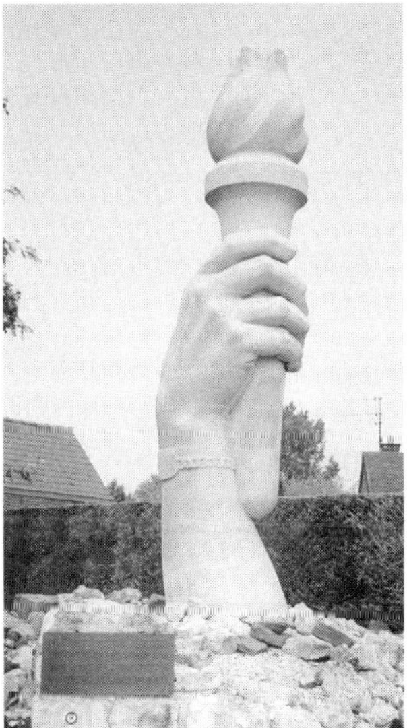

Unusual memorial commemorating the destruction of the village by mining operations.

The Polish Memorial.

The towers of Mont St. Eloi then and now.

Farbus war memorial.

Memorial commemorating all those who fell during the fighting for Farbus.

Farbus. **Turn round and turn left at the cemetery on to the D50 to Willerval. At the roundabout in Willerval, turn left along the D50E1**; 300 yards on the left is the track to Beehive Cemetery, named after a German machine-gun emplacement. **Park the car on the roadside and proceed on foot along the dirt track for about 800 yards to the cemetery**.

Return to the roundabout and follow the D50 to Arleux and, at the junction opposite the memorial, turn left onto the D919 to Bois Bernard. On the right is the large Bois de Fresnoy. **Turn right onto the D33 to Oppy**. In the village centre, on the right, is the village war memorial. Following the road to Oppy, one can see the commanding view the Germans had of their attackers. **Follow the road back to start point.**

Select Bibliography & Further Reading

Bilton, D, *Hull Pals*. Pen & Sword. 1999.

Bilton, D, *The Trench – The full story of the 1st Hull Pals*. Pen & Sword. 2002.

Boraston, Lt Col. J H & Capt. C E O Bax. *The Eighth Division 1914-1918*. Medici Society. 1926.

Bourne, J M. *Britain and the Great War 1914-1918*. Edward Arnold. 1989.

Carver, R B. et al. *A History of the 10th (Service) Battalion The East Yorkshire Regiment (Hull Commercials)*. A Brown & Sons Ltd. 1937.

Clayton, A. *Paths of Glory*. Orion. 2003.

Commonwealth War Graves Commission. *Cemeteries & Memorials in Belgium & Northern France*. Michelin. 2004.

Coombs, R. MBE. *Before Endeavours Fade*. After the Battle. 1983.

Edmonds, Brigadier- General Sir James. *Military Operations – France and Belgium 1916 Volume I*. Macmillan. 1932.

Edmonds, Brigadier- General Sir James. *Military Operations – France and Belgium 1917 Volume II*. HMSO. 1948.

Edmonds, Brigadier- General Sir James. *Military Operations – France and Belgium 1918 Volume II*. Macmillan. 1937.

Edmonds, Brigadier- General Sir James. *Military Operations – France and Belgium 1918 Volume V*. HMSO. 1947.

Falls, Captain C. *Military Operations – France and Belgium 1917*. Macmillan and Co. 1940.

Gerrard, A D. *The Road to Oppy Wood*. Privately published. 1997.

Gliddon, G. *VCs of the First World War – Arras & Messines 1917*. Sutton Publishing. 1998.

Hammerton, J A. *World War 1914 – 1918 Volume 2*. Amalgamated Press. ND.

Jackson, A. *The Accrington Pals, Oppy Gavrelle, May June 1917*. http://www.btinternet.com/~a.jackson/oppy2.html . 2002.

Johnson, J.H. *Stalemate!* Arms & Armour Press. 1997.

Junger, E. *Storm of Steel*. Allen Lane. 2003.

Ludendorff, E. *My War Memories 1914 – 1918*. Hutchinson. 1919.

Macdonald, L. *To the Last Man*. Viking. 1998

Maude, A H. *The history of the 47th (London) Division 1914-1919*. Amalgamated Press. 1922

Michelin. *Illustrated Michelin guide to the Battlefields (1914-1918) – Arras*. Michelin. 1919

Nicholls, J. *Cheerful Sacrifice – The battle of Arras 1917*. Leo Cooper. 1990.

Petre, F L. *The Royal Berkshire Regiment Volume 2*. The Royal Berkshire Regiment. 1925.

Scott, Major General Sir Arthur B, KCB, DSO. *History of the 12th Eastern Division in the Great War, 1914-1918*. Nisbet & Co. ND.

Sheffield, G. *Forgotten Victory.* Headline. 2001.
Sheffield, G & Inglis G. *From Vimy Ridge to the Rhine.* The Crowood Press. 1989.
Sheppard, Capt. E W, OBE, MC. *The race to the sea, September 1914 to October, 1914.* The Army Quarterly Volume 2. Clowes. 1921.
Some of Them. *A Short Diary of the 11th Service Battalion, East Yorkshire Regiment. 1914-1919.* Goddard, Walker & Brown. 1921.
Swinton, Major General Sir Ernest, KBE, CB. *Twenty Years After. Volumes 1 & 2.* Newnes. 1938.
The Snapper. The Regimental Journal of the East Yorkshire Regiment, issues for 1917.
Tallet, K & Tasker T. *Gavrelle.* Leo Cooper. 2000.
Taylor, A J P. *War by Time-table.* Macdonald & Co. 1969.
The Times. *History of the Great War Volume XIV.* The Times. 1917.
The Times. *History of the Great War Volume XV*. The Times. 1917.
The Times. *History of the Great War Volume XX.* The Times. 1919.
Thorold, B. *Invasion – History of the First World War.* Purnell. 1969.
Ward, Major C H D. *The Fifty-sixth Division 1914-1918.* John Murray. 1921.
War Office, *Soldiers Died in the Great War* - Various Volumes. J B Hayward & Son. 1989.
Wilson, T. *The Myriad Faces of War.* Polity Press. 1986.
www.marple-uk.com *Marple War Memorial* book. 2004.
www.purly.demon *History of the 1st (Regular) Battalion Royal Berkshire Regiment. 2004.*
Wyrall, E. *The East Yorkshire Regiment in the Great War 1914 – 1918.* Harrison & Sons. 1928.
Wyrall, E. *The History of The Second Division 1914 – 1918* Volume 2. Nelson. 1921.
4th Hull Battalion. *4th Hull Battalion*. Johnson & Sons. ND.

War Diaries – all unpublished. Held at The National Archive, London.
2 Division, 5 Division, 8 Division, 31 Division, 56 Division, 6 Brigade, 92 Brigade, 99 Brigade, 10 East Yorkshire Regiment, 11 East Yorkshire Regiment, 12 East Yorkshire Regiment, 13 East Yorkshire Regiment, 13 Essex Regiment, 2 Highland Light Infantry, 1 King's Royal Rifle Corps, 1st/4th London Regiment, 17 Middlesex Regiment, 1 Royal Berkshire Regiment, 17 Royal Fusiliers, 22 Royal Fusiliers, 23 Royal Fusiliers, 24 Royal Fusiliers, 1 Sherwood Foresters, 2 South Staffs, 1 Worcestershire Regiment.

INDEX